TCM
IMPORTS

TCM IMPORTS

Timeless Favorites and Hidden Gems of World Cinema

ALICIA MALONE

RUNNING PRESS
PHILADELPHIA

Running Press
Hachette Book Group
1290 Avenue of the Americas, New York, NY 10104
www.runningpress.com
@Running_Press

First Edition: May 2025

Published by Running Press, an imprint of Hachette Book Group, Inc. The Running Press
name and logo are trademarks of Hachette Book Group, Inc.

The Hachette Speakers Bureau provides a wide range of authors for speaking events. To find
out more, go to www.hachettespeakersbureau.com or email HachetteSpeakers@hbgusa.com.

Running Press books may be purchased in bulk for business, educational, or promotional
use. For more information, please contact your local bookseller or the Hachette Book Group
Special Markets Department at Special.Markets@hbgusa.com.

The publisher is not responsible for websites (or their content) that are not owned
by the publisher.

Image credits: Pages 33, 77: Photo 12 / Alamy Stock Photo. Page 251: Album /
Alamy Stock Photo. All other photography courtesy Turner Classic Movies, Inc.

Print book cover and interior design by Katie Benezra and Sheryl Kober

Names: Malone, Alicia, author. | Turner Classic Movies (Firm)
Title: TCM Imports : timeless favorites and hidden gems of
   world cinema / Alicia Malone.
Other titles: Turner Classic Movies Imports
Description: First edition. | New York, NY : Running Press, 2025. |
   Includes bibliographical references and index. | Summary: "Alicia
   Malone, TCM on-air host (including the network's weekly TCM Imports
   series), offers movie buffs and streaming binge-watchers an essential
   guide to some of the greatest cinema from around the world" —Provided
   by publisher.
Identifiers: LCCN 2024027872 (print) | LCCN 2024027873 (ebook) | ISBN
   9780762488483 (paperback) | ISBN 9780762488490 (ebook)
Subjects: LCSH: Foreign films—Catalogs. | Foreign films—Reviews. |
   Foreign films—History and criticism. | Motion pictures—Catalogs. |
   LCGFT: Plot summaries. | Filmographies.
Classification: LCC PN1995.9.F67 M35 2025 (print) | LCC PN1995.9.F67
   (ebook) | DDC 791.43/75—dc23/eng/20240828
LC record available at https://lccn.loc.gov/2024027872
LC ebook record available at https://lccn.loc.gov/2024027873

ISBNs: 978-0-7624-8848-3 (paperback), 978-0-7624-8849-0 (ebook)

Printed in Malaysia

PCF

10 9 8 7 6 5 4 3 2 1

Page ii: *Daisies* (1966)

Page vi: *Pierrot le Fou* (1965)

To our beloved, movie-crazy,
and ever supportive TCM viewers.
Thanks for watching . . .

CONTENTS

INTRODUCTION

In Australia, nearly every movie I watched was foreign. Living on an island so far away from the rest of the world, with a local film and television industry that was relatively small, meant that most of the entertainment I consumed was made elsewhere. Our TV shows came from America and England (part of the reason Australian actors can pull off believable American and British accents) and the multiplexes were filled with Hollywood movies. At the art houses, it was films from France and all over Europe. I grew up not really seeing a distinction between American movies and movies made in, say, Germany—because all movies were foreign, and all taught me about the world.

At Turner Classic Movies, we've used the phrase "opening up a window onto the world" to describe the impact of foreign cinema, and it's true. When you can't travel, or you live in a remote location, movies are a way to visit different countries, learn different customs, meet different people, and travel through time. And with movies being a capsule of the time and place in which they were made, you're not only consuming the story but also everything around it—the politics of the country at that moment, the societal trends, the background and beliefs of the filmmaker, even the history of cinema itself. As the famed film critic Roger Ebert once said, movies can be "a machine that generates empathy," and I truly believe that watching cinema from all over the world opened my eyes to the struggles and triumphs of other people.

It also made me more able to dream of a life outside of Australia. In 2010, I decided I wanted to live where the classic movies I loved were made, and so I moved to Hollywood. Back in Australia, because of all the access to foreign entertainment, I felt as if I was part of the world. But America has felt different, like it is the whole world. To me, there seems to be a distinction here between Hollywood and foreign film, and more than that, a sense that international cinema is something of a scholarly pursuit. It can feel as if you need a film degree before you can talk about what you enjoyed or didn't enjoy about a foreign movie. Or that you must know every film made by Federico Fellini before you're allowed to share your opinion. I've always felt that a good movie is a good movie, no matter where it was made, and throughout my career I have strived to bypass the gatekeepers and make foreign films accessible to everyone.

I got a big chance to do this when I was hired in 2016 to be the host of FilmStruck, the streaming service that combined Turner Classic Movies with the Criterion Collection. What a gift that was—to get to introduce classic Hollywood films and my foreign favorites. I relished every moment, and when FilmStruck prematurely ended in November 2018, I (like so many others) felt bereft. Luckily, TCM allowed me to take over as the host of its weekly series, *TCM Imports*, so I could get my foreign film fix. Every Sunday, late at night, I introduce a film made outside of Hollywood, and in doing so, I have discovered a wealth of exciting movies.

When Cindy Sipala of Running Press approached me to talk about writing a book for the TCM Library, the one gap that I saw in the existing lineup was a book dedicated to foreign film. Or, to be more accurate, "non-American movies," because any book I wrote was always going to include films from Australia and other English-speaking countries. Over the years, I have felt that many of the books on international cinema have been quite academic in nature—important, but adding to the general feeling that watching these movies might be a daunting prospect. I wanted to write a book that was easy to read, that didn't assume any knowledge, but that also gave facts and context around the making of the movie—trivia that would be interesting whether you have seen the film or not.

Once I had the green light, I got out my notebook and started listing all the possible films I could include. When I got to number 289, my stomach sank, and I felt overwhelmed about how I was ever going to narrow my choices down to around fifty films. I knew I didn't want to write a book about the greatest

foreign movies—I don't feel qualified to make that distinction—and choosing just my personal favorites seemed too superficial. I also decided not to write about films that have been examined many times over—because what could I possibly have to say that would add to a conversation about Federico Fellini's *8½* or Akira Kurosawa's *Seven Samurai*? So, I started to think about what kind of book I would love to read. In doing so, I considered how I like to watch movies, and the answer was: seasonally. Every December, I bring out my holiday favorites to watch. In November, it's film noir (for Noir-vember, obviously). October is reserved for horror films. I like watching movies that take place on the beach in summer, and in the snow in winter, and there's nothing I enjoy more than watching a cozy, autumnal movie under a blanket in the fall. It's similar to how our programming team schedules the movies on TCM—on Mother's Day, we have movies about mothers, and so forth.

I got out my list and started organizing films into seasons—either literally (the time setting) or thematically (the feeling it evokes)—and I found that I needed to do more research, more film watching, and more thinking outside of the box. After all of that, what I've ended up with is a list of fifty-two films that is truly eclectic. By choosing films according to a calendar year, I have a mix that means there is (to use a tired saying) something for everyone. There are films most people have heard of, and films that even hardcore cinephiles have never seen. There are movies you could define as being high art and movies that are low art, cult films, and such. There are obvious choices and some weird ones. A few titles I've written about in my previous books, but others were new discoveries for me. It's diverse in genre, but despite my best efforts, the lion's share of these movies were made in France, or by French filmmakers, or by filmmakers from other countries but in a coproduction with France. There are also a lot of white, male directors. Both are reflections of the film industry itself.

The fifty-two movies have been organized into a standard American calendar year, so, if you wanted, you could watch one film a week for an entire year. After watching these films myself, to write this book, I can guarantee you that is a good time. Or you could pop this book on your coffee table, and when you get stuck for what to watch, and get tired of an algorithm choosing your entertainment, you can open to any page and try something new.

Overall, my hope is that this book will inspire you to explore a different side of cinema, to see the world through a new lens and learn to appreciate the wide world of foreign cinema.

Happy watching!
Alicia xx

▶ *Wings of Desire* (1987)

WINTER

(EARLY YEAR)

Amélie

DIRECTED BY **Jean-Pierre Jeunet**

To watch when you . . . need some motivation to start your
"New Year, New You" goals.

France, 2001
Color, 122 minutes, Comedy

Screenplay: Jean-Pierre Jeunet,
Guillaume Laurant

Starring: Audrey Tautou (Amélie Poulain),
Mathieu Kassovitz (Nino Quincampoix),
Serge Merlin (Raymond Dufayel)

> "*Amélie* has a strange feeling of absolute harmony. It's a perfect
> moment. A soft light, a scent in the air, the quiet murmur of the
> city. A surge of love, an urge to help mankind overcomes her."
>
> —Narrator

By the time director Jean-Pierre Jeunet made *Amélie* (2001), he'd already experienced a fair amount of success, though nothing could have prepared him for the phenomenon that *Amélie* would become. Jeunet had taught himself how to use a camera as a teenager and started his professional career directing commercials and short films. Many of these were made in conjunction with artist and designer Marc Caro, and the two parlayed their working relationship into codirecting their first feature, *Delicatessen* (1991). A dark sci-fi comedy about a butcher who murders his workers and sells their meat, *Delicatessen* was an unexpected cult hit, and it heralded the arrival of two bold new voices in French cinema. Jeunet and Caro's second feature was *The City of Lost Children* (1995), another dark fantasy, about a

scientist who steals children's dreams so he can live longer. More acclaim and awards followed, and it was no surprise when Hollywood came calling. The two directors were invited to take charge of the fourth film in the popular *Aliens* franchise, *Alien: Resurrection* (1997), but Marc Caro soon left the production, taking his name off the credits, and the resulting movie failed to become a critical or a commercial success.

Returning to France, and teaming up with writer Guillaume Laurant, Jean-Pierre Jeunet decided to take a big chance—to make a film that was happy. "We wanted to get a smile from the audience," Jeunet said in an interview. "It was just a very small film, and it was risky because I knew I was going to talk about generosity, and it's a risk, because today it's more fashionable to talk about violence."

▲ "She cultivates a taste for small pleasures: dipping her hand into sacks of grain, cracking crème brûlée with a teaspoon . . ." —Narrator

▲▲ Mathieu Kassovitz as Nino Quincampoix   ▲ Audrey Tautou as Amélie

Amélie, made for a modest budget of around $10 million, took France by storm, racing to the top of the box-office charts. The film came to the United States in late 2001, where a post-9/11 audience was eager for escapism. To the astonishment of many, *Amélie* joined the relatively short list of foreign films that have experienced crossover success in America. During its initial release, *Amélie* made just under $175 million at the global box office.

In the more than twenty years since, *Amélie* has earned its fair share of admirers, as well as imitators and critics. The film has inspired a musical, the tone and look of a TV show (*Pushing Daisies*), and even a species of frog (the description of *Teratohyla amelie* explains that, just like the film, "where little details play an important role in the 'joy of living,' amphibians and reptiles may be small but play an important role in the health of our planet"). "Joy of living" is an apt description of *Amélie*, which celebrates the small pleasures in life and reminds viewers of the simple magic that lies in every day.

For the character of Amélie (Audrey Tautou), this discovery changes her life. Born as an only child and starved of love from her distant father and nervous mother, Amélie has grown up to be a sheltered young woman, working as a waitress in a café but struggling to connect with the people around her. This changes when she finds an old tin hidden in her apartment, filled with childhood treasures, and tracks down the owner. Witnessing the joy he experiences when he's reunited with his memories, Amélie decides to become a do-gooder, spreading cheer in elaborate ways—such as encouraging her father to travel by stealing his garden gnome and giving it to a flight attendant, who sends him photos of the gnome having grand adventures all over the world.

On one of Amélie's journeys, she encounters Nino (Mathieu Kassovitz), who accidentally drops a photo album, which Amélie picks up. Inside is a series of photo booth pictures that'd

More Feel-Good Films

The Full Monty (1997, UK)
Life Is Beautiful (1997, Italy)
The Castle (1997, Australia)
Spirited Away (2001, Japan)
The Intouchables (2011, France)

been ripped up and thrown away by the subject but were lovingly reassembled by Nino. As Amélie cooks up a scheme to return the album to Nino, she starts to develop feelings for him but remains too scared to actually talk to him.

It's a sweet story about the power of performing random acts of kindness and the importance of human connection; made even more joyful by the whimsical direction of Jean-Pierre Jeunet, the color-soaked cinematography of Bruno Delbonnel, and a jaunty accordion soundtrack by Yann Tiersen. The film is saturated with visual delights and comedic narration. In one scene, Amélie imagines how useful it would be to have a prompter hiding nearby, whispering comebacks to shy people, as in a theater when an actor forgets their lines.

With its quirkiness, its charming heroine, and its unabashed good heart, *Amélie* can be described as a "feel good" movie—a descriptor that is often used as a pejorative within serious cinephile circles. The movie was denied entry into the 2001 Cannes Film Festival, with festival directors turning it down for official selection. Mathieu Kassovitz, who plays Nino in the film, was on the Cannes jury that year, and told press that if it had been up to him, *Amélie* would not only have been included in the competition, but it also would have won the major award. Despite this snub, *Amélie* was selected to play at the Toronto Film Festival, where it

won the People's Choice Award, and went on to be nominated for five Academy Awards: Best Cinematography, Best Art Direction, Best Sound, Best Original Screenplay, and Best Foreign Language Film.

Amélie was embraced by many film critics, but some weren't charmed by its tone. On the ten-year anniversary of the film, critic Phil Hoad wrote an article for the *Guardian*, saying that even in watching the film a second time, he still found "Audrey Tautou's busybody simpering to the point of psychosis." Even so, he admitted that *Amélie* was an important film, because of the way it was embraced by audiences around the world, becoming "one of the clearest signs of the expansion in non-English language mainstream cinema in the noughties." *Amélie* was an entry point for many audience members who hadn't yet delved into foreign film—an easy-to-watch, fun movie that just happened to have subtitles. However, a valid criticism of *Amélie* is the type of Paris shown in the film. It is a fantasy version, one that only exists in movies like *An American in Paris* (1951). This is a whitewashed Paris, where no social problems—or immigrants—exist.

The huge success of *Amélie* catapulted the then-unknown, twenty-five-year-old Audrey Tautou into worldwide fame. This was something Tautou has never been comfortable with; she is just as shy and introverted as her character. She had grown up in a rural part of south-central France but seemed to be destined to become an actress from birth, with her parents naming her after Audrey Hepburn. After she graduated from university, Tautou's parents sent her to a renowned summer acting course in Paris, though she had wanted to be a painter. Tautou also thought about a career studying primates but decided to give herself one year as an actress to see if she could make it. "I thought,"

◄ Audrey Tautou and director Jean-Pierre Jeunet on the set of Amélie

she said, "'I don't want to keep doing this job, if this job doesn't want me.' I didn't want to spend all my life waiting for the phone to ring and living in a [small] apartment. There are too many other wonderful things to do in life."

During that one year, Audrey Tautou was cast in her first feature film, *Venus Beauty Institute* (1999), and it was on that poster where director Jean-Pierre Jeunet had first spotted her. British actress Emily Watson was already cast as Amélie, but her schedule was tricky, and Jeunet was worried about her French-speaking skills. Tautou ended up being the perfect choice, and her enchanting performance in Amélie led to many more opportunities, including a partnership with the fashion brand Chanel (and a role as its founding designer Coco Chanel in a movie) and being cast opposite Tom Hanks in *The Da Vinci Code* (2006). But Tautou felt she wasn't cut out for Hollywood, saying she wanted to "calm everything down" and that it "wasn't the way I want to live my life." Since then, Audrey Tautou has continued to act in movies in France, but has also managed to maintain a low profile, which suits her perfectly. "I didn't want to have this power," she said, in a very Amélie way. "I understand that nobody understands me, but I can't be someone I'm not."

It is so hard to make a nimble, charming comedy. So hard to get the tone right and find actors who embody charm instead of impersonating it. It takes so much confidence to dance on the tightrope of whimsy. *Amélie* takes those chances and gets away with them.

Roger Ebert, film critic

Ikiru

DIRECTED BY **Akira Kurosawa**

To watch when you . . . want to start the year with a film that will make you reflect on how you're spending your short time on this earth.

Japan, 1952
B&W, 143 minutes, Drama

Screenplay: Akira Kurosawa, Shinobu Hashimoto, Hideo Oguni

Starring: Takashi Shimura (Kanji Watanabe), Nobuo Kaneko (Mitsuo Watanabe), Miki Odagiri (Toyo Odagiri)

> "How beautiful! Truly beautiful. A sunset. I don't think I've really looked at one in 30 years."
>
> —Kanji

The title of the film *Ikiru* (1952) comes from a Japanese word meaning "to live." What exactly it means "to live" is an idea that writer/director Akira Kurosawa explores with this heartfelt film about a man who learns how to live only as he begins to die.

Akira Kurosawa had started his career in the Japanese film industry as an assistant director after studying Western art. He moved to directing his own films in the early 1940s, starting during World War II and continuing through to the American occupation of Japan. These events seeped into his films, and his work during the 1950s gained him international appreciation—particularly with *Rashomon* (1950), which won the major prize at the Venice Film Festival and the Academy Award for Best Foreign Language Film, and *Seven Samurai* (1954), the epic that became a major and enduring influence for filmmakers around the world.

In between, he made *Ikiru*, working for the first time with screenwriter Hideo Oguni—who would go on to be an important collaborator for Kurosawa. According to Oguni, Kurosawa had "wanted to write a story about a person who learns he is dying but finds something to live for in his last days."

The two used Leo Tolstoy's novel *The Death of Ivan Ilyich* for inspiration, and along with their other regular collaborator, writer Shinobu Hashimoto, the trio crafted a screenplay about a regular man named Kanji Watanabe (played by Takeshi Shimura). He is nearing retirement in his job as section chief of the Parks Department, a bureaucratic system full of red tape, where a group of women wanting a park for their children are sent around in a series of hopeless administrative circles.

▶ Takashi Shimura as Kanji Watanabe

Watanabe's son and a daughter-in-law are so focused on getting a share of Watanabe's retirement fund that they don't seem to notice their father's increasingly deteriorating health. His posture is permanently slumped, and he finds it difficult to eat anything but plain noodles. When he visits a doctor, he realizes he only has a few months to live.

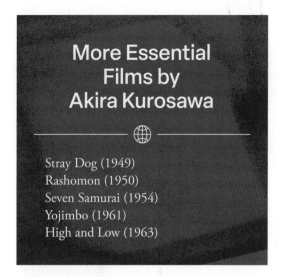

More Essential Films by Akira Kurosawa

Stray Dog (1949)
Rashomon (1950)
Seven Samurai (1954)
Yojimbo (1961)
High and Low (1963)

Watanabe goes through several stages before he accepts the fatality of his illness. He gets depressed and stops going to work. He decides to tell his son but abandons the idea when it becomes clear his son only wants to talk about money. He tries indulging in partying, drinking, and spending money frivolously. He meets up with a young worker from his office, finding her joyful youth infectious. Nothing works to improve his mental state until Watanabe decides to use his final few months (and his job position) to do some good for the community.

Through Watanabe's ordeal, Kurosawa examines the collapse of the family system and the failure of bureaucracy in postwar Japan, in addition to delivering a larger message about appreciating the gift of life—an important one for a country still hurting from the wounds of the war. It takes skill to craft a moral tale without making it feel like medicine, and Takeshi Shimura's mournful face grounds the film, giving the audience a glimpse into all the varied emotions he is silently dealing with. Kurosawa had worked with Shimura before this—including for his directorial debut, *Sanshiro Sugata* (1943)—and while Shimura would appear in many of Kurosawa's acclaimed movies, Watanabe in *Ikiru* would be his most famous role.

Akira Kurosawa's style of filmmaking made his work accessible for audiences outside of Japan. Author and Japanese historian Donald Richie once called Kurosawa "Japan's most Western director," and Kurosawa did have a keen interest in Western art—painting, literature, and American cowboy films. He also had a passion for Japanese folktales and wrote and directed movies with wide-ranging source material from William Shakespeare to Maxim Gorky. Kurosawa's body of work, his skill for directing action, plus his masterful use of framing and editing has led him to become one

▼ Director Akira Kurosawa

◀◀ Akira Kurosawa with fellow directors Francis Ford Coppola and George Lucas in 1980

◀ "How tragic that man can never realize how beautiful life is until he is face-to-face with death."
—Novelist

IKIRU **11**

▲ Mr. Watanabe surveys his good deed.

of the most revered filmmakers in the history of world cinema, and enduringly influential.

Case in point, in 2022: *Ikiru* was remade into the British film *Living*, which changed the setting to 1950s London, with Bill Nighy as the central character. The script was adapted by the acclaimed Japanese author Kazuo Ishiguro, who cited watching *Ikiru* as a child as being a formative artistic experience in his life. He thought it was particularly profound that Watanabe didn't need the wider public to know what he had done for the community, just the act of doing something of service was enough to bring him peace at the end of his life. "Public acclaim may be nice to have," Ishiguro said in an interview, "but, ultimately, it's not worth very much. It's treacherous, fickle, it's usually wrong . . . you've got to take a lonely private view of what is success and failure for you."

The reviews for *Ikiru* almost made it seem like the film was a failure, at least at first. Quite a few critics outside of Japan had objected to the last third of the movie, where the perspective suddenly shifts from following the living protagonist, to observing a wake after his death, where his colleagues debate over Watanabe's good deed. In his review for the *New York Times*, Bosley Crowther wrote that, "the last third of [the movie] is an odd sort of jumbled epilogue in which the charitable act of the deceased man is crudely deconstructed in a series of flashbacks that are intercut with the static action of a tedious funeral." Years later, in 1961, *Ikiru* was given the Golden Laurel Award, which had been created by the famed Hollywood producer David O. Selznick. One of Selznick's assistants had called Kurosawa to tell him about the honor, and added, "Mr. Selznick is of the opinion that it drags a bit, particularly during the funeral scenes. Don't you think we might shorten it a little?"

That perspective shift is a primary reason why *Ikiru* is now lauded as one of Akira Kurosawa's greatest films. Kanji Watanabe finds redemption in community service before his death, only to have his accomplishments questioned by his peers. Eventually, his colleagues realize the selfless act that Watanabe had made, and drunkenly vow to change their ways and do better for the people. This doesn't last long. It's a bittersweet, but realistic, end to Watanabe's tale.

This quiet movie with its critical look at Japanese bureaucracy may not fit with the view many have of Akira Kurosawa—that he was a director of period, samurai action films.

▲ Miki Odagiri as Toyo

But modern-day humanism is a theme that Kurosawa would often return to throughout his five-decade career. As he once said in an interview: "I suppose all of my films have a common theme. If I think about it, though, the only theme I can think of is really a question: Why can't people be happier together?"

Nothing will transcend the fatal X-rays but the sheer radiance of Watanabe's face as he finds belated purpose. Or as he starts to live: *Living* and *Doomed* are the usual English titles for *Ikiru,* and it speaks to the film's subtlety that Kurosawa lets us see them as nearly synonyms.

David Thomson, film critic and historian

Lady Snowblood

DIRECTED BY **Toshiya Fujita**

To watch when you . . . are thirsting for revenge (or a fun grindhouse movie).

Japan, 1973
Color, 97 minutes, Action

Screenplay: Norio Osada, based on
the comic by Kazuo Koike, illustrated
by Kazuo Kamimura

Starring: Meiko Kaji (Yuki Kashima),
Miyoko Akaza (Sayo Kashima), Toshio
Kurosawa (Ryūrei Ashio), Yoshiko Nakada
(Kobue Takemura)

> "Yuki, you will live your life carrying out my vendetta.
> My poor child . . . you are an asura demon."
>
> —Sayo

For inspiration while creating the revenge action thriller *Kill Bill*, director Quentin Tarantino dusted off his copies of a few films from Japan that had starred Meiko Kaji. "Not these beautiful, Technicolor restoration prints," he said in an interview, "but like, my seventh-generation bootlegs from New York's 42nd Chamber of Shao Lin in Times Square." Tarantino was inspired by two characters Kaji had played in the 1970s: one, a prisoner nicknamed "Scorpion" who was featured in a series of action films, and the other, Yuki, an assassin out for revenge in *Lady Snowblood* (1973) and its sequel, *Lady Snowblood 2: Love Song of Vengeance* (1974). Fans of Tarantino have likely heard about Lady Snowblood—its thumbprints are all over *Kill Bill*, albeit with Tarantino's own unique spin—and the multiple mentions of *Lady Snowblood* in interviews

and reviews of *Kill Bill* led to a resurgence in the popularity of the film.

Lady Snowblood started out as a Japanese manga comic book, written by Kazuo Koike, who had previously created the popular manga series *Lone Wolf and Cub*, about an assassin and his son. That series was adapted into a franchise of films in the early 1970s, and following that success, Koike wanted to make a new manga series with a female protagonist. "I'd created enough male assassins," he later said. He decided to write a violent story starring a female assassin, set during a time when women had no power. This character would be "beautiful outside, but a demon inside . . . a beautiful woman with a beautiful sword who turns cutting down people into an art." The fifty-one-issue series featured illustrations by Kazuo Kamimura, and was published in 1972 and 1973 under the

original title of *Shurayuki-hime*, which translates to *Snow White*.

Around that time, Meiko Kaji was becoming a popular actress in Japan. She had started her career at Nikkatsu, an old studio that had first established its reputation by producing period films. In the 1950s, to keep up with the times, the studio had moved into creating "Sun Tribe" (or youth rebellion) films, followed by its "Borderless Action" movies in the 1960s. This encompassed everything from hard-boiled yakuza gangster films to exploitation movies featuring sex and violence. Meiko Kaji had joined the studio in the mid-'60s and gained notice when she was cast in a few of Nikkatsu's *Stray Cat* movies—a wild franchise about a fierce girl gang. By the early 1970s, as audience numbers continued to decrease, Nikkatsu started to make "Roman Porn" (short for "Romantic Porn") films. Those movies were exactly as described, and that was the moment

when Meiko Kaji chose to leave Nikkatsu for its rival, Toei studios, to star in *Female Prisoner #701: Scorpion* (1972) and its subsequent sequels. Not long after that, producer Kikumaru Okada approached Kaji about playing Yuki in his independently produced *Lady Snowblood* adaptation. She was hesitant to say yes because she was tired of action films, but she was intrigued by Kazuo Koike's manga and the story arc of his female character; plus, she liked the idea of singing the theme song of the film, called "The Flower of Carnage" (which would later appear in *Kill Bill*). But what sealed the deal was the opportunity for Kaji to work again with Okada's choice of director for the movie, Toshiya Fujita, who had directed her in two *Stray Cat* films at Nikkatsu studios.

Film historians have noted that Toshiya Fujita was an odd choice to direct *Lady*

▲ Yuki wields her deadly sword.

▲ "All I know is violence." —Yuki

▲ Meiko Kaji as Yuki

Snowblood. Like Meiko Kaji, Fujita started his career at Nikkatsu, working as a publicist, a writer, and an assistant director before getting into the director's chair in 1967. He helmed several of Nikkatsu's youth-oriented films, including three movies featuring Kaji, and built up a reputation for making movies about teenagers feeling alienated from their parents. That was why he didn't seem like an obvious director for the action-packed *Lady Snowblood*, but he brought a stylistic visual flair that had not been seen in his previous movies. In an essay on *Lady Snowblood* for the Criterion Collection website, author Howard Hampton asks, "Can a hired gun also be a visionary—a visionary on demand?!" As Hampton went on to note, nothing in Toshiya Fujita's filmography before or after suggested the

"affinity for the abundant stylistic and attitudinal flourishes" seen in *Lady Snowblood*.

In a similar vein, the screenwriter that producer Kikumaru Okada hired was also not an obvious pick. Writer Norio Osada was a friend of director Toshiya Fujita, though their styles were, as Osada later said, like "oil and water." But Okada had a feeling that their contrasts would serve the film, and together they made bloody movie magic.

The story is set in the Meiji era, a period of great change in the country, as Japan moved away from its feudal past and transitioned into a restored imperial rule with Emperor Meiji in power. *Lady Snowblood* begins in 1874, the seventh year of this turbulent time in Japan, inside a women's prison where a prisoner named

More Japanese Manga Movies

⊕

Lone Wolf and Cub series (1972–1974)
Akira (1988)
Spirited Away (2001)
20th Century Boys series (2008–2009)
Our Little Sister (2015)

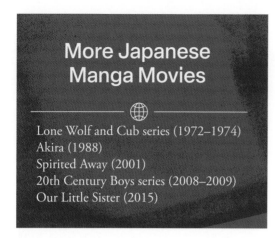

Sayo (Miyoko Akaza) has just given birth to a daughter in a snowstorm, and, of course, names the girl Yuki (meaning "Snow"). The film then flashes back and forth in time—to the present day, where the adult Yuki (Meiko Kaji) is an assassin out for revenge, and to the past, where we see the horrific event that happened to Sayo, explaining why Yuki is avenging her. There are also scenes of a child Yuki training with a master to become an assassin, and we learn that Yuki is not human; she is an "asura," or demon.

Yuki has a list of criminals she is hunting down, whom she is intending to kill, one by one. Her innocent look belies her true strength, and her demure parasol houses her weapon of choice—a sword—which she masterfully uses to dispose of her enemies, complete with great splashes of bright red blood that spurt wildly out of their bodies. Particularly effective are the droplets of red that explode in splashes over the white snow, like a violent work of art by Jackson Pollack. The action is directed as if it's a choreographed dance, with Kaji its elegant center, glaring at her foes with steely eyes before slashing them with her sword. There's also a meta-aspect to the film, with a character (Ryūrei, played by Toshio Kurosawa) creating a *Lady Snowblood* comic, telling Yuki's story in hand-drawn comic panels that flash on the screen as if they are storyboards from the movie.

▶ Miyoko Akaza as Yuki's mother, Sayo

The success of *Lady Snowblood* led to the sequel, *Lady Snowblood 2: Love Song of Vengeance*, which wrapped up Yuki's story. But with Quentin Tarantino's *Kill Bill: Vol. 1* and *Vol. 2,* her legacy lives on, with new generations ready to admire her violent beauty.

It's hard not to wonder—fantasize—about what other *Lady Snowblood* films might have been in store if the series had continued through further permutations. It could have made for a great franchise, like a more radical, quasi-feminist answer to the *Zatoichi* films . . . Yet the mystique these two movies bequeathed may be better: the image of a wraith moving silently down a castle hallway or tossing a corpse from a cliff into the sea, a figure to haunt our eternal art-grind-house dreams.

Howard Hampton, author

The Ascent

DIRECTED BY **Larisa Shepitko**

To watch when you . . . want to be awed
by a powerful and thoughtful war film.

Soviet Union, 1977
B&W, 109 minutes, War

Screenplay: Larisa Shepitko, Yuri Klepikov,
based on the novella by Vasil Bykov

Starring: Boris Plotnikov (Sotnikov),
Vladimir Gostyukhin (Rybak), Anatoly
Solonitsyn (Portnov)

> "I won't betray anyone. Not anyone. There are
> things more important than one's own hide."
>
> —Sotnikov

Director Larisa Shepitko was born in Ukraine in 1938, and following her parents' divorce, she moved to Moscow at the age of sixteen. She'd loved cinema for as long as she could remember and wanted to study at the famous Russian film school, the All-Russian State Institute of Cinematography. When she applied, the enrollment committee told her she should try acting instead, because directing was "too masculine a profession for a woman." But Shepitko was not going to change her mind and insisted that she wanted to be in the directing program. When she was finally accepted, she was the only female student in her class.

During her time at film school, Larisa Shepitko found an important mentor in one of the teachers, Alexander Dovzhenko. He was a Ukrainian filmmaker who was a pivotal figure within Soviet cinema history, working during the silent era alongside famed Russian movie pioneers Sergei Eisenstein (*Battleship Potemkin*, 1925) and Dziga Vertov (*Man with a Movie Camera*, 1929). Shepitko felt a special affinity with Dovzhenko because of their shared Ukrainian heritage and was inspired by the way he used emotion and symbolism in his movies.

Shepitko's determination to be a director was evident right from her graduation film, *Heat* (1963). This turned out to be an apt title—temperatures on the Kazakh steppe location soared to over 120 degrees Fahrenheit, causing film strips to melt. Shepitko fell dangerously sick but refused to quit, and continued to direct from a stretcher. One of the other students in her directing class was Elem Klimov, who helped the ill Shepitko finish *Heat*. He would go on to become internationally famous after releasing his searing, visceral war film *Come and See* (1985),

▸ Boris Plotnikov as Sotnikov

▲▲ "The important thing is to be true to yourself."
—Sotnikov

▲ Vladimir Gostyukhin as Rybak

which would influence Steven Spielberg's war movies *Saving Private Ryan* (1998) and *Schindler's List* (1993). Klimov became infatuated with Shepitko during film school and asked her to marry him several times. Finally, following *Heat*, she said yes—if he promised not to try and influence her work. They married in 1963, and both directors graduated film school to become part of a new generation of young Soviet filmmakers who reshaped Russian cinema post–World War II, along with Andrei Tarkovsky and Sergei Parajanov.

The first feature Larisa Shepitko directed after graduation was *Wings* (1966). This was a bold debut, about a decorated female World War II pilot struggling to adjust to regular life after the war. Around the time of the film's release, the Soviet Union came under the oppressive leadership of Leonid Brezhnev, who enacted a strict censorship of the arts, including literature and film. Shepitko didn't necessarily think of herself as a political filmmaker, but she was interested in exploring ideas about the effects of living under authoritarian rule—a subject she delved into more fully with her 1977 feature, *The Ascent*.

The screenplay, cowritten by Shepitko and Yuri Klepikov, was adapted from a novella by Russian author Vasil Bykov. The film begins as a group of refugees and Russian partisan soldiers flee from Germans in Nazi-occupied Belarus. Hiding in the woods, they realize they don't have enough food to survive, so the Army leader sends out two of his men to find more. These men are Sotnikov (Boris Plotnikov), a young, inexperienced soldier and former teacher who is frail and struggling with a cough. And Rybak (Vladimir Gostyukhin), an older, more experienced, and robust soldier. As they trudge hopelessly through knee-deep snow, they're fired upon by enemy soldiers, and Sotnikov is shot. Rybak does his best to try and help him, but soon, both soldiers are captured by the Nazis and taken to a prison, where they are tortured for information. There, they are faced with a tough choice, and each must decide what price they would be willing to pay to keep their life.

Just prior to making *The Ascent*, Larisa Shepitko and Elem Klimov had their first child, but due to difficulties with Shepitko's spine, she almost didn't survive giving birth. As she described it, "I saw death very closely . . . I could have died because I decided to keep the child. At that time, I was facing death for the first time, and like anyone in such a situation, I was looking for my own formula of immortality." This brush with death started her thinking about ideas of mortality and morality, and this was what she weaved into *The Ascent*, alongside her own childhood memories of the war.

▶ Sotnikov awaits his fate.

"The impression of global calamity," she said, "certainly left an indelible mark in my childhood mind." The shoot was grueling, with Shepitko again battling illness as they filmed in the snow, but she was aided by her crew, and remained determined to finish.

Shepitko's focus on the emotional aspect of the story elevates *The Ascent* from being merely a terrifying war movie to something more—a meditation on what it means to be human.

▲ Director Larisa Shepitko

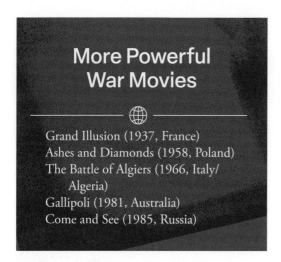

More Powerful War Movies

🌐

Grand Illusion (1937, France)
Ashes and Diamonds (1958, Poland)
The Battle of Algiers (1966, Italy/
   Algeria)
Gallipoli (1981, Australia)
Come and See (1985, Russia)

There's a spirituality to this film, especially as Sotnikov makes peace with his choice, and this is underscored by Shepitko's direction, where she uses dramatic lighting and many close-ups of Sotnikov's face. She also utilizes a handheld camera for the action scenes, and POV shots, where we see the perspective (and sometimes, the hallucinations) of the soldiers. This instinctively makes the viewer feel like we are there, deep in the chaotic madness of the war, freezing in the snow, a gun barrel pointed at our face, and given a horrific choice to either live (but condemn others to death) or die ourselves.

It's easy to see why *The Ascent* was called a masterpiece upon release, winning the prestigious Golden Bear award at the Berlin Film Festival. By that point, Larisa Shepitko was well-known within international film circles, where she cut a glamorous figure and was respected for her work. *The Ascent* took her to new heights of fame and acknowledgment, and her career looked like it was set to soar even higher. But throughout it all, she became preoccupied by death. She visited a fortune-teller in 1978, and afterward, asked her friend to promise that if anything were to happen to her, the friend would look out for her son.

Two years after the release of *The Ascent*, in 1979, Larisa Shepitko was on a location scout for her next movie, when she and five members of her crew were killed in a car accident. Shepitko's promising career was cut tragically short, and the Soviet film industry mourned the loss of such a talent. Following her funeral, director Andrei Tarkovsky reflected in his journal about the shock of her death, writing, "Larisa Shepitko was buried, and so were five members of her team. A car accident. All killed instantly. It was so sudden that no adrenaline was found in their blood." A week after her death, Shepitko's grieving husband, Elem Klimov, returned to her set to finish her film, *Farewell* (1983), and directed a documentary in her honor, titled simply, *Larisa* (1980).

In the years since she died, the name of Larisa Shepitko has become less known than that of her husband, or of her Soviet filmmaking contemporaries—but her work continues to be lauded within cinephile circles. Her list of credits is short, but her impact was enormous, and she poured her heart into every film, living by the motto of her mentor, Alexander Dovzhenko, who once told her: "You have to approach each film as if it were your last."

I see in *The Ascent* Shepitko's relentless search for the source of evil, as well as for the glimmers of divine reality that have not yet been annihilated. I imagine her beside her huge filmmaking instruments, seeking to find meaning in bodies and faces, and in the environment surrounding them—a drive to confront humanity in all its complexity.

Fanny Howe, poet and writer

Force Majeure

DIRECTED BY **Ruben Östlund**

To watch when you . . . feel like a clever comedy that will make you think.

Sweden, 2014
Color, 120 minutes, Comedy

Screenplay: Ruben Östlund

Starring: Johannes Kuhnke (Tomas), Lisa Loven Kongsli (Ebba), Clara Wettergren (Vera), Vincent Wettergren (Harry), Kristofer Hivju (Mats), Fanni Metelius (Fanny)

> ## "You grabbed your phone and your gloves and ran like hell away from me and the kids."
>
> —Ebba

Within a relatively short time, Swedish director Ruben Östlund has become famous for his unique ability to make an audience squirm. Not just by creating uncomfortable situations that you, as a viewer, want to look away from (and like a car crash, you find that you can't), but also by confronting us with the most difficult parts of ourselves. He creates realistic moral quandaries, making them comedic by showing how his characters react, but there's always a moment after watching Östlund's films when you consider what you would do in the same situation.

Perhaps none more so than his 2014 feature, *Force Majeure*. The story follows a Swedish family who take a skiing vacation to the French Alps. While eating lunch at their fancy resort, they see a controlled avalanche, and as it appears to get out of control, the father (Tomas, played by Johannes Kuhnke) runs for his life, taking his iPhone and gloves, but leaving his wife (Ebba, played by Lisa Loven Kongsli) and two kids, Vera (Clara Wettergren) and Harry (Vincent Wettergren), to fend for themselves.

This idea was born out of Östlund's previous career as a ski video director, and his fascination with human social behavior. His parents were both teachers, and his mother was interested in sociological experiments. With the invention of the home video camera, Östlund became curious about recording images, and being an avid skier, he started to take a camera out to the mountains. This became his career for several years—traveling the world in an endless winter to film skiing videos. After that, he chose to study film at the University of Gothenburg, where he had the opportunity to delve into a facet of social studies he was particularly intrigued by: how movies (and now, videos on social media) have changed behavior in the real world. As Östlund put it, he

▶ The happy family starts their skiing trip.

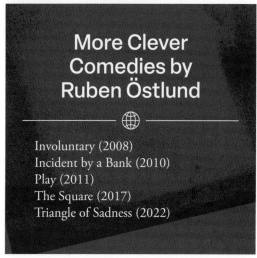

More Clever Comedies by Ruben Östlund

🌐

Involuntary (2008)
Incident by a Bank (2010)
Play (2011)
The Square (2017)
Triangle of Sadness (2022)

wanted to know if "reproduced cinema stereotypes actually inform behavior in reality."

Force Majeure was Ruben Östlund's fourth feature film, after making several short movies, and having two of his features—*Involuntary* (2008) and *Play* (2011)—chosen to screen at the Cannes Film Festival. In his research for *Force Majeure*, Östlund investigated statistics about how people react during and after a big, terrifying event. He found that married couples were more likely to get divorced after airplane hijackings and that more men survived shipwrecks, despite the belief that women and children should be saved first. This was interesting to Östlund—that men might not behave

▲ The avalanche comes. . . .

as bravely as we expect them to, or as they behave in the movies. "Even though we have a culture that teaches men to stand up and be loyal," Östlund said, "when it comes to survival instincts, men are the ones who have the actual ability to survive. I thought that was ironic, a horrifying fact to confront if you're a man, of course, but interesting at the same time." He also heard a story from a friend that seemed to corroborate this. His friend had been vacationing with his girlfriend when a gunman held up a store they were in, and his first instinct had been to leave his girlfriend and hide by himself. Östlund also watched a lot of videos on YouTube

for clues on human behavior, including a search for the "Worst Man Cry Ever" as inspiration for a pivotal scene in the film, and finding one video where a family was eating at a restaurant when an avalanche occurred. "I thought it was so interesting," he said, "to have those three seconds close together, two very different moods: the thing you want to experience, excitement,

and the thing you don't want to experience, fear of death."

How Tomas reacts to the same type of event in *Force Majeure* causes a rift in his family. His children look at him with suspicion because he's now the father who tried to save his own life over theirs. And his wife struggles with why Tomas refuses to own up to his actions.

Meanwhile, Tomas becomes convinced that he did not actually run away from his family, telling their visiting friends Mats (Kristofer Hivju) and Fanny (Fanni Metelius) exactly that. Until Ebba asks Tomas to show them the video, which he took on his phone, and he can't deny it any longer. "One of the most painful things for us humans," Östlund later said, "is to lose face in front of each other. We almost would rather die."

As the family deals with the aftershocks of the avalanche, there remains a feeling that at any moment another disaster could strike.

▲ Kristofer Hivju as Mats

Östlund increases the tension with an intense classical music score, sound effects, and the way he lingers on scenes just a little longer than is comfortable—so the viewer feels as if they should be waiting for something to happen. Most are red herrings, but this family goes through a lot on their vacation, from the avalanche to the uncomfortable conversations about Tomas's reaction, to a gondola swinging violently in the wind, a white-out snowstorm, a rogue drone, and an inept bus driver weaving madly down a steep, curved road. *Force Majeure* premiered at the Cannes Film Festival, where it won the Jury Prize.

▲ Director Ruben Östlund with his Palme d'or award at the 2017 Cannes Film Festival

who have won the award twice—alongside the American Francis Ford Coppola, the British Ken Loach, and one of Östlund's favorite directors, the Austrian master of the psychological drama, Michael Haneke.

What makes *Force Majeure* much more than a clinically accurate depiction of a middle-class marriage in crisis is its keen understanding of how, in modern civilization, people increasingly imagine that they can control nature. But what about human nature? No matter how well we talk the talk of technological mastery and rationality, there are crazy parts of us that remain beyond the reach of language to explain or resolve.

Stephen Holden, film critic

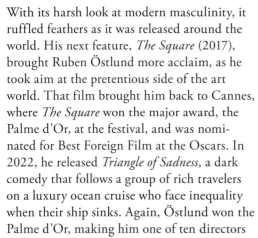

With its harsh look at modern masculinity, it ruffled feathers as it was released around the world. His next feature, *The Square* (2017), brought Ruben Östlund more acclaim, as he took aim at the pretentious side of the art world. That film brought him back to Cannes, where *The Square* won the major award, the Palme d'Or, at the festival, and was nominated for Best Foreign Film at the Oscars. In 2022, he released *Triangle of Sadness*, a dark comedy that follows a group of rich travelers on a luxury ocean cruise who face inequality when their ship sinks. Again, Östlund won the Palme d'Or, making him one of ten directors

The Girls

DIRECTED BY **Mai Zetterling**

To watch when you . . . are having an existential crisis in the dead of winter.

Sweden, 1968
B&W, 100 minutes, Drama

Screenplay: Mai Zetterling, David Hughes, based on a play by Aristophanes

Starring: Bibi Andersson (Liz), Harriet Andersson (Marianne), Gunnel Lindblom (Gunilla)

> ## "What? Yet another woman's revolt?"
>
> —Hugo

When *The Girls* was released in 1968, it was, as director Mai Zetterling wrote in her memoir, "a resounding flop." Audiences were simply not interested in it, and the film was removed from theaters within just three weeks, selling less than twenty-seven thousand tickets in Sweden. This commercial disaster was detrimental to Mai Zetterling's career—her next project was canceled, and she wouldn't have a theatrical movie released in Sweden for eighteen years. Film critics did not hold back with their vitriol toward the movie, particularly male critics. Swedish journalist Bo Strömstedt dismissed *The Girls* as "a case of clogged up menses," while another male reviewer suggested the film would have been better if it had focused on men.

War between men and women is at the center of *The Girls*, with the script by Mai Zetterling and David Hughes taking inspiration from Aristophanes's *Lysistrata*. Their story follows three actresses touring Sweden with a stage version of *Lysistrata*, and we see how the experience of playing their characters changes each of them in profound ways. Liz (Bibi Andersson) is at the center of it all, cast as the titular lead. She begins to take on a warrior role in her own life, pushing back at the suggestion that her husband's work is more important than her own, and refusing to turn a blind eye to his affairs. Marianne (Harriet Andersson) realizes through playing Myrrhine how her sexuality has been used by her older lover for his own pleasure, without committing to her. And Gunilla (Gunnel Lindblom), who plays Kleonike, starts to shed her passivity toward her husband, who hasn't bothered to understand who she really is.

Watching *The Girls* feels like witnessing a rally cry, one that is undoubtedly feminist in its message. The lives of these three women take center stage, while the male characters are caricatures—a Greek chorus who laugh at and demean the actresses from the sidelines. Mai Zetterling expertly uses images, editing, and

▲ Director Mai Zetterling speaking in 1973

sound design to blur fantasy with reality, taking the viewer into the inner thoughts of each of these women. Her filmmaking is self-assured and bold, and with her embrace of surrealism, it's easy to see Zetterling's appreciation for the work of Luis Buñuel, Federico Fellini, and Ingmar Bergman. But to pigeonhole *The Girls* as simply being a woman's picture is to do it a disservice, because alongside gender roles, Zetterling was also taking aim at the Swedish welfare state, and the needless violence of war.

This was also a personal film for Mai Zetterling, who had been an actress herself for twenty years before she'd begun to direct. She started her acting career as a child in her native Sweden, and at just seventeen, she was invited to join the prestigious National Theater. Her

first major film acting role was in the Swedish film *Torment* (also titled *Frenzy*) from 1944, and Zetterling's performance in the British movie *Frieda* (1947) won her a contract with the English production company, Rank Organisation. This arrangement ended up being a disappointment for Zetterling, who found herself cast in a series of roles she disliked. She was placed opposite bankable male stars, such as Dirk Bogarde, Richard Widmark, and Richard Attenborough, but her films still failed at the box office. She decided to give American cinema a try and starred with Danny Kaye in *Knock on Wood* (1954), but she quickly discovered she wasn't cut out for the Hollywood moviemaking machine.

After a brief (and highly publicized) romantic affair with her childhood idol, the actor Tyrone Power, Zetterling married British screenwriter David Hughes in 1958. By this time, she'd

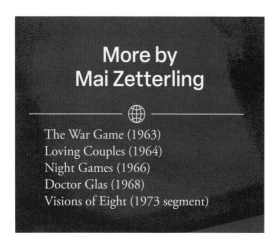

become increasingly frustrated with the roles she was given—typecast as suffering European war survivors or seductive Swedish sexpots—and decided she would change her career. Mai Zetterling made a plan for herself. Over the next five years, she would learn how to be a director.

"I gave up acting," Zetterling later explained, "because I was not a passive person." She challenged herself to learn the technical side of filmmaking, and began her directing career by helming a series of short documentaries for the BBC. Each of these focused on the plight of outsiders in Sweden, and her critical examination of her home country caused controversy. Her first narrative movie was *The War Game* (1963), a short film about two young boys who play a game that turns increasingly violent. *The War Game* was Zetterling's fifth short film, and after it won the Golden Lion award at the 1963 Venice Film Festival, she felt ready to take on her first feature-length movie. Over the course of the next four years, between 1964 and 1968, Zetterling would direct four features in Sweden, starting with *Loving Couples* and ending with *The Girls*. This would become known as her "Swedish Period" and was a moment in time that would bring her both soaring creative freedom and intense critical contention.

Loving Couples (1964) immediately established Zetterling as a confident and uncompromising director who was unafraid to ruffle feathers. Her choice to adapt a novel by Agnes von Krusenstjerna raised eyebrows—von Krusenstjerna was nicknamed "the Swedish Proust," but her frank depictions of sexuality led to a national debate about free speech. *Loving Couples* screened at the Cannes Film Festival, where it was in contention for the prestigious Palme d'Or award. American film critic Kenneth Tynan called it "one of the most ambitious debuts since *Citizen Kane*," but its poster (depicting naked bodies in intimate poses) was banned from being displayed.

After this controversial directorial debut, Zetterling felt that the public's opinion about her had changed. She was no longer the sweet, delicate Swedish actress they'd enjoyed on-screen, but a dangerously outspoken woman director. As she said, she was "not the same any more in the eyes of men," but thought that "the change I had made was positive, and, in the end, the only way." More scandal followed with her next film, *Night Games* (1966), where both the poster and the movie were banned from the Venice Film Festival—despite the poster being an anatomical drawing by the Italian artist Leonardo da Vinci. *Night Games* was also selected to play at a film festival in San Francisco, and Shirley Temple stepped down from her position on the festival's jury in protest, calling the film "pornography for profit" due to its depiction of child sexual abuse. But Zetterling was not a director who aimed to cause controversy simply for publicity's sake. She was determined to confront social taboos head-on, to "look them in the eye," because to ignore them would be more dangerous. Her hope was that her movies would stir up much-needed conversation about gender and class inequality, creating something tangible that her audience could take home with them.

That hope is echoed in *The Girls* by Liz, who, in one scene feels disillusioned with the theater's audience. She stands offstage, watching their faces as they passively sit in their seats, imagining them all to be asleep and snoring

▲ Harriet Andersson, Gunnel Lindblom, and Bibi Andersson in *The Girls*

loudly. At the end of the performance, after giving their bows, Liz strides to the center of the stage and tells the audience to sit back in their seats. She wants to have a dialogue, to hear their thoughts on the play and discuss the themes with them. The entire audience simply stares back at her, not saying a word, causing Liz to become increasingly distraught, while the other actors watch uncomfortably. Eventually,

one of the male actors steps in, stopping Liz from talking, and undermining her intention by making a joke, quipping to the audience, "What? Yet another woman's revolt?"

During the making of *The Girls*, Zetterling had paused production to direct her third feature, *Doctor Glas* (1968). This was to be the only Scandinavian film and the only female-directed movie to screen in competition at the 1968 Cannes Film Festival, but the festival was canceled during its second week. A group of film-makers, including Jean-Luc Godard and François

▲ Mai Zetterling during her acting days, in a publicity still for *Blackmailed* (1951)

Truffaut, had urged for this cancelation, wanting the festival to stand in solidarity with the rising civil unrest happening around the country.

A series of student protests over capitalism had become violent, escalating into riots, with more protests held, the trade unions getting involved, and nationwide strikes enacted. In Cannes, an emergency meeting was called, with Truffaut (who didn't have a film in competition that year) stating, "The radio announces by the hour that factories are occupied or closed. The trains have stopped, and the metro and the buses will be next. So, to announce every hour that the Cannes Film Festival continues is just ridiculous." Godard (also not in competition) said matter-of-factly, "We're talking solidarity with students and workers, and you're talking about dolly shots and close-ups. You're assholes." When Zetterling was allowed to talk, she was met with boos and cheers as she proposed the forming of a committee to make the final decision.

"It's about time that a woman speaks," she said. "You men have declared war, and emotions have conquered reason."

Doctor Glas suffered from the film festival's cancellation, and its box office was disappointing. Following the financial disaster of *The Girls*, Mai Zetterling's creative period in Sweden ended abruptly. But she kept on working, directing documentaries, television movies, and short films, as well as contributing to *Visions of Eight* (1973), an anthology documentary that also featured work by directors Arthur Penn, Miloš Forman, and Kon Ichikawa.

A few years after *The Girls* was released, it found a new life and an appreciative audience, thanks to the rise of second-wave feminism in the early 1970s. By that time Zetterling had also come to embrace the title of "feminist." Despite the provocative messages in her movies, she didn't call herself a feminist until the second wave, when she became a fearless voice for the rights of women in the arts. In 1972, *The Girls* was chosen to open the first International Festival of Women's Films in New York, and its reputation improved—lauded by female critics and established writers such as Simone de Beauvoir, who wrote about her admiration for the film for the French newspaper *Le Monde*. *The Girls* now ranks as the most famous of all of Mai Zetterling's films, and one of the most satisfying to watch.

One of its great qualities is that it doesn't confine us to any one theme, it doesn't lead to any conclusion, but without pointing out, it shows. Through a moment in the lives of three women, we sense what it means to be a woman.

Simone de Beauvoir,
author and feminist activist

In the Mood for Love

DIRECTED BY **Wong Kar Wai**

To watch when you . . . want to languish in the exquisite hopelessness of love.

Hong Kong, 2000
Color, 98 minutes, Romance

Screenplay: Wong Kar Wai

Starring: Tony Leung Chiu Wai (Mr. Chow),
Maggie Cheung Man Yuk (Mrs. Chan)

> "In the old days, if someone had a secret they didn't want to share, you know what they did? They went up a mountain, found a tree, carved a hole in it and whispered the secret into the hole. Then they covered it with mud . . . and left the secret there forever."
>
> —Mr. Chow

Regularly cited as one of the most romantic movies ever made, *In the Mood for Love* (2000) features two main characters who never kiss—or at least, we never see them kiss. It's a film all about restraint and constraint: the restraint they enact on themselves because of the moral constraint they feel from society. This intense suppression of emotions and actions, of keeping secrets hidden within, makes *In the Mood for Love* a highly seductive film.

Director Wong Kar Wai made *In the Mood for Love* as a loose sequel to his 1990 movie, *Days of Being Wild*, though there's little in continuity between the films—beyond the names of two characters. Maggie Cheung Man Yuk and Tony Leung Chiu Wai had appeared in *Days of Being Wild* as Su Li-Zhen and Chow Mo-wan, and in *In the Mood for Love*, their characters also share

those names. But they are different people. Here, Su Li-Zhen is referred to by her married name, Mrs. Chan. She is a secretary to an executive, married to Mr. Chan, a businessman who is constantly traveling. The setting is Hong Kong in 1962, a time that was special to Wong Kar Wai; he moved with his family to the country at around that time, aged five, and had observed his neighbors, who'd also moved from China, starting their own community, complete with their own rituals and their own gossip.

In the film, Mrs. and Mr. Chan rent a room from a well-meaning but nosy landlord; the room is next door to newspaper reporter Mr. Chow and his wife. Later, a question arises—was this planned by their other halves? Do they know each other? There are too many coincidences: Mrs. Chan has a handbag, gifted

▲▲ Tony Leung Chiu Wai and Maggie Cheung Man Yuk in *In the Mood for Love*

▲ "I didn't think you'd fall in love with me." —Mrs. Chan

▲ Maggie Cheung Man Yuk as Mrs. Chan

to her from her husband, which she notes to Mr. Chow is exactly the same as a new handbag Mrs. Chow is using. And Mr. Chow has a tie, picked by his wife, that is very similar to one that Mr. Chan wears to work. The realization that their spouses are having an affair slowly washes over them, and they wonder how it all started—role-playing various scenarios where their spouses meet. But soon, their role-plays start to feel true for them, too.

The silences, the looks that Mrs. Chan and Mr. Chan share, and the double meanings of their words become more important than what is explicitly said. So, too, is the framing of the couple. While the faces of their spouses

are never shown—they are shadowy, ambiguous figures—Mr. Chow and Mrs. Chan are captured in a frame within the frame. They are seen in the reflections of mirrors, through doorways and windows, contained in stairwells and corridors. In short, they are trapped, just like their burgeoning love, with gossip threatening to expose them, and their landlords watching carefully. Mr. Chow and Mrs. Chan decide to push their own happiness aside, saying, "We won't be like them," referring to their spouses.

As inspiration for his sets and costumes, art director, costume designer, and editor William Chang Suk Ping looked to the French doomed romance, *The Umbrellas of Cherbourg* (1964), particularly in the way director Jacques Demy had used bright colors to juxtapose with the

▲ Tony Leung Chiu Wai as Mr. Chow

melancholic tone. With *In the Mood for Love*, Chang Suk Ping wanted to selectively use vivid color, "to contrast," he said, "with the characters' restrained emotions." Mrs. Chan wears a series of brightly patterned, perfectly fitted cheongsam dresses, which stand out against her surroundings, suggesting there is more to this woman than just her roles as the demure wife and the polite secretary. It's hard not to notice the natural sensuality she possesses, especially during the multiple slow-motion scenes of Mrs. Chan walking to buy noodles for dinner. Director Wong Kar Wai and his cinematographers, Christopher Doyle and Mark Lee Ping Bing, use slow-motion beautifully, set to the haunting cello refrain of "Yumeji's Theme," and Nat King Cole singing a Spanish version of "Perhaps, Perhaps, Perhaps." These scenes

heighten the painful desire that is growing between Mrs. Chan and Mr. Chow—becoming a stand-in for the more traditional movie love scene—and are so exquisite to watch that even smoke billowing from Mr. Chow's cigarette

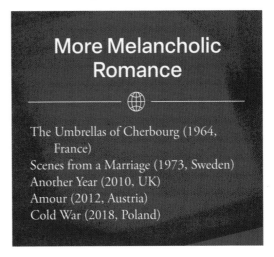

More Melancholic Romance

🌐

The Umbrellas of Cherbourg (1964, France)
Scenes from a Marriage (1973, Sweden)
Another Year (2010, UK)
Amour (2012, Austria)
Cold War (2018, Poland)

becomes mesmerizing. Wong Kar Wai did shoot a sex scene between Mrs. Chan and Mr. Chow but decided against using it.

In The Mood for Love was filmed over fifteen months, with a shooting schedule that ran over for several reasons, one being an economic crisis in Asia following the SARS virus outbreak. The original investors pulled out of the film, and Kar Wai began production for his next movie, *2046*, while trying to find new financiers. Key locations for *In the Mood for Love* were found in Bangkok, Thailand—since Hong Kong in the year 2000 looked very unlike the 1960s Hong Kong that Kar Wai needed.

The longer production schedule allowed for experimentation, with Maggie Cheung Man Yuk saying that she and Tony Leung Chiu Wai would often shoot their scenes a second time, with the dialogue reversed, just to see how it felt. Kar Wai had used a four-page Japanese story as the basis of his plot, and ended up filming so much footage that the movie could be thirty times the length of the final cut. The script was given to the actors a few pages at a time, and they were encouraged to improvise. Wong Kar Wai was grateful for the dedication of his stars, telling an interviewer, "It is exceptional for two Hong Kong actors to spend a year on one project, trying different things with us. For me, the biggest challenge for Tony and Maggie is, I told them, 'This film is not going to be verbal; you are not going to express yourself through dialogue. You have to express yourself through the body, your small gestures, your glances.'"

All the subtlety and ambiguity worked with audiences, and *In the Mood for Love* was well-received by critics around the world, playing at film festivals and picking up many awards—including Best Actor for Tony Leung Chiu Wai

▲ Director Wong Kar Wai joins cinematographer Christopher Doyle on the set of *In the Mood for Love*.

at the Cannes Film Festival. In the years since its release, the film has continued to grow in esteem, and now stands as one of the most romantic—and most beautiful—movies ever made.

This film is a sweet kiss blown to a time long since over, a time that may have existed only in the movies, with ballads recorded in mono while hand-sewn clothing lay perfectly over the bodies of stars.

Elvis Mitchell, film critic

Wings of Desire

DIRECTED BY **Wim Wenders**

To watch when you . . . need to believe in the beauty of humanity.

Germany, 1987
B&W and Color, 127 minutes, Fantasy

Screenplay: Wim Wenders, Peter Handke

Starring: Bruno Ganz (Damiel), Solveig Dommartin (Marion), Otto Sander (Cassiel), Curt Bois (Homer), Peter Falk (himself)

> "It would be rather nice coming home after a long day to feed the cat, like Philip Marlow. To have a fever and blackened fingers from the newspaper. To guess, instead of always knowing. To be able to say 'ah' and 'oh' and 'hey' instead of 'yea' and 'amen.' Or to feel how it is to take off shoes under a table and wriggle your toes barefoot, like that."
>
> —Damiel

At the end of *Wings of Desire* (1987), there is a dedication to several film-making "angels," namely Yasujirō Ozu, François Truffaut, and Andrei Tarkovsky. That director Wim Wenders thought to include this dedication proves his immense love of cinema, which has guided him throughout his career of making films in America, Japan, Europe, and his native Germany.

Wim Wenders was born in Düsseldorf, Germany, as Ernst Wilhem Wenders. Growing up in a Catholic house, he briefly entertained the idea of becoming a priest, but his interest in photography and obsession with American B movies, Westerns, and rock and roll led him in a different direction. While at film school in Munich, Wenders drew on his knowledge of Americana to inform his student films, and a few years after graduating, he made a trilogy of road movies directly inspired by American road films such as *Easy Rider*. His first English-language film, *The American Friend* (1977), gave him the opportunity to cast several filmmakers that he deeply admired, including the directors Samuel Fuller and Nicholas Ray. Wenders would go on to collaborate with Ray as the codirector of *Lightning over Water* (1980), a documentary about Nicholas Ray's career. And he would also direct films made with other cinema luminaries—Francis Ford Coppola

produced *Hammett* (1982), Michelangelo Antonioni starred in *Chambre 666* (1982), and Samuel Fuller acted (again) in *The State of Things* (1982). But the breakout film for Wenders came in the middle of his career with *Paris, Texas* (1984), his version of the American Western. This visually striking movie placed Wenders firmly on the cinematic map, and showed a trait that would continue to make his work successful—a unique ability to direct art house movies that were accessible to (and popular with) a wide audience.

After spending eight years in America, Wim Wenders decided to return home to Germany, choosing to live in Berlin. As he started to think about what this city represented to the world, he thought about the wall that divided the city into two, and the battle scars from the war that were still very much present. Berlin was haunted by its past and unable to move into the future while the wall remained in place; but as he walked around the city, Wenders couldn't help but notice all the statues that watched him from above. "I saw angels all over," Wenders said, "as monuments or sculptures or reliefs in public places, more than in any other city. I was really looking for a story that could help me to tell the city's story. I certainly didn't want to make a documentary about Berlin . . . Eventually my night reading

▲ Bruno Ganz as Damiel

being populated by angels, and the angels I photographed and encountered all over the city, led me to the realization that I wouldn't find any better characters for my project . . . the idea opened so many possibilities to look into so many different lives, because these angels could be anywhere. They could cross the bloody wall. They could meet anybody and be perfect witnesses of life in the city of Berlin."

Witnessing and observing is exactly what the angels do in *Wings of Desire*. To help create the script, Wenders contacted an esteemed writer, whom he called his "archangel," Peter Handke. He is an Austrian novelist, poet, and filmmaker who won the Nobel Prize for Literature in 2019, for his "influential work that with linguistic ingenuity has explored the periphery and the specificity of human experience." He was the perfect choice to shape Wenders's idea, though Wenders said that Handke didn't have time to write a script, so instead, they spent time talking about the story. Later, Wenders began to receive envelopes filled with suggestions for dialogue from Handke.

Wenders filled up multiple notebooks with thoughts and ideas and knew from the

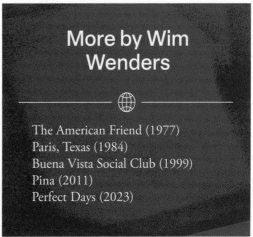

More by Wim Wenders

The American Friend (1977)
Paris, Texas (1984)
Buena Vista Social Club (1999)
Pina (2011)
Perfect Days (2023)

film in black-and-white, because it made sense to him that angels wouldn't know what colors are. He started filming before working out the finer details, trusting that the movie would reveal itself, and knowing he had a veteran cinematographer by his side who could make magic happen. That was Henri Alekan, the legendary cinematographer and director who had photographed the lush French fairy tale *Beauty and the Beast* (1946), directed by Jean Cocteau.

The story follows Damiel and Cassiel as they roam Berlin, listening to everyday people and their worries. They can't change the outcome for them, but just by bearing witness to their struggles, they offer unseen comfort. By observing and listening, the angels show unconditional and nonjudgmental love to those around them, but soon Damiel starts to get involved with a trapeze artist named Marion, and longs to become human, so he can properly love her.

start who he wanted to cast as the three main characters: Bruno Ganz as the angel Damiel, Otto Sander as the angel Cassiel, and Solveig Dommartin as the human, Marion. Photos of the three actors hung on his wall while writing, and Wenders also decided to shoot most of the

The only humans that can see (or sense) the angels are children and the Hollywood actor Peter Falk, who plays himself. Wim Wenders wanted to have a notable figure playing themself in the film and had thought of using a novelist or a painter. He asked his assistant director, Claire Denis (who would become an acclaimed

▲▲ Peter Falk talks to an angel in *Wings of Desire*.
▲ Otto Sander as Cassiel

director in her own right), for suggestions, and she thought of Peter Falk. He was well-known at the time as the star of the TV show *Columbo*, but Denis had admired him in the films he made with John Cassavetes and Elaine May. Those movies had required improvisation, so Falk was not worried about the lack of a finished script. He and Wenders spent a weekend getting to know each other, and Falk improvised dialogue, with Wenders also encouraging him to sketch the actors around him—as he often did in real life.

When it was released, *Wings of Desire* became a smashing success—much more than was expected from an art house movie. The striking visuals, cool soundtrack (including the band Nick Cave and the Bad Seeds, who appear in the film), and the theme of finding beauty in everyday life moved audiences around the world. It was also popular in Germany, where moviegoers appreciated Wenders setting the film in Berlin, showing the city as it was in 1987, and intercutting that with archival footage from World War II. Just two years after *Wings of Desire*, Berlin would change again when the wall was finally taken down. Wim Wenders won Best Director at the Cannes Film Festival for *Wings of Desire*, and went on to direct a sequel, called *Faraway, So Close* (1993). Hollywood also remade *Wings of Desire* in 1998, under the title *City of Angels*, starring Meg Ryan and Nicolas Cage.

Wings of Desire was a different film for Wim Wenders, who was known for being part of the New German Cinema movement. This had started in 1962, when several German filmmakers, such as Alexander Kluge, Haro Senft, and Edgar Reitz, created the Oberhausen Manifesto, declaring, "The old film is dead. We believe in the new one." They were advocating for a new type of cinema language, becoming tired of the postwar films in Germany, which were conventional and had lost their political bite. This movement lasted from the 1960s into the 1980s and gave birth to several exciting new talents—such as Rainer Werner Fassbinder, Werner Herzog, Margarethe von Trotta, and Wim Wenders.

▲ Director Wim Wenders and Peter Falk talk on the set of *Wings of Desire*.

Wenders had something of Frank Capra or Powell and Pressburger with this tale of benevolent angels, and also something of Marcel Carné or even T. S. Eliot's "The Waste Land." Perhaps *Wings of Desire* has dated a little, but it is a cinema of ideas, almost an essay movie, and utterly distinctive.

Peter Bradshaw, film critic

Jeanne Dielman, 23 Commerce Quay, 1080 Brussels

DIRECTED BY **Chantal Akerman**

To watch when you . . . can put aside all distractions
and be absorbed into a mesmerizing film.

Belgium/France, 1975
Color, 201 minutes, Drama

Screenplay: Chantal Akerman

Starring: Delphine Seyrig (Jeanne
Dielman), Jan Decorte (Sylvain Dielman)

"Life with my aunts was dull. I didn't feel like getting married,
but it seemed to be 'the thing to do,' as they say. My aunts
kept saying, 'He's nice. He's got money. He'll make you happy.'
But I still couldn't decide. But I really wanted a life of my own,
and a child. Then his business suddenly hit the rocks, so I
married him. Things like that happened after the war."

—Jeanne Dielman

Once a decade since 1952, *Sight and Sound* magazine has published a list of the "Greatest Films of All Time." The one hundred listed movies are decided by a poll, with more than one thousand film critics, filmmakers, academics, curators, distributors, writers, and archivists participating from all over the world. For fifty years straight, *Citizen Kane* (1941), directed by Orson Welles, held the top spot, but dropped down to number two in 2002 and 2012, with Alfred Hitchcock's *Vertigo* (1958) taking number one. In 2022, all of this changed. *Vertigo* was pushed to number two and *Citizen Kane* to number three, with a little-known movie made by a female director jumping from its number thirty-six place in the 2012 poll to being named the Greatest Film of All Time in 2022.

That film was *Jeanne Dielman, 23 Commerce Quay, 1080 Brussels* (1975), directed by Chantal Akerman. It's a three-hour meditation on the domestic work of women, a mesmerizing study of time, and the type of movie that was—for many years following its successful initial release—known within academic spheres but not widely outside of them. *Jeanne*

Dielman's place at the top of the respected *Sight and Sound* poll was the first time that a female director had held the number one spot, and marked the change that has happened over the past few decades, as critics have begun to consider movies made by women more

▲ Delphine Seyrig as Jeanne Dielman

seriously. As film scholar Laura Mulvey said of the results, "The arrival of *Jeanne Dielman* at the top of the 2022 *Sight and Sound* poll signals an amazing shift in critical taste. Given the status of the poll, the film will attract a new audience, drawn, first, by curiosity to this latest addition to the list of great films in cinema history; and then, held enthralled by the

extraordinary daring cinema of a great woman director."

The film itself is simple, at least on the surface. The story follows a single mother named Jeanne Dielman (Delphine Seyrig), as she goes about her life over the course of three days. On the first day, we see that Jeanne is a meticulously neat woman. Her hair is perfectly coiffed, everything in her apartment has its place, and she moves about her space with

▲ On day three, Jeanne's routine is off.

mechanical precision. Jeanne's routine is quickly established within the first two days: She wakes her son Sylvain (Jan Decorte) for breakfast, visits the grocery store, cleans her apartment, prepares dinner, and while the potatoes are boiling, she accepts clients for her job as a sex worker.

On the second day, something happens inside her bedroom with one of her clients. We don't see exactly what it was, but when Jeanne returns, there is a sense that something is wrong.

Her hair is mussed, she forgets to turn on a light, and overcooks her potatoes—staggering from room to room holding the pot, unsure of what to do. Day three becomes more chaotic for Jeanne, and there are several moments when she sits and just stares, blankly. She is a woman who likes to be in control, and the film ends with Jeanne taking drastic action to get that control back.

▲ Jeanne goes about her daily routine, peeling potatoes.

▲ Director Chantal Akerman in 1976

Jeanne Dielman is worthy of being called "the Greatest Film of All Time," but it is also a demanding watch, requiring complete and unwavering attention. Chantal Akerman uses minimal cuts, with long takes that show Jeanne doing everyday tasks, such as peeling her potatoes and washing dishes. Her camera is fixed, there are no close-ups or reverse angles, and the shots are never voyeuristic, with Akerman explaining that she wanted her framing to "respect [Jeanne's] space, her, and her gestures within it." This slow pace will test the patience of many viewers, but this film can't be understood if caught in glances while also looking at a phone. The experience is not unlike viewing a video piece in an art museum—you need to give yourself over to fully appreciate it. Modern-day audiences used to quick edits and wall-to-wall action might feel uncomfortable at first, willing something—anything—to happen. But the pace allows Akerman to introduce viewers to Jeanne's world, letting them become absorbed in the details of her routine. The action is so understated for much of the movie, that when slight changes start to happen, the shift feels seismic.

Chantal Akerman was born in Brussels in 1950 to a Jewish family that had suffered greatly during the war. Her mother and grandparents had been sent to Auschwitz, with only her mother, Natalia, returning. Natalia and Chantal forged a close relationship over their lives, with Natalia appearing in some of Chantal's movies, and Chantal once described *Jeanne Dielman*

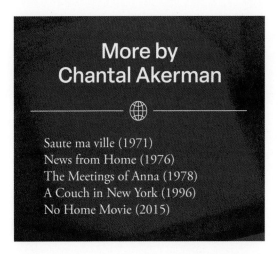

as a love letter to her mother. As she said, she wanted to elevate a woman's domestic work to high art, explaining, "I do think it's a feminist film because I give space to things which were never, almost never, shown in that way, like the daily gestures of a woman. They are the lowest in the hierarchy of film images. A kiss or a car crash come higher, and I don't think that's accidental. It's because these are women's gestures that they count for so little."

At the age of fifteen, Chantal Akerman had decided she wanted to be filmmaker after watching Jean-Luc Godard's *Pierrot le Fou* (1965), and she began to study at film school, but being eager to start making movies, she dropped out after only a few months. One of her first features was the experimental documentary *Hotel Monterey* (1972), and it was during a screening of that movie at a festival when Akerman met the actress Delphine Seyrig. She cast Seyrig as the lead in her next feature, *Jeanne Dielman, 23 Commerce Quay, 1080 Brussels*. The budget was small, with a crew made up almost entirely of women, and the movie became an unexpected success. It premiered at the 1975 Cannes Film Festival, and the twenty-five-year-old Akerman found herself at the center of great acclaim, with the *New York Times* calling her film the "first masterpiece of the feminine in the history of the cinema."

Akerman was uncomfortable with such high praise and found the success of *Jeanne Dielman* difficult to live up to. She felt pressure not to repeat herself, going on to make movies in all different genres—including *No Home Movie* (2015), a documentary that featured conversations with her mother, recorded shortly before Natalia passed away in 2014. Chantal Akerman had a hard time recovering from her mother's death. As she grieved, she also struggled with depression, and eventually took her own life in 2015 at the age of sixty-five. Her life was tragically cut short, but her work continues to influence filmmakers today. Perhaps Nicola Mazzanti, the director of the Royal Belgian Film Archive, summed up her legacy the best, when she said about Chantal Akerman, "There are filmmakers who are good, filmmakers who are great, filmmakers who are in film history. And then there are a few filmmakers who change film history."

Chantal Akerman's unwavering and completely luminous adherence to a female perspective (embedded in the film itself and its director's vision) combined with her uncompromising and completely coherent cinema to produce a film that was both feminist and cinematically radical. One might say that it felt as though there was a before and an after *Jeanne Dielman*, just as there had once been a before and after *Citizen Kane*.

Laura Mulvey, film theorist

SPRING

Ali: Fear Eats the Soul

DIRECTED BY **Rainer Werner Fassbinder**

To watch when you . . . feel like watching a romantic
film that is not predictable or formulaic.

Germany, 1974
Color, 92 minutes, Romance

Screenplay: Rainer Werner Fassbinder

Starring: Brigitte Mira (Emmi), El Hedi ben
Salem (Ali), Irm Hermann (Krista). Rainer
Werner Fassbinder (Eugen)

"Fear eat soul."

—Ali

Director Rainer Werner Fassbinder made a huge impact on postwar German and world cinema. He once said: "I'd like to be for cinema what Shakespeare was for theatre, Marx for politics and Freud for psychology: someone after whom nothing is as it used to be." And while he may have said that jokingly, it wasn't far from what would happen. Because, as soon as Fassbinder started making movies, he did not slow down, becoming instantly prolific and directing around thirty-five feature films across all different genres between 1969 and 1982. He also directed TV shows, TV miniseries, made-for-TV movies, plays, and short films, and he helped on film projects with other directors. Fassbinder had a keen interest in exploring themes of oppression, and his socially conscious movies tackled difficult subjects head-on. Sadly, this breakneck pace would catch up to him, and his heart gave out at the age of thirty-six, after years of abusing drugs and alcohol.

What he left behind was a wealth of challenging films, written by, directed by, produced by, and often starring himself. Fassbinder had started juggling these multiple roles right from the beginning. When he was sixteen, he left school to join an avant-garde theater troupe in Munich, where he wrote, directed, and acted in their productions. After just two months, he was named the company's director, and being a naturally subversive individual, Fassbinder renamed it, calling it an "anti-theater" company, and produced many controversial and political plays. The troupe of actors all lived together, and a few would go on to star in Fassbinder's movies. Directing movies was always his goal, and in 1969, Fassbinder made his feature film directorial debut with *Love Is Colder Than Death*.

After that, he was off to the races, directing multiple movies a year, with his initial style being inspired by the French filmmakers Jean-Luc Godard and Jean-Marie Straub, and the German playwright Bertolt Brecht. Though praised by critics, Fassbinder's early films failed to connect with audiences. But in

1971, Fassbinder had a life-changing experience when he met the German American director Douglas Sirk at the Munich Film Museum. Sirk had made a series of successful melodramas for Hollywood in the 1950s, which had been derided at the time as being "weepies" and "women's pictures." It took many years for his lush movies to be taken seriously by film scholars, but he was hugely influential for many directors, including the American Todd Haynes and Rainer Werner Fassbinder. For Fassbinder, meeting Sirk and watching six of his films, "removed the fear I had of 'selling out,'" he said. "Sirk gave me the courage to make films for the public. Before that I believed that serious work meant shunning the Hollywood model . . . but Sirk, no matter how one regards his films, made me understand that it was possible to pursue this path." Fassbinder also wrote an essay about his appreciation for the films he had seen at the

▲ Brigitte Mira as Emmi and El Hedi ben Salem as Ali

▲ "When we're together, we must be nice to each other. Otherwise, life's not worth living." —Emmi

▼ Irm Hermann and Rainer Werner Fassbinder in *Ali: Fear Eats the Soul*

museum, writing, "Sirk has made the tenderest films I know, they are the films of someone who loves people."

Douglas Sirk was a master at creating films that looked beautiful on the surface, but tackled real social issues underneath. *All That Heaven Allows* (1955) was about a wealthy widow whose love affair with a younger working-class man caused scandal in her small town, while *Imitation of Life* (1959) examined race relations. Fassbinder combined those two themes for *Ali: Fear Eats the Soul* (1974), which became the first of his movies to bring him international critical acclaim. His screenplay follows an older German widow, named Emmi (Brigitte Mira), whose children have all married, leaving her alone and lonely. She finds comfort in a younger Moroccan immigrant, who is known as Ali (El Hedi ben Salem), and quickly, the two decide to get married. This union shocks her family, including her daughter Krista (Irm Hermann) and Krista's husband (played by Rainer Werner Fassbinder). Emmi's neighbors and coworkers are also not supportive, and the pressure on the couple builds as the people around them reveal their intolerance and racism.

Ali: Fear Eats the Soul is obviously inspired by Douglas Sirk's *All That Heaven Allows*, and what Fassbinder had written about Sirk's film rings true here: "This is the kind of thing Douglas Sirk makes movies about. People can't live alone, but they can't live together either. This is why his movies are so desperate." But this is not a copy of Douglas Sirk or a remake of *All That Heaven Allows*. Rainer Werner Fassbinder made the idea his own, updating the story to involve a much more complex relationship between Emmi and Ali, and placing it in 1970s Germany—where tensions around immigrants and foreign workers were running high, and the Munich massacre was still fresh in everyone's minds. That was the deadly attack that happened during the 1972 Olympics, where a Palestinian terrorist group killed members of the Israeli

More Essential Fassbinder Films

🌐

The Bitter Tears of Petra von Kant
(1972)
World on a Wire (1973)
Fox and His Friends (1975)
Lola (1981)
Veronika Voss (1982)

▲ Director Rainer Werner Fassbinder

Olympic team. Fassbinder had also been inspired by a story one of his characters had told in his earlier movie, *The American Soldier* (1970). In that film, a hotel maid talks about a cleaning woman named Emmi, who had a relationship with a Turkish immigrant named Ali, but later was found strangled to death, the letter *A* imprinted into her throat from a signet ring. Fassbinder took the names from that story but explained that he wanted to give the couple more hope. "I want to give the young Turk and the old German the chance to live together," he said. "Now I'm more interested in showing the ways people can resist and how they manage in spite of everything."

Ali: Fear Eats the Soul is an emotional film, somewhat of an outlier in Fassbinder's work. Fassbinder himself could be volatile and difficult, with his personal and sexual relationships being described as violent and sometimes abusive. Many of his movies explore ideas of the immense cruelty humans can inflict on each other, but in *Ali: Fear Eats the Soul*, he shows compassion toward Emmi and Ali, making the audience feel the unfairness of their situation and desperately wish they could live happily ever after. But Rainer Werner Fassbinder was always a realistic filmmaker, and he declares his intention in the opening titles of *Ali: Fear Eats the Soul*, with a title card that simply reads: "Happiness is not always fun." You have been warned.

> Both a wonderful demonstration of how film form creates meaning—the isolating framing and composition, the deliberately stiff performance style—and a moving, unusual, odd-couple romance that highlights the hypocrisies and prejudices of society. This reworking of Douglas Sirk's *All That Heaven Allows* manages to be both more emotionally involving (while somehow remaining detached) and much bleaker than the original.
>
> David Morrison, cinematographer

Bicycle Thieves

DIRECTED BY **Vittorio De Sica**

To watch when you . . . feel like having a good ol' cathartic cry.

Italy, 1948
B&W, 89 minutes, Drama

Starring: Lamberto Maggiorani (Antonio), Lianella Carell (Maria), Enzo Staiola (Bruno)

Screenplay: Vittorio De Sica, Cesare Zavattini, Suso Cecchi D'Amico, Gerardo Guerrieri, based on a novel by Luigi Bartolini

"I've been cursed since the day I was born."

—Antonio

Considering the amount of influence the Italian Neorealism cinematic movement has had on world cinema, it's surprising that it only lasted roughly ten years. The movement sprung up in the mid-1940s in postwar Italy, when filmmakers took their cameras out of the studios and into the bombed-out streets. They wanted to move away from simple escapism, to capture the real struggles working-class Italians were facing following the war. There had also been criticism leveled at the Italian film industry: Their commercial movies had no style of their own; they were simply copying American movies. All this led to a burst of innovation and creativity, as a group of directors decided to strive for authenticity, often casting first-time actors in lead roles.

The vital creative forces within the Italian Neorealism movement included Roberto Rossellini (*Rome, Open City*), Federico Fellini (*La Strada*), Luchino Visconti (*La Terra Trema*),

and Vittorio De Sica (*Bicycle Thieves*). De Sica had been an actor before he started directing, and made his film debut while he was still a teenager. Quite quickly, he proved himself in his own country to be a talented actor, with enough romantic charm to rival Hollywood's Cary Grant. De Sica would continue to act in films until the end of his life, but in 1940, he turned to directing, and after the war, his movies reflected the personal and collective pain of the Italian people—especially in his neorealist films *Shoeshine* (1946), *Bicycle Thieves* (1948), *Miracle in Milan* (1951), and *Umberto D.* (1952).

For *Bicycle Thieves*, De Sica worked with his frequent collaborator, the screenwriter Cesare Zavattini, who had approached him with a novel written by Luigi Bartolini. Zavattini thought they could turn it into something, and the two worked with a few screenwriters to adapt the book into a screenplay. Their story follows a father named Antonio (Lamberto

Maggiorani). He is desperate to provide for his family and eagerly accepts a job pasting posters on walls around Rome. A bicycle is needed, so Antonio pawns his family's linen collection to get one, but on his first day of work, his bike is stolen. This is a devastating event for Antonio, who can't afford to buy a new bike, or to lose his job. Frantically searching the city to find it, Antonio is joined by his young son, Bruno (Enzo Staiola), and slowly becomes willing to do just about anything to get his bicycle back.

When Vittorio De Sica was looking to finance *Bicycle Thieves*, he had approached the Hollywood producer David O. Selznick. Selznick was interested but told De Sica he would only give him the money if he cast Cary Grant in the lead as Antonio. It's difficult to imagine the suave Grant playing the desperate Antonio, and De Sica said no, because he wanted to use first-time actors. De Sica was

▲ First-time actor Lamberto Maggiorani as Antonio

looking for everyday men and women who would be believable in these roles, and in his search, he discovered Lamberto Maggiorani. He was a thirty-nine-year-old steelworker who had never acted before—and had no plans to—but had been spotted by De Sica when Maggiorani had brought his son to the auditions.

Maggiorani had hoped his son would be cast as Bruno in the film, but he ended up with the lead role himself. He accepted though he was anxious about acting, and was incredibly nervous and shy on the set. That was exactly what De Sica had wanted, knowing that Maggiorani's anxiety would translate as the anguish Antonio feels over his stolen bike. De Sica had thought that Maggiorani was perfect, because of "the way he moved, the way he sat down, his gestures with his hands hardened by work. He had the hands of a working man, not an actor." And De Sica's own experience as an actor helped him while directing Maggiorani, noting, "The man in the street, particularly if he is directed by

▲ Antonio's search for his stolen bicycle seems impossible.

◀ Enzo Staiola as Bruno

someone who is himself an actor, is raw material that can be molded at will."

In the end, the hardest part to cast in *Bicycle Thieves* wasn't the lead, but the role of Antonio's son, Bruno. By the time production began, Vittorio De Sica still hadn't found the right child for the part. One day, while filming on the real streets of Rome, De Sica spotted a boy among the hordes of people who had gathered to watch. "I turned around in annoyance at the onlookers who were crowding around me," De Sica said, "and saw an odd-looking child with a round face, a big funny nose and

wonderful lively eyes." That was Enzo Staiola, who was nine at the time and was the perfect choice for Bruno, with his beautifully expressive face becoming the emotional heart of the movie.

Even though *Bicycle Thieves* was filmed with nonprofessional actors and on real locations, Vittorio De Sica had carefully planned and directed the film, and unlike some of the Italian neorealist films, there was no improvisation involved. The movie had a larger budget

▲ Lamberto Maggiorani and Enzo Staiola in *Bicycle Thieves*

▲ "You live and you suffer." —Antonio

More to Explore in Italian Neorealism

⊕

Ossessione (1943)
Rome, Open City (1945)
La Terra Trema (1948)
Bitter Rice (1949)
La Strada (1954)

than most others from the movement, and a big crew of paid professionals and volunteers. Amongst those volunteers was a young Sergio Leone, who would go on to become a pioneer himself in the subgenre of the Spaghetti Western—directing Clint Eastwood in *A Fistful of Dollars* (1964), *For a Few Dollars More* (1965), and *The Good, the Bad and the Ugly* (1966). When Leone joined the crew of *Bicycle Thieves,* he was sixteen, and De Sica talked him into being an extra—he plays a priest who takes shelter from a storm next to Antonio.

    Bicycle Thieves was received enthusiastically by critics at film festivals around the world. When it came to the United States, its screenplay was nominated for an Academy Award and was given an honorary Oscar for Best Foreign

▲ Director Vittorio De Sica

Film. For this American release, the movie was given the title *The Bicycle Thief*. Many historians still refer to the film as this, but the original title of *Bicycle Thieves* fits better with Vittorio De Sica's intention for the film. He wasn't making a movie about one bicycle being stolen by one thief; he was showing the lengths that all humans will go to in order to survive.

By the mid-1950s, the Italian Neorealism movement had waned, with directors like Federico Fellini further adapting the style into something more fanciful and audiences gravitating to stories with optimism. Italian cinema also needed to compete with Hollywood movies, which returned to screen in the country after the war, and even Vittorio De Sica started directing movies that had more commercial appeal. But the influence of neorealism would be felt for decades to come, inspiring the French New Wave in the 1960s, as well as young Italian filmmakers like Ermanno Olmi. With his film *Il Posto* (1961), Olmi built upon the style of Italian Neorealism, using a first-time actor and real locations; but making it modern, focusing on the alienation young people were feeling in the 1960s. In the end, as Federico Fellini reportedly said, "For Italian cinema, neorealism was just the beginning."

During the course of its telling in the brilliant director's trenchant style, it is full and electric and compelling as any plot-laden drama you ever saw. Every incident, every detail of the frantic and futile hunt is a taut and exciting adventure, in which hope is balanced against despair.

Bosley Crowther, film critic

My Brilliant Career

DIRECTED BY **Gillian Armstrong**

To watch when you . . . need some inspiration to chase your dreams.

Australia, 1979
Color, 100 minutes, Drama

Screenplay: Eleanor Witcombe, based on a novel by Miles Franklin

Starring: Judy Davis (Sybylla Melvyn), Sam Neill (Harry Beecham), Wendy Hughes (Aunt Helen)

"Gertie, don't you ever dream that there's more to life than this? Don't you want to meet people who talk about books and words and have visions? I can't settle for a new dress, a picnic, now and then, living out in the bush for the rest of my life. I might just as well be dead."

—Sybylla

The title *My Brilliant Career* could describe director Gillian Armstrong. With this 1979 feature film, she kickstarted her own brilliant career, and became the first female director to make a movie in Australia in around fifty years. Armstrong was part of the first class from a new national film school, established to reinvigorate the local film industry in Australia, which had virtually ground to a halt. After graduation, she made several short films, and worked as an assistant to filmmaker Fred Schepisi. One of Armstrong's shorts, *The Singer and the Dancer* (1977), had caught the attention of producer Margaret Fink, who had recently discovered the novel *My Brilliant Career* when it was republished in 1965. Fink had considered asking Roman Polanski to direct, but once she met Gillian Armstrong, she knew Armstrong was the right director to bring the book to the big screen.

Author Miles Franklin was really Stella Maria Sarah Miles Franklin, a young woman who was twenty when she first published *My Brilliant Career* in 1901. She had completed the book in 1899, but it took two years before she found a publisher who would take it on. Franklin's work caused controversy in her native Australia, because of her focus on unruly women rejecting society's traditional roles. Screenwriter Eleanor Witcombe was brought on to adapt Franklin's book for Armstrong's film, and even in 1979, Franklin's story still felt revolutionary. The script follows Sybylla Melvyn, a headstrong young woman with wild red hair and a twinkle

▲ Judy Davis as Sybylla

in her eye, living in rural Australia around the turn of the twentieth century. Like all young women, she is expected to marry, and she seems to fall in love with a good prospect—a handsome property owner named Harry Beecham (played by Sam Neill). But Sybylla is determined to have a brilliant career as a writer, or an opera singer, or a pianist, anything other than just being a wife. She chooses independence and self-discovery over marriage, and as the character narrates at the start of the film, this is "the story of my career,

my brilliant career. I make no apologies for being egotistical because I am."

Judy Davis plays Sybylla in only her second film role, and her first as the lead. Armstrong had to push to cast the relative newcomer, but Davis more than proved herself, giving a tour-de-force performance that earned her worldwide attention. You could say that with this film, Davis also launched her own "brilliant career"—one that is continuing and includes two Oscar nominations to date, for *Husbands and Wives* (1992) and *A Passage to India* (1985).

Davis's performance as Sybylla, plus Armstrong's energetic direction, Witcombe's script, the Oscar-nominated costumes by Anna Senior, and the beautiful cinematography by Don McAlpine turned *My Brilliant Career* into a hit around the world. The film was chosen to screen in competition at the 1979 Cannes Film Festival, alongside Terrence Malick's *Days of Heaven*, *The Tin Drum* by Volker Schlöndorff, and Francis Ford Coppola's *Apocalypse Now*—which won the major award. *My Brilliant Career* also became an important film within the Australian New Wave, the cinematic boom spurred on by government grants created to encourage new filmmakers. Gillian Armstrong would be the only woman working as a director during the Australian New Wave, but she didn't realize the importance of this achievement until much later. Thanks to the new access to funding in the 1970s, Armstrong hadn't encountered the same types of difficulties getting her films financed as many other female directors around the world had. However, she did face sexism during the production of *My Brilliant Career*, with the press asking her condescending

questions like, "How will the crew hear your small voice?"

After the film's success, Armstrong battled with the label of "female filmmaker," feeling that it limited what she could do. The scripts she received in the wake of *My Brilliant Career*, as she said, were all "women achievers—first woman to fly a plane, climb a mountain, ride a camel." She fought against being typecast as a director who

▲ "I make no apology for being egotistical . . . because I am!" —Sybylla

could only make movies about women, though Armstrong would continue to direct films that featured complex female characters—such as her most famous movie to date, a 1994 adaptation of Louisa May Alcott's *Little Women*, starring Winona Ryder and Susan Sarandon.

About a decade later, Gillian Armstrong noticed that her success hadn't opened doors for female directors in her country. Once she saw the exact percentage of working women directors in Australia—around 16 percent between 1970 and 2014, despite film school graduates being approximately 50 percent female—she became determined to speak up. In the years since, thanks to Armstrong's vocal support and a general awareness of gender inclusion in the film industry, those numbers have grown to around 31 percent.

▲ Sam Neill as Harry

▲ Director Gillian Armstrong

◄ "I'd be obliged to you, sir, if you'd take yourself out of the way; unless you want me foot in your big, fat face." —Sybylla

More from Gillian Armstrong's Brilliant Career

Starstruck (1982)
Mrs. Soffel (1984)
Little Women (1994)
Oscar and Lucinda (1997)
Charlotte Grey (2001)

Throughout it all, Gillian Armstrong has worked, though more sporadically than her fans would like. Of particular note is a creative documentary about the Australian-born Hollywood costume designer, Orry-Kelly, called *Women He's Undressed* (2015). And she's continued to lend her voice to encourage female filmmakers to enter the Australian film industry, saying pointedly in a 2016 interview, "There won't be equality until there are as many mediocre women directors as there are mediocre men."

Like most of Armstrong's films, *My Brilliant Career* subverts movie genres and viewer expectations. It has the meet-cute and the larkiness of a romantic comedy but ultimately reveals itself as a bildungsroman.

Carrie Rickey, film critic

Daisies

DIRECTED BY **Věra Chytilová**

To watch when you . . . feel like causing a ruckus.

Czechoslovakia, 1966
B&W and Color, 76 minutes, Drama

Screenplay: Věra Chytilová, Ester
Krumbachová, Pavel Juráček

Starring: Jitka Cerhová (Marie I), Ivana
Karbanová (Marie II)

"Do you care?"

—Marie II

"I don't care."

—Marie I

In the fifty-odd years since its release, *Daisies* (1966) has become one of the most important films made during the Czech New Wave cinematic movement. Even in its time, the film was hugely popular, released in what was then Czechoslovakia and experiencing success with local audiences and critics. This reaction to *Daisies* brought it to the attention of the Communist government, who then banned the film from theaters. Interestingly, their objection was not because *Daisies* shows two young girls running wild, rejecting society's standards for women; but due to one scene that involved a food fight. During the 1960s, Czechoslovakia was suffering from food scarcity, and the government cited the film's "food wastage" as the reason for its ban. Director Věra Chytilová

had already added a dedication to the end credits of her film, overlaid on top of war footage, which stated: "This film is dedicated to all those whose sole source of indignation is a trampled-on trifle," rather than the real issues facing her country.

The Czech New Wave lasted only a few years, beginning around 1963 and ending just after the Soviets invaded Czechoslovakia in 1968. The local film industry had been under the control of the Communist government since 1948, and movies produced during the 1950s were, by and large, propaganda. They were filmed in a Soviet social-realist style, with straightforward narratives, blatant messages about communist values, and happy endings. But by the 1960s, established directors such as Vojtěch Jasný (who had at first supported the

Party) felt they needed to speak out against the oppressive communist rule, and they started to sneak anti-communist messages into their movies—disguising them from the censors using fantasy and metaphor.

During the five or so years of the Czech New Wave, the country experienced a burst of creativity from young filmmakers who were eager to speak out against the government and take risks with their storytelling. Many of these filmmakers had studied at the national film school in Prague, FAMU, where teachers had surreptitiously screened movies that students weren't able to watch otherwise—films from the French New Wave and the Italian Neorealist movement. These graduates came out of FAMU in the late 1960s, ready to take what they had learned and experiment, much like Jean-Luc Godard or Federico Fellini before them.

▲ Jitka Cerhová as Marie I and Ivana Karbanová as Marie II

weaved documentary and narrative together to tell parallel stories about two very dissimilar women.

Daisies was Věra Chytilová's second solo feature, and she pushed the boundaries of filmmaking even further. The plot is simple: two young, bored women—the brunette Marie I and blond Marie II (played by first-time actresses Jitka Cerhová and Ivana Karbanová)—decide that because the world is spoiled, they might as well act spoiled. They go on a series of adventures, seen through various vignettes, where they ditch the social mores expected of women and run rampant eating, destroying, and annoying everything and everyone around them. They use older men for free dinners, which they scoff down without any care about how attractive they seem, then leave the men alone at

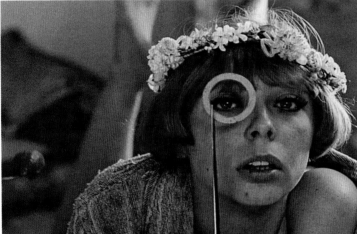

Věra Chytilová had applied to study at FAMU at the age of twenty-eight, after working as a clapper girl at a film studio. The only female student in her class, she reportedly shocked her male peers with her confidence and ferocious nature. She was excited to experiment with her student films, using nonprofessional actors and nonlinear storytelling, which carried over into her career after graduation. Chytilová's first feature film as a director was the aptly titled *Something Different* (1963), where she

▲▲ The two Maries cause trouble.

▲ Marie II

the train station. In their revolt against society, they rip apart the symbols of wealth and power: money, food, possessions, and the male ego.

Marie I and Marie II are dangerous because they have freed themselves from expectations, rebelling against the male-dominated society that treats them like objects, deciding that they do not need men to complete their lives. In this way, it's easy to see *Daisies* as a bold feminist film, made by a director who often told stories about women and created new representations for female characters on the screen. But Věra Chytilová did not call herself a feminist. She rejected the title and resented it being attached

More from the Czech New Wave

Courage for Every Day (1964)
Loves of a Blonde (1965)
The Shop on Main Street (1965)
Closely Watched Trains (1966)
All My Good Countrymen (1969)

to her work without her consent. Instead, she saw herself as an individual who made statements about her country, not her gender.

Whether you watch *Daisies* as being an attack on the patriarchy or an attack on the communist ideals of the former Czechoslovakian government, it remains smart, entertaining, and sneakily funny. Věra Chytilová said that her film was "about people's ability to destroy things, which is the opposite of creativity, yet there is a certain creative attractiveness within destruction." And Chytilová's creativity in telling her story about destruction is impressive. *Daisies* is filled with striking images, sudden switches from black-and-white to color, jump cuts, montages that compare the girls' antics with war footage, and surreal fantasy sequences where the Maries talk about everything from romance to death.

Daisies was banned from being screened in Czechoslovakia about a year after its initial release. The government hadn't understood what Věra Chytilová's film was about, but according to director Jan Němec—whose movie *A Report on the Party and Guests* (1966) was also banned—they "had a feeling that its celebration of anarchism or revelry was dangerous." *Daisies* had a brief return to theaters in 1968 during the Prague Spring, where protests led to a short period of liberalism in the country. That ended when the Soviet Union and other members of the Warsaw Pact invaded and put another restrictive government in its place. Filmmakers and other artists, many of whom had been blacklisted from working, fled the country—but Věra Chytilová remained.

The leading members of the Czech New Wave had included Miloš Forman, František Vláčil, Jan Němec, Evald Schorm, Jiří Menzel, Věra Chytilová, and more. Chytilová was the only woman who worked during the cinematic movement, and she was able to release one more film in theaters, *Fruit of Paradise*, in 1970. She was never officially classified as a blacklisted director, but the government made it impossible for her work in her home country for nearly a decade. To make money, she would sometimes direct commercials under pseudonyms, and in the mid-1970s, she wrote a passionate letter to the Czech president, imploring, "I want to work!"

Her ban was lifted in 1976, allowing Chytilová to finally get back to directing. She went on to be a teacher and found more success in the documentary genre. When she passed away in 2014, Věra Chytilová was remembered as an uncompromising artist who made bold films at a time when it was dangerous, and never regretted her career. "I was daring enough to want to do what I wanted," she explained, "even if it was a mistake."

What ensues is 76 minutes of pure rebellious chaos. From bilking men of industry for good food to disrupting reputable couples at a nightclub, the Maries commit to hedonistic pleasures, while trying to find signs of their own existence.

Marya E. Gates, film critic

Spring in a Small Town

DIRECTED BY **Fei Mu**

To watch when you . . . want to experience a poetic drama
from China that has been criminally underseen.

China, 1948
B&W, 98 minutes, Drama

Screenplay: Li Tianji

Starring: Wei Wei (Yuwen), Yu Shi (Dai
Liyan), Li Wei (Zhang Zichen), Zhang
Hongmei (Xiu), Cui Chaoming (Lao Huang)

> "Anyone walking along this wall feels as though they've left the world behind. The eyes do not see. The mind does not think."
>
> —Yuwen

When *Spring in a Small Town* was released in China in 1948, it was met with controversy. This was not because of its risqué story—about a wife who flirts with the idea of running away with her former lover—but due to the way director Fei Mu had told that story; he didn't take the type of political stance that was expected of films made at that time. Later, *Spring in a Small Town* was forgotten, lost until around 1980 when film archives in China were reopened and the movie was rediscovered. Now, it is regularly cited as being one of the greatest Chinese films ever made.

It's difficult to pinpoint exactly when the film industry began in China, though many sources point to a 1905 film recording of a Beijing Opera titled *The Battle of Dinguinshan*

as being the first Chinese movie. Following that, silent film production started in earnest, with the city of Shanghai as its hub, and the film industry flourished during the 1930s, now called Chinese cinema's "Golden Age." Shanghai was one of the first ports in China to open to Western trade, and with that came an influx of foreign influence and open-mindedness that was important to the arts. Films such as *The Highway* (1934, sometimes also titled *The Big Road*) and *Street Angel* (1937) pushed boundaries of cinematic innovation, and despite the films being subject to heavy censoring by the nationalist government in power at the time, the stories explored the idea of equality between genders and classes.

The second Sino-Japanese war changed everything, as China started to fight back against

▲ Li Wei and Wei Wei as two former lovers in *Spring in a Small Town*

the increasing Japanese presence in the country. This war lasted from 1937 until 1945 and included World War II. A decade's worth of conflict caused immense damage to the country and its people, leaving behind massive destruction to property and the death of around 20 million Chinese. Many of the films made during this time were also inadvertently destroyed, and movies produced in the years directly after reflected on the devastation left behind by war.

Spring in a Small Town was one of those movies, set in the then present-day in a village that had suffered from bombings. The script, written by Li Tianji, follows a once-prosperous husband and wife, who are now living in the ruins of their former glory. These ruins are both literal (the crumbling house) and figurative (their unhappy marriage). The wife, Yuwen (Wei Wei) narrates the film, detailing her unhappiness and her loveless union to Dai Liyan (Yu Shi), who suffers from depression and a variety of ailments, some real, some imagined. Yuwen looks forward to her daily grocery shopping, where she can spend time walking along the collapsing city wall. The only other bright spot in her day is the energetic presence of Liyan's younger sister (Zhang Hongmei), who lives with them, along with their faithful helper Lao Huang (Cui Chaoming). Suddenly, Wei Wei's life changes with the arrival of an unexpected guest, Zhang Zichen (Li Wei), Liyan's old friend and Yuwen's former lover. He represents a rare glimpse of hope and a chance

More Forbidden Love

Brief Encounter (1945, UK)
La Belle et La Bête (1946, France)
The Night Porter (1974, Italy)
The Handmaiden (2016, South Korea)
Portrait of a Lady on Fire (2019, France)

at happiness for Yuwen, but she needs to decide if she's willing to destroy her marriage to get it.

Fei Mu directs this emotional story in a serene way, using long takes, a delicate moving camera and getting restrained performances from his cast. There are little to no close-ups in Fei Mu's work; he utilizes wide shots and narration for emotional insight, and except for his use of fades in editing—sometimes midscene—his style is purposely understated and reserved. His lyrical style has now been compared to the likes of the French director Max Ophüls, the Japanese Kenji Mizoguchi, or Wong Kar Wai from Hong Kong. (About Fei Mu, Wong Kar Wai once said, "From my point of view, there has been only one 'film poet' in Chinese film history, and that is Fei Mu who made *Spring in a Small Town*. I definitely don't deserve the title of 'film poet.'")

For *Spring in a Small Town*, authenticity and realism were paramount for Fei Mu, who said he wanted the movie to feel "lifelike, truthful, and honest." He shot on real locations within around three months, using just five actors and cutting the original screenplay by two-thirds to fit the modest budget. He advised his cast to forget about the words on the page and most of the sound live to capture natural acting moments (rather than rerecording it later in a controlled environment). To Wei Wei, Fei Mu gave her the direction that any "inflamed emotions must be kept under control." Wei Wei delivers a beautiful performance, one that was so believable that reportedly Li Wei, the actor who plays her character's former lover Zhang,

fell in love with her on the set. His feelings were not reciprocated, and his obsession grew so stifling that Wei Wei needed to flee to Hong Kong to escape him.

In 1949, the Chinese Civil War ended, and the Communist Party came into power. Fei Mu—and many other artists of the time—escaped artistic repression by moving to Hong Kong. He had been born in Shanghai in 1906, and as a child he was highly intelligent—excelling at school and becoming fluent in English, French, German, Italian, and Russian. Fei Mu

was interested in movies from a fairly young age, later saying he watched over a thousand films, both Western and Chinese. He was also an avid reader, often staying up late to read books in the dark, a habit that reportedly caused him to lose sight in his left eye. While at school, he made friends with two other movie-obsessed boys who would also become directors—Zhu Shilin and He Mengfu—and together they created a film magazine. Fei Mu's father was determined that

▲ *Spring in a Small Town*

he would have a sensible career, so even with his dreams of directing movies, he took a job as an accountant at a mining company, though he continued to watch movies and write about cinema whenever he could.

By 1930, Fei Mu decided he could no longer put off his dreams and went against his father's wishes, telling him he was going to be a filmmaker. His mother was eventually supportive, and she tried her best to change his father's mind, though it caused a rift in his family. Fei Mu later told his daughter that he never regretted his decision. "I loved my job," he said, and "worked hard to achieve my goals without complaints." He had started in the film industry as an editor, often also translating for subtitles. In 1932, he was offered a job as an assistant to the legendary director Hou Yao. A pioneer in Chinese cinema, Hou Yao wrote the first film theory book in the country and became a mentor to Fei Mu.

After that experience, Fei Mu felt ready to direct, and made his directorial debut in 1933 with *Night in the City* (also called *City Nights*). The film was a critical and commercial hit, and Fei Mu quickly became prolific—*Spring in a Small Town* was his third movie released during the year of 1948. It wasn't a success upon first release and was criticized for not having a political message—most Chinese films at the time took a heavy-handed, Communist stance. Fei Mu's decision to focus on the individual, rather than the collective, was controversial, but he was more interested in exploring the psychological repercussions of forbidden love. Even with the marriage between Yuwen and Liyan, he didn't judge his characters, instead showing the true hopelessness of their situation.

In 1950, Fei Mu tried to come back to China, but was interrogated about his decision to leave for Hong Kong. Ironically, he'd once directed the person who questioned him: actress Lan Ping. She had married the Chinese communist leader Mao Zedong in 1939, and changed her name to Jiang Qing. For a time, with Mao in power, she became the most influential woman in China. Fei Mu was upset at his treatment by her and went back to Hong Kong. Sadly, he never made another film following his three in 1948; he suffered a fatal heart attack in 1951. He died at his desk, aged forty-four, where he had been writing a script for a future movie. After his death, Fei Mu and his movies were largely forgotten—they weren't accessible to audiences in the West, and in China they had been disavowed for their lack of political stance. This finally started to change in 1980, when China opened its film archives and made a new print of *Spring in a Small Town*, among others. Slowly, Fei Mu's beautiful movie was rediscovered, and in 2005, the Hong Kong Film Awards Association named *Spring in a Small Town* the "greatest Chinese film of all time." Modern film critics and filmmakers started to write and speak about its merits, with director Zhang Yimou being one of the first, summing up its impact by saying: "A film like *Spring in a Small Town* has not been surpassed by many urban films to this day. It's a rare masterpiece in Chinese film history."

For reasons no one can explain, everyone is drawn to taking walks by the ruined city wall. Perhaps there is something about damaged limits or vulnerable barriers. There is a captivating subtlety in the glances, smiles, brief hand-holdings; it has an inspired emotional fluency and candour. This is a film to fall in love with.

Peter Bradshaw, film critic

Dilwale Dulhania Le Jayenge

DIRECTED BY **Aditya Chopra**

To watch when you . . . want to experience the charm of a popular Bollywood romantic musical, one that rewrote the rules and pushed traditional boundaries.

India, 1995
Color, 181 minutes, Romance

Screenplay: Aditya Chopra, Javed Siddiqui

Starring: Kajol (Simran Singh), Shah Rukh Khan (Raj Malhotra), Amrish Puri (Chaudhry Baldev Singh), Anupam Kher (Dharamvir Malhotra), Farida Jalal (Lajwanti "Lajjo" Singh), Parmeet Sethi (Kuljeet), Pooja Ruparel (Chutki)

"I was wrong, Simran. I forgot women have no right to make promises either. They're born to sacrifice themselves for men. But men don't sacrifice anything for women. Nor will they."

—Lajjo

It's impossible not to smile while watching *Dilwale Dulhania Le Jayenge* (1995), a Bollywood romance so beloved that it's affectionately known by its acronym *D.D.L.J.* This musical premiered in October 1995, and in the thirty years since, it has rarely left Indian screens. One theater in Mumbai plays the three-hour movie daily for patrons who return to reexperience its magic. *D.D.L.J.* also reflects a pivotal point in Indian history, made during a period of economic growth—both in the country and the film industry—and at a time when modern young women were questioning old traditions around love.

Hindi cinema began in the 1930s in Bombay (now Mumbai) and quickly grew to rival, and then eclipse, Hollywood, in terms of the sheer number of movies produced and the level of fame achieved by its stars. The nickname "Bollywood" was coined as a play on "Hollywood" and "Bombay," and refers to the Hindi-language section of the Indian film industry. An estimated eight hundred films are produced every year across all genres—including action, Western, comedy, romance, and the "masala" or "mashup" films, comprising multiple genres. But no matter the genre, most Bollywood films are musicals. The musicals of Bollywood are not inspired by

Hollywood's versions; instead, they have their own unique way of incorporating song and dance into the plots, with little realism required. Mostly, this is a way for characters to express love and desire, without needing to be explicit with dialogue. India also produces movies in other major languages, such as Bengali, Telegu (those movies are nicknamed "Tollywood" films), and Tamil (nicknamed "Kollywood"), but Bollywood remains the largest segment. Its popularity extends beyond India, with Bollywood fans living across the globe, and several of its stars also experiencing fame in Hollywood.

The idea for *D.D.L.J.* came from a first-time filmmaker, the twenty-three-year-old Aditya

▲▲ Kajol as Simran

▲ Shah Rukh Khan as Raj

▲ Simian and Raj meet, and it's not love at first sight.

Chopra. As is often the case in Bollywood, Chopra's family was in the business—his father, Yash Chopra, was a highly respected director and producer, and Aditya worked for years as an assistant director on his productions. Yash Chopra's film company, Yash Raj Films, would go on to produce *D.D.L.J.*, but Aditya brought a new perspective to the industry. He wanted to make a different sort of romantic film, one that would ask questions about what it means to be Indian.

The story follows two college-age, second-generation Non-Resident Indians (NRIs), Simran Singh (Kajol) and Raj Malhotra (Shah Rukh Khan), who are both living in London. Raj is a carefree prankster who failed university, but his easygoing father (Anupam Kher) doesn't mind. Meanwhile, Simran dreams of finding her one true love, and though her mother (Farida Jalal) supports her fantasies, her father (Amrish Puri) is traditional and has already promised her to the son of his friend in India. Simran has little say in the matter, but before the wedding, she convinces her father to let her go on a train trip across Europe with friends. That's where she meets Raj, who is also traveling around Europe. As many romantic comedies go, at first Raj and Simran can't stand each other, but slowly they fall in love. After their vacation, they have to face reality, but Raj follows Simran to India, hoping to get into the good graces of her family so she can marry him instead.

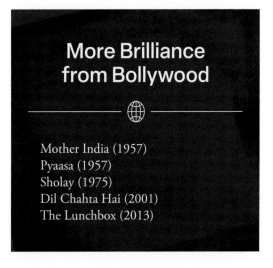

More Brilliance from Bollywood

🌐

Mother India (1957)
Pyaasa (1957)
Sholay (1975)
Dil Chahta Hai (2001)
The Lunchbox (2013)

▲ One of the popular dance numbers in *Dilwale Dulhania Le Jayenge*

Arranged marriages and love-based marriages have long been a staple of Bollywood cinema, but up to this point the storyline usually went one of two ways. As Kajol explained to the *New York Times*, prior to *D.D.L.J.*, there were "films that celebrated marriages and everybody was involved from uncles to aunties, or it was 'us against the world, we will fight it out, we will live together, die together.' I think *D.D.L.J.* came up with a very simple thought— to say that maybe we can walk a line." Rather than choosing to abandon Simran's family, Raj sets out to win over her father, wanting to have his approval before they marry. The full title, *Dilwale Dulhania Le Jayenge*, translates to *The Brave-Hearted Will Take the Bride*, and in choosing the difficult course, the NRI Raj proves himself to be more Hindustani than the man Simran is set to marry.

In this way *D.D.L.J.* was unique, because it refused to show the NRI characters as being out of touch. Simran and Raj may have been born in London, but they have retained the same values (or better) as those in India. In her book, *Dilwale Dulhania Le Jayenge: A Modern Classic*, Anupama Chopra writes about the wide appeal of this theme. "*D.D.L.J.* worked as a fantasy for Indian audiences both inside and outside India," she wrote. "It told Indians that an Indian is a hybrid who easily enjoys the material comforts of the West and the spiritual comforts of the East. For the local audience, the film offered a lifestyle to aspire to. But the film also reassured the home audience that while their expatriate brethren might enjoy the affluence of the West, their hearts ached for the lost homeland . . . Like fusion clothes and fusion food, *D.D.L.J.* presented a fusion lifestyle."

With the central tension being Simran's upcoming arranged marriage and her burgeoning love for Raj, *D.D.L.J.* was also able to explore the role of Indian women in the modern-day 1990s in an explicit way—while also keeping the patriarchal status quo. In one scene, Simran's mother tells her about a promise she made to herself when Simran was a baby, that Simran would grow up to have more autonomy than she did, in all ways. But then, she adds sadly, she realized that she (as a woman) did not have the power to make that kind of promise, even to herself. Later, Simran asks Raj to run away with her and elope. But he convinces her to stay so he can win over her father, who ultimately has the final say on her life. "Simran is an amaanat (property) to be passed from Baldev [her father] to Raj," Anupama Chopra writes. "But the film is distinctive in that it fleshes out its female characters, and at least records these dissenting voices. Lajjo [Simran's mother] and Simran are keenly aware of their position."

Many scenes in *D.D.L.J.*, reflect the changing ideals from the older generation, who followed the rules, to the younger, who wanted to create their own lives and wear fashionable Western clothes. During the 1990s, as the economy grew in India, the youth experienced a greater financial power than their parents had, and, with the introduction of satellite television, they had access to Western TV shows, channels like MTV, and Hollywood movies. *D.D.L.J.* attempted to bridge the gap between generations, combining the changing youth with all their independence and modernity, while also reaffirming the traditional ideals of family coming first.

In between, there are plenty of vivid songs and energetically choreographed dances shot across Europe. The composing team of brothers Jatin and Lalit Pandit teamed up with lyricist Anand Bakshi and singer Lata Mangeshkar to come up with a soundtrack that would go on to be a bestseller. Practically everyone involved in the creation of *D.D.L.J.* would experience success; the film was an instant hit and catapulted its two stars, Kajol and Shah Rukh Khan, to enormous fame.

Shah Rukh Khan (nicknamed "King Khan"), went on to build a lucrative career out of playing sensitive male heroes who, like Raj, were respectful to their female love interests and helped them out with domestic chores. This has made him a beloved figure in Bollywood cinema, where he has broken stereotypes

surrounding male film characters. *D.D.L.J.* was "the film that established Shah Rukh Khan as a guy who can romance in a way that we had never seen before," said Anupama Chopra in an interview. "Here's a guy who's in the kitchen with the women. Here's a guy who keeps Karva Chauth [a Hindu day of fasting for women] with his girlfriend. He's telling the aunt which sari to buy. And none of this means that he's any less manly. It's just that he's secure enough to be all of those things and to be in places that are traditionally female."

Three decades after its initial box office run, *Dilwale Dulhania Le Jayenge*, and its stars, continue to enchant audiences. It holds the record for being the longest-running film in Indian cinema history, and screenings of the movie attract viewers of all ages. Its enduring success still manages to surprise those involved in the film, including its lead star. "I have had so many people," Kajol said, "who told me that we have made our children sit down and watch *D.D.L.J.*, we've made our grandchildren sit down and watch—and I was like, 'there are grandchildren now?' Children I am fine with. But grandchildren?"

India has done as much for the movies as America, and there are as many great Bollywood films as there are great Hollywood films. Not to have seen *Mother India, Pyaasa* or *Sholay* is not to have seen *Gone With the Wind, Casablanca* or *Star Wars*. And not to have seen *D.D.L.J.* is to have missed out on the good feelings that flow from one of the greatest feel-good films.

Scott Jordan Harris, film critic

Cinema Paradiso

DIRECTED BY **Giuseppe Tornatore**

To watch when you . . . want to be reminded of
the simple power of going to the movies.

Italy, 1988
Color, 124 minutes (Theatrical
Version), Drama

Screenplay: Giuseppe Tornatore,
Vanna Paoli

Starring: Philippe Noiret (Alfredo),
Jacques Perrin (adult Salvatore), Marco
Leonardi (teen Salvatore), Salvatore Cascio
(child Salvatore), Antonella Attili (young
Maria), Agnese Nano (Elena), Leopoldo
Trieste (Father Adelfio)

"Life isn't like in the movies. Life . . . is much harder."

—Alfredo

Watching *Cinema Paradiso* (1988) is akin to receiving a warm hug. Over the years, this Italian drama has been called "sentimental" or "saccharine" by critics, but whether that is true or not, sometimes, you just need to satisfy your sweet tooth with a film that makes you feel good.

Anyone who has joyfully spent hours in the dark, escaping the real world to sit with strangers in front of a flickering big screen will relate to this film, because at its heart it is a love letter to the cinema. With a memorable score by Ennio Morricone, the story follows Salvatore, who we first see as an adult (played by Jacques Perrin). He's a well-known film director who receives news that a childhood friend named Alfredo has died. The movie then flashes back in time to the young Salvatore (Salvatore Cascio) in his small Sicilian hometown. The local movie theater

is the Cinema Paradiso, and this is where the whole village gathers—to yell at the screen, to smoke, to play practical jokes, to fall in love, to escape the aftermath of World War II, and to watch the wide range of films on offer, everything from John Ford's *Stagecoach* (1939) to Luchino Visconti's *La Terra Trema* (1948). The town's priest (Leopoldo Trieste) watches the films before they are screened, noting any inappropriate scenes, which the projectionist, Alfredo (Philippe Noiret), must edit out.

Young Salvatore (or "Toto" as he is called by everyone in town) peeks his head cheekily through the curtains to watch the priest's reactions to the movies, gleefully giggling away, before running up to join Alfredo in the projection booth. Toto's father hasn't returned from the war, so Alfredo becomes his paternal figure and friend, teaching him how to load the film and run the projector. Toto looks at the whirring

celluloid in wonder, completely captured by the magic of movies, especially when Alfredo manipulates the projector to show a film on the wall of the town's square, so those who couldn't get into the theater can still watch it.

After a tragedy befalls Alfredo, Toto looks after him and takes over as the cinema's projectionist. When he is a teen (played by Marco Leonardi), he falls in love with a beautiful girl named Elena (Agnese Nano), but her parents won't allow them to be together. Toto becomes increasingly miserable, and Alfredo encourages him to leave the town and find a different life.

"Don't come back," Alfredo tells him. "Don't think about us. Don't look back. Don't write. Don't give in to nostalgia. Forget us all." Toto keeps that promise for thirty years, until he hears about Alfredo's death. Now an adult, Toto returns to his hometown, and after attending the funeral, he visits the now-run-down theater. Later, back in Rome, he watches a special movie that Alfredo has left him.

▲ Philippe Noiret as Alfredo and Salvatore Cascio as "Toto"

That scene is beautiful, and likely to make you cry—or at least, feel moved—and sums up the central themes in the movie. *Cinema Paradiso* is as much about the relationship between Alfredo and Toto (how those who have the most impact on your life may not be the ones you expect) as it is about lost love, and, importantly, the enchanting experience of going to your local movie theater. This is a message that is perhaps even more relevant today than it was back in 1989—following the COVID-19 pandemic lockdown, many independent movie theaters couldn't reopen. The ones that did have struggled to get audiences back in the same numbers they experienced before 2020, with moviegoers now used to watching films at home. But these movie theaters, situated on the Main Streets of America, are often the lifeblood of a small town, driving the local economy and acting as a gathering place

▲▲ "Who else around here could run a projector? Nobody. It takes an imbecile like me. I never had any luck." —Alfredo

▲ "I choose my friends for their looks, my enemies for their intelligence." —Alfredo

for the community—just like the theater in *Cinema Paradiso*.

Director Giuseppe Tornatore partly filmed *Cinema Paradiso* in the same small town in Sicily where he had grown up. In cowriting the script, he had drawn on his own life for inspiration. He began his career as a photographer and started to direct stage plays as a teenager. Later, he transitioned to television, directing TV documentaries—with his interest in documentaries coming from an admiration of Italian Neorealism. Tornatore's feature film directorial debut came in 1986 with *The Professor*, and his work was soon noticed by Franco Cristaldi, a producer who had worked on the controversial Pietro Germi film *Seduced and Abandoned* (1964) and had been married to the actress Claudia Cardinale.

Cristaldi encouraged Tornatore during the process of *Cinema Paradiso*, and Tornatore had imagined his film to be a eulogy (of sorts) to historic, small-town movie theaters, which were being torn down or replaced by multiplexes. The film industry in Italy was also struggling in the late 1980s, and when *Cinema Paradiso* first opened in 1988, it was a box-office failure. But Franco Cristaldi wasn't willing to give up on the picture and suggested to Giuseppe Tornatore that he go back to the edit room, cut the film down, and reshape it a little. That version (now called "The Theatrical Version") was premiered at the 1989 Cannes Film Festival, where it picked up a Grand Jury Prize and rave reviews. *Cinema Paradiso* soon became a worldwide sensation and a box-office hit, and though some American critics were lukewarm when it was released in the United States in 1990, it did win the Best Foreign Language Film Oscar at the Academy Awards.

In 2002, Giuseppe Tornatore released a director's version (called "The New Version"), where he added fifty-one minutes of footage. And while critics are still mixed on whether *Cinema Paradiso* is too conventional or an appealing crowd-pleaser, the one aspect they seem to all agree on is that it's the theatrical version that remains superior.

Anyone who loves movies is likely to love *Cinema Paradiso*, and there is one scene where the projectionist finds that he can reflect the movie out of the window in his booth and out across the town square so that the images can float on a wall, there in the night above the heads of the people . . . I realized the same thing this movie argues: Yes, it is tragic that the big screen has been replaced by the little one. But the real shame is that the big screens did not grow even bigger, grow so vast they were finally on the same scale as the movies they were reflecting.

Roger Ebert, film critic

More Movies About Movies

8½ (1963, Italy)
Contempt (1963, France)
Day for Night (1973, France)
Through the Olive Trees (1994, Iran)
One Cut of the Dead (2017, Japan)

An Angel at My Table

DIRECTED BY **Jane Campion**

To watch when you . . . want to marvel at a remarkable, true story.

New Zealand, 1990
Color, 158 minutes, Drama

Screenplay: Laura Jones, based on the autobiographies of Janet Frame

Starring: Kerry Fox (adult Janet), Iris Churn (Mum), K. J. Wilson (Dad), Karen Fergusson (teenage Janet), Alexia Keogh (young Janet)

> ## "Over the next eight years, I received more than 200 applications of electric shock treatment. Each one equivalent in fear to an execution."
>
> —Janet

An Angel at My Table (1990) screened at the Venice Film Festival, where it won the Silver Lion prize. To win the second-place award at such a renowned film festival is an impressive achievement for any film, let alone for the first New Zealand film to ever screen at Venice. However, the audience at the Venice Film Festival weren't happy with the result. "It was not the best film at the festival," explained director Jane Campion, "but it was the most loved. When it was awarded the second prize, the Silver Lion, the crowd wouldn't allow the head of the jury to announce the winner. For ten minutes they chanted, 'Angel, Angel, Angel.'"

An Angel at My Table tells the true (and disturbing) story of writer Janet Frame. She grew up a shy and awkward kid in her hometown in New Zealand, and her anxious behavior led doctors to incorrectly diagnose her with schizophrenia. Frame believed the doctors and endured eight years inside mental institutions and more than two hundred electroshock therapy treatments before she finally had her diagnosis reexamined. Janet Frame wrote about her horrific experience in a three-part autobiography—*To the Is-land*, *An Angel at My Table*, and *The Envoy from Mirror City*—released between 1982 and 1984. Director Jane Campion had discovered Frame's earlier work, with Frame's novel, *Owls Do Cry*, having a particular impact on her as a teenager. She liked how Frame had given a voice to teenage girls, which was, as she said, "poetic, powerful and fated." Inspired by Frame, Campion would go on to explore the inner lives

▶ Karen Fergusson, Alexia Keogh, and Kerry Fox as the three Janets, with the real Janet Frame

▲ Alexia Keogh as the young version of Janet

of misunderstood women and girls in her films, weaving in similarly complex family dynamics.

When Frame's first book in her autobiographical series, *To the Is-land*, was published, Jane Campion was studying filmmaking at a school in Australia, and she decided that she wanted to make the book into a movie for television. Frame was open to an adaptation but asked Campion to wait until the other two books in the series had been released. Frame promised her that she wouldn't sell the rights to any other director.

In the meantime, Campion started her filmmaking career. After directing several shorts (including *An Exercise in Discipline: Peel*, which won Best Short Film at the 1982 Cannes Film Festival), she made her first feature for Australian television, with *2 Friends* (1986) being about a friendship between two teenage girls. By the time Campion released her first theatrical feature, *Sweetie* (1989), Frame's three books had been published, and Campion was ready.

She initially conceived her adaptation to be a television miniseries, with the adapted screenplay by Laura Jones following Janet Frame from childhood, through her teen years, and into young adulthood. The character of Janet is played by three different actors—all with Frame's naturally unruly, curly red hair. Alexia Keogh is the striking face we first see as the young Janet, living with her siblings and poor family in a tiny house. Then, Karen Fergusson takes over as the teenaged Janet, who suffers through the grief of losing two of her sisters to separate drownings, the scary seizures experienced by her brother, and the general struggles of being a teenage girl who wants to fit in. Frame's writing talent is evident from a young age, and she continues to write as she grows up; with Kerry Fox (in a remarkable debut) playing Janet as she leaves school and tries to deal with her incorrect medical diagnosis of schizophrenia.

When *An Angel at My Table* was picked up for theatrical release, Jane Campion worked to condense her miniseries into a feature-length film. She worried that her stylistic choices—using the standard television direction of close-ups and medium shots—would seem boring on a big screen, but, as critics have noted, the simplicity of her framing perfectly suited Janet Frame's straightforward, no-nonsense writing style. Critic Amy Taubin wrote in an essay for the Criterion Collection's website, "The modesty of Frame's style demanded an act of self-effacement on the part of the filmmaker, who brilliantly channeled her onto the screen." Plus, as Campion herself explained, she was more interested in "what sorts of sensations and feelings and subtleties you can get through your story and can bring out through performances," than making any grand style statements with her camera.

Right from the start, Jane Campion's films and her directorial choices were so self-assured and uniquely her own, it's hard to believe that she hadn't imagined that she could be a film director. "I just thought," she said, "in the most unconscious fashion, that women don't have those sorts of careers, and if you're a talented woman you just support a talented man." Though, Campion did grow up with a creative family in Wellington, New Zealand—her father directed theater productions and her mother was an actress. She hadn't wanted to follow their footsteps into the performing arts, studying visual arts in London and Sydney. But soon, she felt that painting wasn't enough to hold all her thoughts and decided to try her hand at filmmaking.

The film industry in New Zealand was small, with documentaries being the focus since the 1940s. It was only during the 1970s that narrative features and dramas started to be made in more significant numbers, but female filmmakers were rare—the first feature film to be made by a woman in New Zealand came in 1984, with *Trial Run*, directed by Melanie Read. Campion had begun her filmmaking career in Australia (*Sweetie* is an Australian film) but with *An Angel at My Table* she made her mark around the world as a New Zealand director of note.

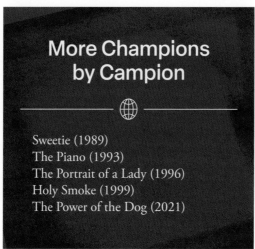

More Champions by Campion

Sweetie (1989)
The Piano (1993)
The Portrait of a Lady (1996)
Holy Smoke (1999)
The Power of the Dog (2021)

Following the film's successful screening at the Venice Film Festival, the positive critical reviews came flooding in. Vincent Canby wrote for the *New York Times* that "the movie records the world as Janet sees it, sometimes incredibly beautiful and often frightening." And Roger Ebert said it was "strangely engrossing from beginning to end . . . It tells its story calmly and with great attention to human detail, and, watching it, I found myself drawn in with a rare intensity." The film and its protagonist weren't universally praised—a few male critics thought that the character of Janet should, essentially,

▲ Kerry Fox as the adult Janet

"lighten up." When asked about this years later, Jane Campion said, in her typically honest way, "I know that the (male) critical response in America was highly mixed and not great. Maybe they just don't like dumpy redheads. Or, more basically, those men probably find women very threatening and difficult, unless they're packaged like sex objects."

The success of *An Angel at My Table* led to a resurgence in the popularity of Janet Frame and her work, with her books being published in multiple languages. Meanwhile, Jane Campion took a few years to make her next film, but it was a smash hit. *The Piano* (1993) was a highly acclaimed period drama starring Holly Hunter,

Harvey Keitel, and a young Anna Paquin, and it won the Palme d'Or award at the 1993 Cannes Film Festival (shared with *Farewell My Concubine* from China). That made Jane Campion the first female director to win Cannes's major prize, and with the film's eight Academy Award nominations, Campion was only the second woman to be nominated for Best Director. She would do it again with *The Power of the Dog* (2021), becoming the eighth woman nominated for an Oscar for Directing, and the first to have two nominations to her name. Throughout her continuing career, Jane Campion has been a true trailblazer, breaking records and glass ceilings, and creating unforgettable movies along the way.

Director Jane Campion has taken on the most difficult challenge of the movies: the description of a profound inner life by means of the wholly external imagery of the cinema.

Dave Kehr, film critic and museum curator

Late Spring

DIRECTED BY **Yasujirō Ozu**

To watch when you . . . are struggling to embrace change in your life.

Japan, 1949
B&W, 108 minutes, Drama

Screenplay: Kôgo Noda, Yasujirō Ozu,
based on a novel by Kazuo Hirotsu

Starring: Chishû Ryû (Shukichi Somiya),
Setsuko Hara (Noriko Somiya)

> "Being with you like this is my greatest happiness.
> Please, Father, why can't we stay as we are?
> I know marriage won't make me any happier."
>
> —Noriko

It's difficult to know where to start with a filmmaker such as Yasujirō Ozu. This Japanese director has multiple masterpieces to his name, each one worthy of study and appreciation. He started early, being a cinephile from a young age, and worked at Shochiku Studio as an assistant cameraman and assistant director in 1923 at twenty years old. Ozu directed his first film in 1927 and immediately built up an impressive body of work by releasing two or three films every year throughout the 1930s, making everything from comedies to gangster films. During the war, he was sent to Singapore to direct propaganda movies, and once he returned, Yasujirō Ozu finally made his mark as an internationally renowned director with *Late Spring* (1949).

In many ways, *Late Spring* is emblematic of Ozu's postwar style, featuring a deceptively simple plot that focuses on family dynamics and carefully composed visuals that draw the viewer in. Ozu wrote the script with his regular screenwriter, Kôgo Noda, adapting a novel by Kazuo Hirotsu. This would be their first of their many "shomin-geki" or "modern family drama" films. Most of these explored the relationship between a parent and a child and featured seasonal titles—which were less about the setting for the plot and more about the feeling the season evoked. Like the end of spring, *Late Spring* is about inevitable change—here in the relationship between a father and daughter. Setsuko Hara stars as Noriko, an unmarried twenty-seven-year-old who lives at home with her widowed father, Shukichi (played by Ozu regular Chishû Ryû). She is perfectly happy to take care of him and their house, remaining adamant that she does not want to get married. But her father worries about

▲▲ Setsuko Hara as Noriko   ▲ Chishû Ryû as Shukichi

her, and as pressure mounts for Noriko to settle down with a husband, she realizes that their lives will never be the same.

Late Spring is set during the time when Japan was under American occupation. The film itself was subject to censorship by American authorities, who had objected to its depiction of a traditional Japanese arranged marriage. All mentions of the allied forces and the destruction caused during the war had to be taken out, but the occupation still lingers in the background—in the way the children play American baseball, in shots of signs written in English, and the presence of Coca-Cola ads.

Yasujirō Ozu became famous for his sparse yet emotional storytelling and his unique visual style. This is easy to see in *Late Spring*, with every frame intricately composed and perfectly symmetrical. Many of his shots are filmed from a low angle, with the camera positioned on the ground—to that the viewer is watching the action while sitting on a Japanese tatami mat. Conversations are often recorded head-on, with the characters looking at the camera, as if, when they're speaking to one another, they're really communicating to us. And in between the dialogue scenes are serene shots of everyday objects and life—such as boats floating on the water, empty train tracks, or a teapot. These transitional moments became known as Ozu's "pillow shots." That term was coined by critic Noël Burch, because just like "pillow words" in poetry, they take the viewer from one mood to another. They're also seemingly used as metaphors for the emotions the characters are going through, beneath their polite exteriors. Because of

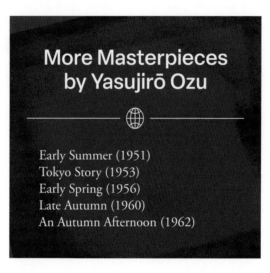

More Masterpieces by Yasujirō Ozu

🌐

Early Summer (1951)
Tokyo Story (1953)
Early Spring (1956)
Late Autumn (1960)
An Autumn Afternoon (1962)

this, Ozu's pillow shots have been endlessly speculated over by film scholars and casual fans alike—and none more than one shot in *Late Spring*.

During the scene in question, Noriko and her father lie in their beds on the last night of their vacation together, not long before Noriko is due to be married. In the darkness, she speaks about a mutual friend, and how wrong she was to call his new marriage "filthy." But she admits that she also finds the idea of her father getting remarried "distasteful." Shukichi doesn't answer and Noriko smiles as she sees that he has fallen asleep. Then, the scene suddenly cuts to a shot of a vase, sitting in an alcove, and then back to Noriko. The realization that she will have to go through with the wedding and let go of her father seems to dawn on Noriko as she stares solemnly into the darkness. The scene ends with a shot of the vase. Ozu gave no explanation about his use of pillow shots, or the meaning of this vase—leading cinephiles to have debates about it ever since. To American filmmaker Paul Schrader, the vase was an example of Ozu's focus on stasis, but to others, it symbolizes tradition, femininity, or even Noriko's absent mother.

The release of *Late Spring* in 1949 was met with critical acclaim in Japan. It took a few more decades before the work of Ozu would find appreciation in the United States, but when it finally did, *Late Spring* was heralded as one of the best of his films, alongside his highly esteemed *Tokyo Story* (1953). Following *Late*

◀ "Marriage may not mean happiness from the start. To expect such immediate happiness is a mistake." —Shukichi

Spring, Yasujirō Ozu slowed down his output, focusing on directing an average of about one film a year—each in his careful, exacting style. Then, in the late 1950s, Ozu and screenwriter Kôgo Noda decided to revisit *Late Spring*, reimagining it as *Late Autumn*. As in *Late Spring*, the plot of *Late Autumn* is about a single parent who wants their unmarried child to find a spouse. But rather than examining the relationship between a father and a daughter, it's a mother and a daughter. And in a nice nod to *Late Spring*, Setsuko Hara stars in *Late Autumn*, this time as the worried parent.

As Noriko in *Late Spring*, Setsuko Hara is mesmerizing—somehow portraying her as being both demure and daring. Noriko is quiet but offers her blunt opinions freely, with her constant giggles softening the blow. In this way, she represents the struggles for many young women in Japan at this time, who felt they were caught between tradition and modernity. The turning point for Noriko happens during a Noh theater performance. She and her father are enjoying the

production, until Noriko spots a young widow who might end up being her father's future wife, sitting in the audience. The sight of her seems to trigger a realization in Noriko that she has no choice, she will have to marry and her father will move on. Life is about to change one way or another. Her father sits beside her, unaware of the shift in her mood, and as her effervescent smile and natural joy drains from her face, Noriko becomes serious and guarded.

Late Spring was the first time Setsuko Hara was directed by Yasujirō Ozu, but even before this success, she was one of Japan's most popular actresses—having featured in approximately sixty prior films. Hara would go on to make five more movies with Ozu, including the so-called Noriko trilogy—she played different characters also called Noriko in *Early Summer* (1951) and *Tokyo Story*. In 1962, at the age of forty-two, Setsuko Hara abruptly retired from film acting, choosing to live the rest of her life away from the harsh glare of show business.

The difficulty with Ozu is not in appreciating his films . . . [but] in describing an Ozu work in a way that doesn't diminish it, that doesn't reduce it to an inventory of his austere techniques, and that accurately reflects the unsentimental humanism of his discipline.

Vincent Canby, film critic

▲ Director Yasujirō Ozu

Pan's Labyrinth

DIRECTED BY **Guillermo del Toro**

To watch when you . . . want to swap a brutal reality for a beautiful and dark fantasy.

Mexico/Spain, 2006
Color, 118 minutes, Fantasy

Screenplay: Guillermo del Toro

Starring: Ivana Baquero (Ofelia), Maribel Verdú (Mercedes), Sergi López (Vidal), Ariadna Gil (Carmen)

"A long time ago, in the underground realm, where there are no lies or pain, there lived a Princess who dreamed of the human world. She dreamed of blue skies, soft breeze, and sunshine. One day, eluding her keepers, the Princess escaped."

—Pan

The year 2006 was great for the "Three Amigos"—the nickname for the long-time friends and Mexican directors Guillermo del Toro, Alejandro G. Iñárritu, and Alfonso Cuarón. Each director released a critically acclaimed film that year, and each of those films were nominated for at least one Academy Award. Cuarón was nominated for three Oscars for *Children of Men*, Iñárritu's *Babel* won Best Original Score, and del Toro's *Pan's Labyrinth* was nominated for six Oscars, including Best Foreign Film, winning three for its cinematography, makeup, and art direction. This was quite an achievement for a trio of filmmakers born in Mexico, who each found their own crossover success in America. As directors, they have vastly different styles, yet they freely collaborate and support one another. During a

2023 event honoring the three directors at the Academy Museum, Iñárritu put it simply, saying that while he thought it was a blessing to be a filmmaker, "it's so tough and so lonely to walk this path." As he added, he felt lucky to have "two friends that can hold you in failure and can celebrate with you in success. These two guys—without them, I would not exist."

Like Alejandro G. Iñárritu and Alfonso Cuarón, Guillermo del Toro had started his directing career in Mexican television. But unlike his amigos, del Toro's passion lay in the macabre. This had started at an early age—as a boy in Guadalajara, he had caught an episode of the TV show *Outer Limits* and became both scared and fascinated by the monsters he saw on his screen. Much of his time at high school was spent making horror movies with a Super-8

▲ Ivana Baquero as Ofelia

▲▲ Doug Jones as the Pale Man   ▲ Doug Jones again as the faun

camera and using household items as special effects and props. After graduation, he studied filmmaking at the University of Guadalajara, then an interest in monster makeup led him to a course run by the legendary artist Dick Smith. During the 1980s and '90s, del Toro set up his own special effects company, working as a makeup artist while also directing TV on the side. He taught at film workshops and set up the Mexican Film Festival in Guadalajara, but all the while, he was dreaming of directing a horror movie for the big screen.

That dream came true with *Cronos* (1992), a dark and original vampire tale. The critical and commercial success of *Cronos* caught the attention of Hollywood. Del Toro was hired to direct *Mimic* (1997), but he struggled to work within the American studio system. Around the same time, del Toro's growing fame in Mexico made him a target of criminals. In 1997, his father was kidnapped for ransom money, and del Toro and his brothers negotiated his release after seventy-two days. Following that ordeal, and with an eye on forging a career making bigger movies, del Toro took his family to Los Angeles.

Pan's Labyrinth came after Guillermo del Toro had made three successful films—one independently, *The Devil's Backbone* (2001), and two with Hollywood studios, *Blade II* (2002) and *Hellboy* (2004). By this time, del Toro had figured out a way to bring his own style to commercial films and how to use those earnings to fund movies he was truly passionate about. *Pan's Labyrinth* was born out of del Toro's love for fairy tales, and the way they can make sense of the real world. "Fantasies and stories," del Toro has said, "have the same weight in shaping who we are [as real experiences do]." With this script, he wanted to create a tale that felt familiar—as if it had been retold many times before and since.

His dark fable is set a few years after the end of the Civil War in Spain, when the country was ruled by dictator Francisco Franco and

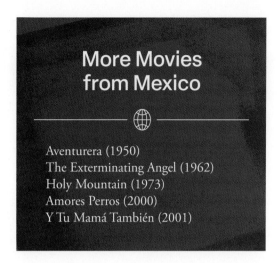

More Movies from Mexico

Aventurera (1950)
The Exterminating Angel (1962)
Holy Mountain (1973)
Amores Perros (2000)
Y Tu Mamá También (2001)

groups of rebels were doing their best to fight fascism. Ivana Baquero stars as twelve-year-old Ofelia, a dreamy young girl who loves to read and adores her mother. Ofelia's father has died, and her mother, Carmen (Ariadna Gil), has remarried the fascist Captain Vidal (Sergi López). Pregnant with Vidal's child, Carmen arrives with Ofelia at the captain's estate, and then falls deathly ill. Finding no affection from her authoritarian stepfather, and with her mother bedridden, Ofelia retreats to a world of fantasy—where she is a princess charged with undertaking three dangerous tasks to regain her throne, at the behest of a faun named Pan. He is played by a del Toro favorite, the contortionist and actor Doug Jones, who also plays the terrifying Pale Man in the film.

The script is an allegory for the traumas of war, though del Toro was, purposely, not heavy-handed in his messaging. In the years since the film's release, Ofelia's fantasies have been studied for symbolism and mined for meaning—which is a testament to del Toro's vivid imagination. He created a rich world filled with unforgettable monsters who haunt beautiful landscapes. It's never made clear whether Ofelia is imagining this world, or if it is really happening, and that was exactly what del Toro had intended. "I wanted the audience to experience a movie," he said, "in which they were not sure if the fairy tale

elements were real or not. But, I was sure. As far as I'm concerned, they're real."

This is a film that could have only come from the mind of Guillermo del Toro. His influences are varied and mixed, from a childhood spent in Mexico to an adulthood in America, plus his love of horror, fantasy, fairy tales, and most of all, being a bona fide cinephile. Movies are in his DNA, and his adoration of the work of Terry Gilliam, Luis Buñuel, Alfred Hitchcock, and Victor Erice's *The Spirit of the Beehive* (1973)

▲ "You're getting older, and you'll see that life isn't like your fairy tales." —Carmen

are sewn into the fabric of his films. It's impossible to separate initial influence from end product, because all of this is what makes up Guillermo del Toro himself.

Weaving real life into film fantasy is a common trait among the work of the Three Amigos. As del Toro said about himself, Alejandro G. Iñárritu, and Alfonso Cuarón, "For the three of us, one thing we have in common is that we don't have a difference between filmography and biography. We make movies that reflect our lives." And in Guillermo del Toro's case, movies that reflect our inner lives, inside our deepest imaginations.

A hot-tempered yet methodical fable in which fantastical and human calamity run hand in hand, the movie has the matter-of-fact magic and fearsome intercourse with historical blood of an Isaac Bashevis Singer or a Gabriel García Márquez story.

Michael Atkinson, film critic

▲ Director Guillermo del Toro gives direction to Doug Jones.

▶ Director Guillermo del Toro in 2023

All About My Mother

DIRECTED BY **Pedro Almodóvar**

To watch when you . . . want to see a vibrant
film celebrating mothers and women in all their glory.

Spain, 1999
Color, 101 minutes, Comedy

Screenplay: Pedro Almodóvar

Starring: Cecilia Roth (Manuela), Penélope
Cruz (Sister Rosa), Marisa Paredes
(Huma Rojo), Antonia San Juan (Agrado),
Candela Peña (Nina), Rosa Maria Sardá
(Rosa's mother)

"To Bette Davis, Gena Rowlands, Romy Schneider . . . To all
actresses who have played actresses. To all women who act.
To men who act and become women. To all the people
who want to be mothers. To my mother."

—Director's Dedication

Pedro Almodóvar said it best, when he described the bulk of his work as being "the cinema of women." For over five decades, Almodóvar has been making movies that put women front and center, with female protagonists who are messy, complicated, and emotional. He's brought those pushed out to the fringes of society into the spotlight, with plenty of queer and trans female characters in his work. He allows his characters to express the full breadth of their femininity, and, importantly, hires trans actresses to play trans women. And throughout his career, Almodóvar has made plenty of movies celebrating mothers of all kinds, and none more heartfelt than *All About My Mother* (1999).

As his dedication card in the credits explains, Almodóvar created *All About My Mother* to be a love letter to actresses, female performers of all kinds, and mothers—including his own. During the production of *All About My Mother*, Almodóvar's mom, Francisca Caballero, was unwell, and a few months after the film was released, she passed away. Penélope Cruz, who stars in this film (and many others by Almodóvar), said she felt lucky that she had the chance to meet his mother. "It helped me to understand," Cruz told the *New York Times*, "the way [Pedro] is and the fascination he has for women." Caballero had made cameos in several of Almodóvar's previous films, inspiring many of his characters along the way.

Pedro Almodóvar grew up with his family in a small village in the wine region of La

Mancha in Spain. His father had tried his hand at winemaking but hadn't been successful, and the family struggled for money. Because of that, Pedro's father was determined that he would get a sensible job when he grew up, with a secure income. But Pedro had fallen in love with movies at a young age, and after graduating high school, he announced to his parents that he was moving to Madrid to become a filmmaker. When Pedro arrived in the Spanish capital, he found that the film schools had been shut down by Spain's dictator, Francisco Franco. He remained undeterred and undertook his own education, visiting movie theaters at night and watching films from all over the world—movies from the French New Wave, Italian Neorealism, American film noir, and B movies made by the American producer/director Roger Corman. By day, he had a job at a phone company and used that money to buy a Super-8 camera to start making short films.

▲ Penélope Cruz as Rosa

In 1975, when Francisco Franco died, Pedro Almodóvar found himself at the center of a cultural explosion called La Movida. After so many years of being repressed under dictatorship, the young citizens of Madrid came out onto the streets in droves, celebrating with hedonistic parties and feeling a newfound freedom to express themselves fully. Men, women, and nonbinary people dressed up, wearing bright colors and trying on different identities—men in lipstick, women in dog collars—anything went, and everyone was welcomed.

▲ Cecilia Roth as Manuela

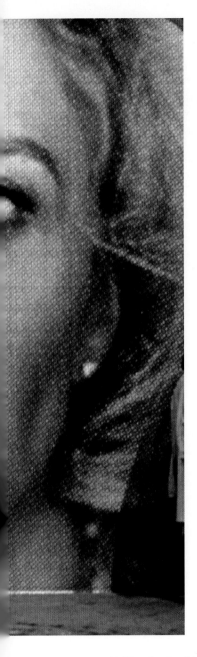

La Movida only lasted for a few short years, but its wild sensibility became ingrained in Pedro Almodóvar, who took the colors, the queerness, the freedom, the sexuality, and the open-mindedness, and put it into his movies.

The first feature that gained Almodóvar international notice was *Women on the Verge of a Nervous Breakdown* (1988), which won the Oscar for Best Foreign Language Film. He would win a second time for *All About My Mother*, his fourteenth feature. This marked a turning point in Almodóvar's career, a transition of sorts from his boundary-pushing and often explicit early films like *Tie Me Up! Tie Me Down!* (1989) to dramas that were more mature, though still quite edgy for the time. With a screenplay written by Almodóvar, *All About My Mother* follows Manuela (Cecilia Roth), who loses her son in a tragic accident, and travels to Barcelona to find his estranged father, Lola. She bumps into her old friend, Agrado (Antonia San Juan) and encourages her to get off the streets. Agrado introduces Manuela to a nun named Sister Rosa (Penélope Cruz), and Manuela agrees to look after Rosa when she falls pregnant. Manuela also starts working as a personal assistant to a stage actress performing in a production of *A Streetcar Named Desire*. The actress is Huma Rojo (Marisa Paredes), who explains that she gave herself that first name after being inspired by Bette Davis and the way she smoked cigarettes ("humo" translates to "smoke" in Spanish).

A Streetcar Named Desire, Bette Davis, and *All About Eve* (1950) all factor into the story, with Almodóvar also weaving in the idea of women performing in their daily lives. "Life is filled with these miniature plays," he said, "where people are forced to act or fake, and women are naturally born actresses." Many scenes take place inside Huma's dressing room, which to Almodóvar is the "center of the female universe. I very much like to see the actresses when they are making up or getting dressed. It's very intimate. They talk. It seems to me that women can't lie in a dressing room or in the toilet or in the kitchen. These are spaces in which you can only say the truth."

Almodóvar looks at the female characters in *All About My Mother* through a nonjudgmental and compassionate lens, inviting the audience to do the same. Manuela is racked

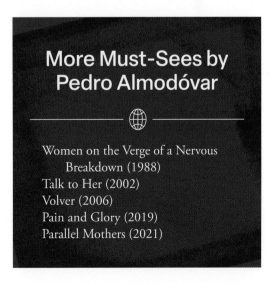

More Must-Sees by Pedro Almodóvar

Women on the Verge of a Nervous Breakdown (1988)
Talk to Her (2002)
Volver (2006)
Pain and Glory (2019)
Parallel Mothers (2021)

▲ Marisa Paredes as Huma

with grief over her son's death but finds a new family of women to "mother" in Barcelona, including the female identifying Agrado. Agrado is a bright spark in this movie, brought to life with a hilarious performance by Antonia San Juan. In one scene, Agrado walks onto a stage and delivers a monologue about her life that is, at turns, funny and heartbreaking. She speaks about the price of her plastic surgeries, saying, "It costs a lot to be authentic. And one can't be stingy with these things, because you are more authentic the more you resemble what you've dreamed of being."

All About My Mother was released in Spain in April 1999, and a month later it played at the Cannes Film Festival. This was Pedro Almodóvar's first film to be selected to screen at the prestigious festival, and he took home the

Best Director Award. The movie continued to pick up awards in many different countries and was greeted with positive critical reviews when it made its way to the United States. Almodóvar won the Oscar for Best Foreign Film at the Academy Awards in 2000, and this second time on the Oscars stage was made even more special because two of his close friends and collaborators, Penélope Cruz and Antonio Banderas, presented him with the statuette. They were unable to conceal their excitement when they announced *All About My Mother* as the winner, with Cruz opening the envelope and screaming, "PEDRO!" Once onstage, Almodóvar gave Cruz and Banderas a big hug, dedicating his Oscar to everyone in Spain who had stayed up late to watch the awards. "This is for Spain," Pedro Almodóvar said. He continued his speech, but soon the band started to play, and he was still thanking people as Antonio Banderas jokingly pulled him off the stage.

Gay filmmakers like Almodóvar may be providing a last refuge for decent parts for women, and for wholehearted melodrama in our hyperironic age.

Ella Taylor, film critic

▲ Pedro Almodóvar directs Antonia San Juan for Agrado's monologue.

Went the Day Well?

DIRECTED BY **Alberto Cavalcanti**

To watch when you . . . feel like a surprising action film set in a cozy English village.

UK, 1942
B&W, 92 minutes, War

Screenplay: John Dighton, Diana Morgan, Angus MacPhail, based on a story by Graham Greene

Starring: Leslie Banks (Oliver Wilsford), Valerie Taylor (Nora), Marie Lohr (Mrs. Fraser), Harry Fowler (George), Basil Sydney (Major Ortler), David Farrar (Lieutenant Jung)

"They wanted England, these Jerries did, and this is the only bit they got. The Battle of Bramley End, the papers called it. Nothing was said about it until after the war, and old Hitler got what was coming to him."

—Charlie Sims

There are many surprising moments in *Went the Day Well?*, a British war propaganda film from 1942; but one particularly memorable scene involves an older woman, a Nazi soldier, and a hatchet. The woman, a postmistress named Mrs. Collins (Muriel George), is being held hostage by the German, and he demands that she serve him dinner. Suddenly, she throws pepper into his face, grabs a hatchet, and brings it down on him with all her might. It's astonishingly brutal, but also exhilarating, as the folksy villagers in a sleepy English town turn into vigilantes to fight back against the German paratroopers who hold them captive.

The title *Went the Day Well?* is similarly deceiving, sounding like a lovely greeting that one neighbor may say to another. In fact, it's a line from a British poem that was published in newspaper columns announcing the dead during World Wars I and II. The full poem reads: "Went the day well? We died and never knew. But well, or ill, freedom, we died for you." The plot is loosely based on a magazine story written by Graham Greene called "The Lieutenant Died Last," and the adapted script was cowritten by John Dighton and Angus MacPhail with Diana Morgan, who was the only female writer in residence at Ealing Studios.

It begins in a graveyard, with a local villager who speaks directly to the camera. He points out a few gravestones and remarks on how odd it is to have German names in an English village. From there, the film flashes back to Saturday, May 23, a spring day that starts out like any other in the small (fictional) village of Bramley End. We meet several of the

▲ Nazis posing as British soldiers take over Bramley End.

▲ The townspeople are held hostage.

locals and observe their daily routines—which are suddenly interrupted with the arrival of a group of English soldiers. They are put up in various houses of the local people, but as they settle in, one villager, Nora (Valerie Taylor), starts to notice a few discrepancies in the way the soldiers act and questions whether they are who they claim to be.

Nora's intuition proves correct. The soldiers reveal themselves to be Nazis, and they take the townspeople hostage. This town, however, is not about to sit back and let that happen, and they decide to fight, with several of the villagers losing their lives in the process. Again, this is somewhat

surprising for a 1940s war film—in addition to the hatchet incident, the vicar is shot in the back, some of the nicest characters are brutally killed, the genteel women of the town take up arms, and Nazis threaten to shoot all the children at dawn. It's almost as if Quentin Tarantino took a time machine back to the 1940s, injecting his brand of bloody anarchy into a stately British drama. But

the slightly surreal tone, the brutal realism, and the beautiful visuals were all the product of its director, Alberto Cavalcanti—credited under the single name of Cavalcanti.

Cavalcanti was born in Brazil, but started his film career in Paris, designing sets during

▲ Valerie Taylor as Nora and Leslie Banks as Oliver

▲▲ The locals arm up to fight back.

▲ German paratroopers infiltrate the sleepy English village.

the 1920s for surrealist and avant-garde French filmmakers. His own directorial debut came in 1926 and was similarly experimental. Called *Nothing but Time*, the film involved Cavalcanti taking a camera out to the streets of Paris, capturing the city from dawn to dusk, then adding surreal touches and special effects. He moved to England in the early 1930s and directed a series of documentaries. And even when Cavalcanti switched to directing narrative features at Ealing Studios, he used a documentary-like visual style, with moments of surrealism mixed in among the realism.

Went the Day Well? was produced by the historic Ealing Studios. Ealing was established in 1902, with the first soundstages being built in 1931 under the guidance of theater producer Basil Dean, who created them for his film company Associated Talking Pictures. Ealing now has the distinction of being the longest continual running movie studio in the world, and it really flourished in the late 1930s, when producer Michael Balcon took over. He increased movie production, helped to encourage the careers of several up-and-coming filmmakers such as Alfred Hitchcock, and established Ealing's reputation for producing films with high production values.

As World War II loomed, Ealing started to hire documentary filmmakers (such

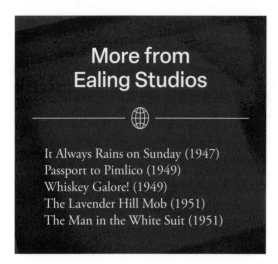

More from Ealing Studios

It Always Rains on Sunday (1947)
Passport to Pimlico (1949)
Whiskey Galore! (1949)
The Lavender Hill Mob (1951)
The Man in the White Suit (1951)

▲ Director Alberto Cavalcanti

as Cavalcanti) to bring a sense of realism to their war dramas and propaganda movies. The initial idea for *Went the Day Well?* was to warn the British public about the dangers of Nazi Germany, and when it was released in England in 1942, it worked as a morale booster for the local audience—celebrating the "stiff upper lip" of British people, who face adversity with strength. *Went the Day Well?* was also released in the United States, coming to America two years later, in 1944, under the title *48 Hours.*

Eighty years on, *Went the Day Well?* continues to surprise film lovers—during the 2020 COVID lockdown, director Edgar Wright asked Martin Scorsese if he had any favorite British films. Scorsese sent him back a voice note listing fifty titles, including *Went the Day Well?* Wright sent the list to his friend, Quentin Tarantino, and the two formed an unofficial "quarantine movie club" to make their way through Scorsese's selections. Wright commented on the experience of watching *Went the Day Well?* in an interview with film critic Mark Kermode, noting how he had seen Cavalcanti's work in the anthology film *Dead of Night* (1945) and *They Made Me a Fugitive* (1947), but had missed *Went the Day Well?* "Strangely," Wright said, "I hadn't seen *Went the Day Well?* before I made *Hot Fuzz*, despite the fact that it's a rural semi-action film in which Thora Hird wields a

machine gun. It's really dark. On paper, some older British movies may sound sort of twee and cozy, yet they're anything but. That was the real revelation for me, especially with Ealing films like this, or *Nowhere to Go*, *It Always Rains on Sunday*, and *Pink String and Sealing Wax*. This is the darker side of Ealing."

Propaganda this may have been, but how extraordinary, in 1942—with the war far from won—playfully to imply that the home-front manners of British decency could easily be an insidious veneer.

Peter Bradshaw, film critic

The Passion of Joan of Arc

DIRECTED BY **Carl Th. Dreyer**

To watch when you . . . are curious to see a masterpiece of silent cinema.

France/Denmark, 1928
B&W, 81 minutes, Drama

Screenplay: Carl Th. Dreyer,
Joseph Delteil

Starring: Renée Falconetti (Joan), Eugène Silvain (Pierre Cauchon), André Berley (Jean d'Estivet)

> "You claim that I am sent by the Devil. It's not true. To make me suffer, the Devil has sent you . . . and you . . . and you . . . and you."
>
> —Joan

The first thing that strikes you about *The Passion of Joan of Arc* (1928) is the cinematography. Danish director Carl Theodor Dreyer and his cinematographer, Rudolph Maté, utilize multiple close-ups of Renée Falconetti's compelling face to immerse the viewer into the mental anguish of a young woman put on trial by suspicious men and sentenced to death. For a film that is almost one hundred years old, it remains astonishing and transcendent—well worthy of being called one of the greatest films made during the silent era.

Prior to directing films, Carl Th. Dreyer had many different occupations. He worked as a clerk and a pianist before a job in journalism introduced him to film and theater; then he became a theater critic. Finally, Dreyer entered the film industry in 1913 as a writer of intertitles for silent films. He branched out from there, writing scripts, finding books and plays to adapt, and working as an editor. Dreyer's directorial debut came in 1919 with *The President*, based on a novel that he had found and adapted, and he continued to adapt various literary sources for his next several projects. The opportunity to direct *The Passion of Joan of Arc* came to him through a French film company called Société Générale des Films. Run by a wealthy Frenchman, the company agreed to give Dreyer an initial budget of seven million francs—a huge number for the time. Société Générale des Films wanted to make a

▲ Renée (Maria) Falconetti as Joan of Arc

film about a historic French figure, and Dreyer suggested Joan of Arc, having become interested in her after her canonization in 1920.

There were quite a few protests about a Danish director being the one who would bring the French saint's story to the big screen, but Dreyer did extensive research, taking a year of preproduction to study the transcripts of Joan's trial. He hired the editor of the 1921 publication of those transcripts, Pierre Champion, as a historic consultant, and carefully planned the shoot, deciding that he would film the script in sequence. A giant re-creation of Rouen castle—the site of Joan's imprisonment—was built. Production designers Hermann Warm and Jean Hugo strived to get the details as historically correct as possible, using medieval illuminated manuscripts for reference. Dreyer also focused on authenticity in casting, choosing stage actress Renée (Maria) Falconetti for her "rustic" looks, and asking her to cut her hair short—and then, to shave it—for the production. Falconetti and the other actors were forbidden to wear makeup, with Dreyer later writing, "In order to give the truth, I dispensed with 'beautification.' My actors were not allowed to touch makeup and powder puffs." Interestingly, while the sets, acting, and look of the actors were important to him, Dreyer wasn't as worried about the costumes being accurate. "A thorough study of the documents from the rehabilitation process was necessary," wrote Dreyer, "[but] I did not study the clothes of the time, and things like that. The year of the event seemed as inessential

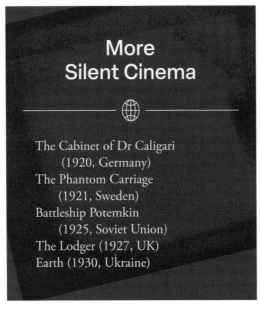

More Silent Cinema

The Cabinet of Dr Caligari (1920, Germany)
The Phantom Carriage (1921, Sweden)
Battleship Potemkin (1925, Soviet Union)
The Lodger (1927, UK)
Earth (1930, Ukraine)

to me as its distance from the present. I wanted to interpret a hymn to the triumph of the soul over life."

A "hymn" is an apt way to describe this mesmerizing and spiritual film, which follows the nineteen-year-old Joan of Arc (Renée Falconetti) as she is put through a harrowing trial by Bishop Pierre Cauchon (Eugène Silvain) over accusations of heresy. She is interrogated about her visions, whether she consorts with the Devil, and why she wears men's clothes; all the while being pressured to sign a confession that would deny her own truth. On the thirtieth of May, 1431, she was judged as being guilty and was burned at the stake.

On the set, Dreyer chose not to direct in the usual way of silent films—where music was played, and the actors were instructed by the director. Instead, he kept his set silent, and only gave his actors limited direction, recording multiple takes until he found the moments of truth that he was after. Dreyer explained that he would begin each day by watching the "bad" takes from the day before, saying, "We would examine it, we would search and we always ended by finding, in that bad take, some little fragments, some little light that rendered the exact expression, the tonality we had been looking for. It is from there that we would set out again, taking the

▶▶ "Dear God, I accept my death gladly but do not let me suffer too long." —Joan

▶ Antonin Artaud as Jean Massieu

best and abandoning the remainder." His use of rapid editing and close-ups was intentional—the camera focuses often on Falconetti's wide, pleading eyes—and in doing away with the usual establishing shots, which would introduce the audience to the space, Dreyer created a disorientating, claustrophobic feeling, designed so viewers would feel the walls closing in on the increasingly helpless Joan.

By the time *The Passion of Joan of Arc* was released, silent films were on their way out. Even though several silent filmmakers (such as Dreyer and the German F. W. Murnau) were working at the height of their artistry, the introduction of sound was a novelty for audiences of the late 1920s, who flocked to see their favorite actors talk. "Silent film was not ripe for replacement," wrote the German film theorist Rudolph Arnheim in 1930, "It had not lost its fruitfulness, but only its profitability." This is true of *The Passion of Joan of Arc*, because while Dreyer had created his film—with its final budget of nine million francs—to screen for a wide audience, it was admired by critics but was not a commercial success. Adding to its woes was a fire at UFA studios in Berlin in 1928, which destroyed the original negative. Dreyer was distressed by this loss, and re-created his movie as best as he could, editing outtakes together to make a second version. Unfortunately, the highly flammable nitrate film stock in use at the time led to many fires in storage facilities, and this secondary print was believed to have been destroyed in a fire in 1929. But in 1951, a copy of the second version was discovered by a film historian, and amazingly, thirty years after that, in 1981, a Danish print of the original was found at a Norwegian mental institution. These negatives were used to do an extensive restoration in 1985 that added back the French intertitles. By that time, *The Passion of Joan of*

▲ The expressive face of Renée (Maria) Falconetti

◀ Director Carl Th. Dreyer

Arc was being lauded as one of the greatest films of all time.

Its reputation has only increased since then, with much acclaim given to Renée Falconetti's remarkable performance in her second and final film role. Following *The Passion of Joan of Arc*, the Danish film industry struggled, so Dreyer needed to get private financing to make his next movie, *Vampyr* (1932). He continued to direct films whenever he could until the mid-1960s, creating more meditations on religion that would be critically acclaimed: *Day of Wrath* (1943) and *Ordet* (1955). In between, he went back to journalism, and even managed a movie theater for a time. When he died in 1968, Carl Th. Dreyer had built a filmography of

movies that are all different from one another, but undeniably come from his singular vision. Somehow, they each—especially *The Passion of Joan of Arc*—feel timeless, as if they could be from our time, or from no time at all . . . suspended in the air, like a dream.

▼ Carl Dreyer's close-ups focus on the faces of Joan and the men putting her on trial.

One of the greatest of all movies . . . No other film has so subtly linked eroticism with religious persecution. Falconetti's Joan may be the finest performance ever recorded on film.

Pauline Kael, film critic

SUMMER

La Dolce Vita

DIRECTED BY **Federico Fellini**

To watch when you . . . could do with a cool summer dip in the Trevi fountain in Rome.

Italy, 1960
B&W, 174 minutes, Tragicomedy

Screenplay: Federico Fellini, Ennio Flaiano, Tullio Pinelli, Brunello Rondi

Starring: Marcello Mastroianni (Marcello Rubini), Anita Ekberg (Sylvia), Anouk Aimée (Maddalena), Yvonne Furneaux (Emma)

> ## "By 1965 there will be total depravity. How squalid everything will be."
>
> —Travestito

In hindsight, 1960 was a year filled with movies that would shake up the old conventions of cinema. In France, *Breathless* and *The 400 Blows* kicked off the Nouvelle Vague. In the UK, director Michael Powell shocked audiences (and just about ended his career) with *Peeping Tom*, while in the United States, Alfred Hitchcock also shocked with his thriller *Psycho*. Swedish filmmaker Ingmar Bergman won the Academy Award for Best Foreign Film with *The Virgin Spring*, and competed at the 1960 Cannes Film Festival—where the Italian director Michelangelo Antonioni's *L'Avventura* incited boos and hisses from the audience, and fellow Italian Federico Fellini won the major prize for *La Dolce Vita*.

La Dolce Vita translates to "the sweet life," but the life of the protagonist, journalist Marcello Rubini (Marcello Mastroianni), is anything but sweet. Though he regularly indulges in hedonistic nighttime pleasures, his is an empty life, partying with vapid celebrities and socialites, and churning out celebrity gossip instead of challenging himself by finishing his novel. Seen today, the debauchery in *La Dolce Vita* seems tame, but in its time it was shocking, and it predicted the obsession with fame that would emerge over the following few decades. This film also gave the word "paparazzi" to the world—a photographer in *La Dolce Vita* is called Paparazzo, played by Walter Santesso.

With *La Dolce Vita*, director Federico Fellini was turning his camera inward, to spoof the celebrity scene he had become part of in Rome. Born in the seaside city of Rimini, Fellini loved to draw, and he escaped his hometown for Florence, for a job illustrating comic strips and proofreading. He enrolled in the University of Rome, intending to study

▲ Marcello Mastroianni as Marcello and Anita Ekberg as Sylvia

law, but he skipped classes to work as a cartoonist and writer of satirical short stories. At nineteen, his long-held fascination with circuses led to a stint with a traveling vaudeville troupe, where Fellini painted sets, wrote sketches, and did menial tasks. The year he spent with the troupe would be a meaningful one, with Fellini later calling it "perhaps the most important year of [his] life" for the way it allowed him to see Italy and learn more about himself. "It was the kind of experience that few young men are fortunate enough to have," he said. "A chance to discover the character of one's country and, at the same time, to discover one's own identity."

By 1942, Fellini was back in Rome, writing scripts for radio, then for films. He avoided being drafted into World War II by hiding out at his aunt's house. Following the war, he opened

a store, called the Funny Face Shop, where he drew caricatures for Allied soldiers to send back to their families. That was where he met the director Roberto Rossellini, who visited the shop and eventually invited Fellini to work with him on a film project—which would turn out to be *Rome, Open City* (1945). Directed by Rossellini and written by Fellini with Rossellini and Sergio Amidei, *Rome, Open City* was a landmark Italian Neorealist picture, and it helped to kick off the whole movement toward realistic cinema.

Fellini and Rossellini worked together on his follow-up film, *Paisan* (1946), but by 1950, Fellini felt ready to get into the director's chair himself. He made his own mark on Italian Neorealism by injecting a touch of surrealism into the style. In doing so, his first international breakthrough, *La Strada* (1954), marked the beginning of the end of the cinematic movement. This poetic story followed a young clown, played by Fellini's wife, Guilietta Masina, who

▲ "There are three things I like most: love, love, and love." —Sylvia

▲ The famous scene at the Trevi fountain.

joins a circus, and it won the Best Foreign Film Academy Award at the Oscars. More acclaim and Oscars followed with *Il Bidone* (1955) and *Nights of Cabiria* (1957), but on *La Dolce Vita*, Fellini would shapeshift again—creating a three-hour savage satire of celebrity culture, starring his alter ego, the actor Marcello Mastroianni, in a role that would make Mastroianni an international star.

The screenplay is complex, written by Fellini with three of his regular screenwriting collaborators, Tullio Pinelli, Ennio Flaiano, and Brunello Rondi. Set over a week, the action follows Marcello as he works (and plays) in Rome. It comprises seven stories, which each feature a night scene (the party) and a dawn scene (the aftermath). There's also a prologue, a few

interludes, and a surreal epilogue. Throughout these episodes, the journalist Marcello encounters and reencounters several personalities, who were based on real figures—most memorably a Swedish-American Marilyn Monroe type of

▲ Federico Fellini directing on the set of La Dolce Vita

Fantastic Federico Fellini Films

🌐

La Strada (1954)
Il Bidone (1955)
Nights of Cabiria (1957)
8½ (1963)
Amarcord (1973)

actress, played by Anita Ekberg, who takes a famous dip in the Trevi fountain. She is a bright spark in this tragicomedy, where nobody seems to be having any fun. Fellini makes the viewer feel compassion for the characters who are the most naïve, but he also reveals the seemingly moralistic ones to be monsters underneath. All the hedonism builds to a disturbing party scene—one that caused much controversy in 1960—where Marcello tries to drunkenly convince his fellow partygoers to have an orgy.

The Vatican objected to *La Dolce Vita* when it was released, as did the Italian government, and the film was banned in several countries. But despite (or perhaps, thanks to) the scandal that it caused, *La Dolce Vita* was a hit. It was to be the most commercially successful film directed by Federico Fellini and won the major prize at the Cannes Film Festival. This critical acclaim was soon eclipsed by the reaction to Fellini's next feature, the autobiographical *8½* (1963), again

starring Marcello Mastroianni as a version of the director. Fellini would continue to find success internationally over the rest of his career, culminating with an honorary Oscar in 1993 "in recognition of his cinematic accomplishments that have thrilled and entertained worldwide audiences." Federico Fellini died from a heart attack later that same year, with his wife of fifty years, Guilietta Masina, by his side.

▲ "Once I had ambitions, but maybe I'm losing everything. I forgot everything." —Marcello

After a dozen years of neorealism, which cataloged the privations of postwar Italy, Fellini reinvented Rome as a caravan of dreams or nightmares, debauched, pathetic, yet perfidiously appealing, a tourist attraction and also a recruitment station for the inferno.

Gary Giddins, film critic

Black Girl

DIRECTED BY **Ousmane Sembène**

To watch when you . . . want a shorter film that still packs a big punch, featuring a complex (and compelling) message.

Senegal, 1966
B&W, 59 minutes, Drama

Screenplay: Ousmane Sembène, based on a story by Ousmane Sembène

Starring: M'Bissine Thérèse Diop (Diouana), Anne-Marie Jelinek (Madame), Robert Fontaine (Monsieur)

> **"I spend my life between the kitchen and my bedroom. Is that living in France?"**
>
> —Diouana

The original title of the landmark 1966 drama by Ousmane Sembène is *Le Noire de…* The direct English translation would not be *Black Girl*, but instead, *The Black of…* This title infers a type of possession, using language more commonly associated with slavery—implying white ownership of a Black person. It's appropriate for *Black Girl*, as Sembène looks at a type of Black indentured servant, one confined by the lingering prejudice of the white French following the independence of Senegal.

Ousmane Sembène arrived at directing relatively late into his life, making *Black Girl* at the age of forty-three. He had grown up in Senegal but migrated to France during his twenties—reportedly, illegally stowing away on a boat to get there. Senegal had been under French rule virtually since the French had begun trading in the country during the fourteenth century, but in 1960, Senegal was finally given

independence. In the meantime, Sembène had taught himself to read and write in French and started to use his own experiences and beliefs to write books—such as his 1956 novel *The Black Docker*, which drew on his time working on the docks of Marseilles and examined the ill treatment of African immigrants. Following Senegal's independence, Sembène began to visit his home country more frequently, and during those trips, he noted how the scars of colonialism had continued to inflict damage on the native population. He also realized that his work could have more of an effect if it were filmed, rather than written. "I realized with a book," Sembène later said, "especially in Africa where illiteracy is known to prevail, I could only touch a limited number of people. I became aware that film, on the contrary, was likely to reach broad masses."

Sembène enrolled in a film school in Russia to learn directing and worked at the Gorki

film studio in Moscow. When he returned to Senegal, Sembène made his directing debut with *Borom Sarret* (1963), a short film about a horse cart driver in Dakar, which looked at the poverty remaining after Senegal's independence. This short was the first sub-Saharan African film to have been made by a Black African, and Sembène made more history with his second movie (and first feature), *Black Girl*.

    Black Girl was the first movie to be made by a sub-Saharan African director, and Sembène had based the script on one of his own short stories. It's a deceptively simple film, only an hour long, shot in black and white. M'Bissine Thérèse Diop plays Diouana, who we first see on a boat traveling from Dakar to Antibes in France. She is joining a white family in France for their

summer vacation, and while she's expecting to look after the children of the family, she discovers that it's only the husband (Robert Fontaine) and the wife (Anne-Marie Jelinek) who are in the house. Once there, Diouana becomes a prisoner, locked in the house ("for her own safety")

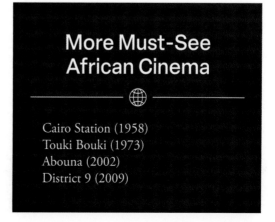

More Must-See African Cinema

Cairo Station (1958)
Touki Bouki (1973)
Abouna (2002)
District 9 (2009)

▲ "Maybe they'll show me the city. Maybe we'll go to Cannes, Nice, Monte Carlo . . ." —Diouana

▲ M'bissine Thérèse Diop as Diouana

and expected to cook and clean as their maid. Through flashbacks and voice-over, Diouana tells her story, explaining how she got this job, and how different it was for her to work for the family back in Dakar. We see how excited she was for the chance to travel to France, and how she imagined shopping for dresses that would make her relatives jealous. Her reality is very different. She is essentially a slave, with the couple (and their friends) either berating or exoticizing her. Diouana is seen as an "other," and slowly, she loses her spark and self-esteem.

The white French couple are abhorrent, though Ousmane Sembène does not judge any of his characters. Instead, he's attempting to show how years of colonialism have shaped the prejudices and expectations of people—both white and Black. The couple, especially the wife, has an inbuilt feeling of superiority over Diouana, and in turn, Diouana is compliant and silent because

she's used to acting subservient to survive. Sembène gives Diouana back her voice with the voice-over, allowing the viewer to hear the inner turmoil that lies behind her stoic face. The flashbacks of Diouana in Dakar are heartbreaking because we can see just how lively and confident she used to be. But with Diouana's dreams of a more glamorous life in France, Sembène is also examining how colonialism, with its capitalist goals, has affected her, too.

Black Girl features a remarkable performance by first-time actress M'Bissine Thérèse Diop. She has limited dialogue in the film but manages to convey Diouana's range of emotions with her expressions, her body, her hair, and her costumes. Sembène had discovered Diop after she had been photographed in Senegal. She was attending art school, where one of her classes had involved acting, but she was more focused on dressmaking at the time. Sembène pitched her the idea, and Diop was interested in trying something new—and also offered to make the dresses that her character would wear in the movie. Following *Black Girl,* Diop would act in a few more movies, working with Ousmane Sembène again on *Emitai* (1971). Sembène himself also appears in *Black Girl,* making a cameo as a writer in Dakar, complete with his ever-present pipe.

Prior to *Black Girl,* there was not much of a film industry in Africa, and depictions of native Africans were usually made by colonial ethnographers. Even if these ethnographers were well-intentioned, such as the French filmmaker Jean Rouch, Africans themselves couldn't freely share their own stories. This was something Ousmane Sembène had felt strongly about, saying, "If Africans do not tell their own stories, Africa will soon disappear." In 1963, after the independence of Senegal, France had set up a cinema bureau within the Senegalese Ministry of Cooperation, which invited African filmmakers to submit scripts for financing. *Black Girl* was the only script that was rejected from funding—reportedly because of its subject matter—but Sembène was not going to back down, and he put together a tiny budget himself to make it happen. Sembène had been particularly driven to tell a story of multiple oppressions—throughout the film, Diouana experiences prejudice because she is a native African, racism because she is Black, and sexism because she's a woman.

Black Girl screened at the Cannes Film Festival, where it virtually went unnoticed amongst the flashier styles of the French New Wave and its imitators. Sembène's style was closer to Italian Neorealism in its simplicity, and its focus on the struggles of everyday people. But soon, *Black Girl* picked up critical acclaim and went on to win awards internationally. With its success, more films in Africa (directed by Africans) started

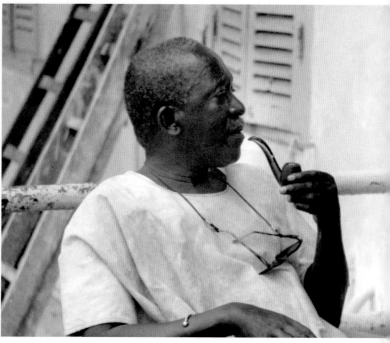

▲ Director Ousmane Sembène

to be made. Ousmane Sembène died in 2007, and his legacy as the first sub-Saharan African director to make a feature-length film, along with his subsequent body of work, earned him the title "the father of African cinema."

Black Girl is thus, in some ways, a documentary after the fact, an attempt to trace an awful, easily forgotten event to its source and to emphasize its political implications. The fate of an individual . . . is used to illuminate larger issues of identity, exploitation and displacement.

A. O. Scott, film critic

The Young Girls of Rochefort

DIRECTED BY **Jacques Demy**

To watch when you . . . feel like dancing through your troubles in the pastel-colored streets of a small town in France.

France, 1967
Color, 126 minutes, Musical

Screenplay: Jacques Demy

Starring: Catherine Deneuve (Delphine Garnier), Françoise Dorléac (Solange Garnier), Gene Kelly (Andy Miller), George Chakiris (Étienne), Grover Dale (Bill), Jacques Perrin (Maxence), Danielle Darrieux (Yvonne Garnier), Michel Piccoli (Simon Dame)

"We are a pair of twins, born in the sign of Gemini . . ."

—Delphine and Solange

During his lifetime, the films of director Jacques Demy went largely unappreciated. He was part of the explosion of new talent who formed the French New Wave, but while his movies were just as daring and innovative, Demy's style made him an outsider within the cinematic movement. The filmmakers of the French New Wave, such as Jean-Luc Godard, François Truffaut, Alain Resnais, and Claude Chabrol, used their experimental, avant-garde filmmaking to confront real issues happening in France, while Jacques Demy's films were something else. They were in a world all their own, with a heightened realism that blurred into fantasy. And his movies weren't shot with handheld cameras on black-and-white film; they were an explosion of color. Demy's two musicals, *The Umbrellas of Cherbourg* (1964) and *The Young Girls of Rochefort* (1967), were also dismissed because of the obvious inspiration he took from the Technicolor classic musicals of MGM. But many of the New Wave directors who were taken more seriously, such as Godard and Truffaut, had looked to Hollywood for inspiration, most particularly in the landmark gangster movies *Breathless* (1960) and *Shoot the Piano Player* (1960). And while Demy's movies may have looked happy and bright, that was merely the surface. Lying below, among the romance, there was plenty of melancholy, tragedy, and suffering to be found.

▲▲ Catherine Deneuve as Delphine and Françoise Dorléac as Solange
▲ The sisters perform an homage to *Gentlemen Prefer Blondes* (1953).

▶ Catherine Deneuve and Françoise Dorléac were sisters in real life.

In the 1960s, Demy was not considered to be radical enough to take a place within the French New Wave, but that started to shift following his death in 1990, thanks to his wife, the filmmaker Agnès Varda. She worked hard to keep his legacy alive, overseeing restorations and rereleases of his films, and offered her own perspective on his life and place in cinema history with films like *Jacquot of Nantes* (1991) and *The World of Jacques Demy* (1995). In 1993, Varda released a documentary about the making of *The Young Girls of Rochefort*, called *The Young Girls Turn 25*. In it, she travels back to the location of the film with some of the cast, to reflect on its legacy and her own memories of being on set. As she says, in a typically playful Agnès Varda fashion, "The memory of happiness is perhaps also happiness."

Demy had the opportunity to make *The Young Girls of Rochefort* after the huge commercial success of his previous musical, *The Umbrellas of Cherbourg*. That film had won the Palme d'Or at the 1964 Cannes Film Festival and was also nominated for five Academy Awards. *The Umbrellas of Cherbourg* was unusual in that it was entirely sung—with no dialogue—set to haunting music composed by the legendary Michel Legrand. Demy and Legrand had been close collaborators for many years, and they next decided to create a companion piece to *Cherbourg, The Young Girls of Rochefort*. The two worked together on a score, and this time decided it would be a more traditional musical, with dialogue scenes inserted in between the songs.

The *Umbrellas of Cherbourg* star Catherine Deneuve was cast, alongside her real-life sister, Françoise Dorléac. They play artistic twins named Delphine and Solange, who live in the small town of Rochefort, but have big dreams. The action takes place over a single weekend, when a fair has come to town, bringing dancers Étienne (George Chakiris) and Bill (Grover Dale), who ask the twins to perform on their stage. But the bigger theme of the movie is missed connections and second chances. Delphine, Solange, and their mother, Yvonne (Danielle Darrieux), each unknowingly has an ideal partner living in the town,

whom she keeps missing. For Yvonne, it's her
long-lost love, Simon Dame (Michel Piccoli),
who had asked her to marry him years before,
but she said no, because she thought "Madame
Dame" sounded ridiculous. Delphine dreams
of an ideal love not realizing she is the dream

woman of a soldier and artist named Maxence
(Jacques Perrin), whose painting of Delphine
hangs in a local gallery. And Solange bumps
into a visiting American named Andy Miller
(Gene Kelly), who she instantly recognizes as
her one true love but doesn't know he is the

composer she had requested to meet, to hear her composition.

Throughout *The Young Girls of Rochefort*, Jacques Demy pays homage to iconic Hollywood musicals, including *An American in Paris* (1951) and *West Side Story* (1961). The casting of musical performers Gene Kelly and George Chakiris in key roles acts as a further nod to his admiration for the genre. Both Kelly and Chakiris, as well as fellow American Grover Dale, had to learn how to phonetically speak and sing in French, though their voices were ultimately dubbed by French singers and actors. The only member of the cast who sings her own songs is Danielle Darrieux. The cast also had the extra

▲ George Chakiris and Grover Dale play the "carnies" who visit the town of Rochefort.

challenge of recording the entire film in both French and English. Two versions of *The Young Girls of Rochefort* were created, but the English version wasn't well-received and was taken out

More Musicals from France

🌐

Le Million (1931)
French Cancan (1955)
Black Orpheus (1959)
A Woman Is a Woman (1961)
The Umbrellas of Cherbourg (1964)

of circulation. Today, that version is nowhere to be found, save for a short clip, on YouTube.

Filming took place between May and August of 1966 in the actual town of Rochefort, where the shutters on the windows surrounding the town square were painted in shades of pastel colors for the production. In the sweltering summer heat, the cast learned the dance choreography by Norman Maen. The sweat and fatigue are evident in Agnès Varda's *The Young Girls Turn 25*, as stars Deneuve and Dorléac performed multiple takes of their finale musical number, one that pays homage to Marilyn Monroe and Jane Russell in *Gentlemen Prefer Blondes* (1953).

Dorléac had found success in film before her younger sister Catherine. Their family had advised Catherine not to use their surname of Dorléac, to create her own path, and though she later regretted not keeping her original name, Catherine Deneuve forged a successful, enduring career as a versatile film actress, where she was directed by Jacques Demy several times. Working with Demy, Deneuve said, made her realize that "the most important thing was to do the things you want with people you trust and whose ideas don't seem too conventional." Denueve also acted for a variety of unconventional filmmakers all over the world, such as Luis Buñuel, Lars von Trier, Roman Polanski, and François Truffaut. And with *The Young Girls of Rochefort*, Demy proved his unconventionality, because among all the music, the dancing sailors with pom-pom hats, and the color palette of neon and pastel pinks, blues, and yellows, there's melancholy to be found, and the story even includes a brutal ax murder.

The Young Girls of Rochefort was to be the first and final film to star sisters Françoise Dorléac and Catherine Deneuve. Tragically, just before the release of *Young Girls*, in 1967, Dorléac died in a car accident. She had completed one last film, *Billion Dollar Brain* (1967), but wasn't able to experience the type

▲ Director Jacques Demy

of international stardom she was seemingly on the cusp of. Following the accident, Catherine Deneuve was inconsolable, but has later said that out of her sister's films, *The Young Girls of Rochefort* remains the only one she can bear to watch. "We were very close," Deneuve later told an interviewer, "and shooting that film brought us even closer, back to a place and way we had been when we were much younger. Life can give you some terrible knocks, and there's not a happy ending every time. But I do believe in them. I am very optimistic. I am still very romantic about life."

The vexing yet unmistakable triumph of this movie is that it somehow manages to be both more artificial and more realistic than we expect our musicals to be.

Jonathan Rosenbaum, film critic

Purple Noon

DIRECTED BY **René Clément**

To watch when you . . . dream about living "la dolce vita" in Italy over summer, even if it requires a little murder and some con artistry.

France/Italy, 1960
Color, 117 minutes, Thriller

Screenplay: René Clément, Paul Gégauff, based on a novel by Patricia Highsmith

Starring: Alain Delon (Tom Ripley), Maurice Ronet (Philippe Greenleaf), Marie Laforêt (Marge Duval), Bill Kearns (Freddy Miles)

"I might not look it, but I've got lots of imagination."

—Tom Ripley

The most fascinating character in *Purple Noon* (1960) is Tom Ripley, a con artist who insinuates himself into the life of a rich playboy, studying him and eventually stealing his identity. Ripley was the creation of author Patricia Highsmith, who featured Tom Ripley in five of her crime novels, nicknamed the "Ripliad." *The Talented Mr. Ripley*, published in 1955, was her first Ripley adventure, and remains her most famous. To date, the book has been adapted into several motion pictures—such as *Purple Noon* from 1960, directed by the French René Clément, and *The Talented Mr. Ripley* from 1999, by the British Anthony Minghella—and it inspired the TV series *Ripley* in 2024. Patricia Highsmith passed away before she could see Anthony Minghella's version, but she did approve of René Clément's. In particular, she liked the casting of Alain Delon as Tom Ripley. This was Delon's first major film role and was the one that would make him a star.

In many ways, Alain Delon was an unexpected movie star. Born into a tumultuous home, Delon grew up as a troublemaker—he was expelled from six schools and quit altogether at the age of fourteen. He then enlisted in the French Navy and served in the First Indochina War, but a few years later was dishonorably discharged. Delon seemed destined to drift between various low-paying jobs, until he befriended the actor Jean-Claude Brialy. Brialy was about to attend the 1957 Cannes Film Festival, and invited Delon to join him. At the festival, Alain Delon's startling good looks caught the attention of many producers, directors, and talent scouts, and when he returned to Paris, Delon was cast in his first feature film—*Quand la femme s'en mêle* (1957). More film roles followed, and it was in his fourth feature, *Faibles Femmes* (1959), that director René Clément spotted him. "Delon did not really shine in it," Clément later said in an interview. "Nonetheless, there was something

▲ Alain Delon as Tom Ripley

that interested me in certain ways." That "something" convinced Clément that Alain Delon should play Tom Ripley.

In both the book and in *Purple Noon*, Ripley and his playboy friend, Philippe Greenleaf, are Americans. That they are played here by French actors (Alain Delon and Maurice Ronet) and speak French to each other wasn't a great concern for René Clément. He thought that giving the actors an American accent would be "a useless addition," and perhaps distract viewers, taking them out of the story. Instead, it's assumed that Tom Ripley and Philippe Greenleaf (as he's called here) are bilingual, both having spent time in

France, with Philippe lounging around Europe on his family's dime.

When we first meet Tom and Philippe in *Purple Noon*, they are soaking up the sun in Rome, enjoying their endless free time. Then, Philippe spots an American friend named Freddy Miles (Bill Kearns), who makes it obvious he doesn't like Tom Ripley. Freddy is suspicious of Tom's intentions and looks down on him for not having any money of his own. "I have my own dough," Freddy says pointedly. And Tom replies, "I have other people's."

After a drunken night of privileged debauchery, Tom and Philippe head back to Philippe's apartment, where his girlfriend Marge (Marie Laforêt) is angrily waiting. Tom leaves them

▲ Ripley plans his dark deeds.

to reconcile and begins to put on Philippe's clothes, looking in the mirror and kissing his image, speaking to himself as if he were Philippe talking to Marge. As the story goes on, it's not clear whether Tom wants to be Philippe or wants to be with him. Tom's ambiguity also extends

to his past, with little background information given about him. He shares childhood memories with Philippe, but Philippe tells Marge that he never knew Tom before Italy. "What I like," René Clément explained, "is that neither Greenleaf nor Ripley told me *everything* [while making the movie]. I like that . . . I like the attitude of being somewhat led by your characters,

because it seems to me to provide a guarantee of authenticity."

All of this ambiguity also serves to increase the audience's unease about the character. There's a slipperiness to him, with Ripley always on the edge of doing something dangerous. Undoubtedly, he has psychopathic tendencies, but in looking at this world through the icy-blue eyes of Delon, you can't help but sympathize with him—as he tries on different roles and copies what he sees, Philippe's life of easy luxury just out of his reach. Phillipe is also revealed

▲ Maurice Ronet as Philippe and Marie Laforêt as Marge

to be a horrible character, torturing everyone around him, particularly his long-suffering girlfriend, Marge.

On set, René Clément was pleased to find that Alain Delon was up to the challenge of taking on such a complicated character. Despite his newness to acting, Delon threw himself into the role and improvised many scenes, with Clément yelling ideas and instructions to him from the sidelines. The director viewed the script as being like "a score that is missing any indication of tempo. You have to breathe life into it. It demands an element of improvisation." This

also suited the character of Tom Ripley because he, too, improvises his way out of difficult situations. Alain Delon imbues his Ripley with both childlike excitement and a dangerous

More Alain Delon

Rocco and His Brothers (1960)
L'Eclisse (1962)
The Leopard (1963)
Le Samouraï (1967)
La Piscine (1969)

▲ "Why bother having money when you can spend other people's?" —Philippe

▲ Director René Clément works on the set of *Purple Noon*.

allure, creating a compelling performance that shows talent beyond his handsome looks. But his looks are also part of it, with cinematographer Henri Decaë languishing on Delon's tanned face and sweaty body. There is something unsettling about seeing a dark crime committed in broad daylight, and Decaë's sun-soaked cinematography juxtaposes the bright light and beautiful colors of the Italian coast with the horrors of dead bodies and cruel murder.

Rather than resting on his looks and playing simple roles in commercial movies, Alain Delon continued to challenge himself with complex characters for a variety of acclaimed filmmakers. He followed *Purple Noon* with Italian director Luchino Visconti's *Rocco and His Brothers* (1960) and went on to work consistently in Europe and Hollywood, gaining more recognition with his roles in *L'Eclisse* (1962),

The Leopard (1963), *Le Samouraï* (1967), and *La Piscine* (1969), while also trying his hand at producing and directing. *Purple Noon* might have put Alain Delon on the map as a star to watch, but he quickly proved that this impressive performance was not a fluke.

This is a film that can hardly be watched without nagging waves of desire and envy—all the better to become complicit in the desires and envies of the murderous hero. By the end of the film, we do not simply understand Tom Ripley; we want what he wants.

Geoffrey O'Brien, film critic

Cléo from 5 to 7

DIRECTED BY **Agnès Varda**

To watch when you . . . feel like strolling around Paris
in the summer, contemplating your life.

France, 1962
B&W and color, 89 minutes, Drama

Screenplay: Agnès Varda

Starring: Corinne Marchand (Cléo),
Antoine Bourseiller (Antoine), Dominque
Davray (Angèle), Dorothée Blank
(Dorothée), Michel Legrand (Bob)

> "Today, everything amazes me.
> The people's faces next to mine . . ."
>
> —Cléo

Director Agnès Varda plays with a few different ideas in her 1962 film, *Cléo from 5 to 7*, the dominant being how time can feel. Film critics have described this as Varda comparing objective time (the actual minutes passing on a clock) with subjective time (that time can feel painfully long or sometimes, tragically short, depending on the circumstance). For the central character of Cléo (Corinne Marchand), her perception of time changes as she strolls the streets of Paris for two hours, waiting to hear medical results that will tell her if she has cancer.

Cléo from 5 to 7 was the second feature-length film directed by Agnès Varda, following her boundary-pushing debut feature, *La Pointe Courte* from 1955. Collective wisdom dictates that the avant-garde cinematic movement known as the French New Wave officially began in 1960 with the release of two films: *Breathless* by Jean-Luc Godard and *The 400 Blows* by François Truffaut. But to look at *La Pointe Courte* now is to see many of the techniques that would later become synonymous with that movement. Such as, a mix of a documentary style of filming with narrative storytelling, experimental editing, and real locations. Historically, the work of Godard and Truffaut has been more widely known and studied in film courses than Varda's, but within the last decade there has been a new appreciation for her work, and a celebration of her place within film history. In particular, the ways in which Varda's first film is an important precursor to the French New Wave. As film critic Georges Sadoul said, *La Pointe Courte* was "truly the first film of the nouvelle vague [New Wave]."

Agnès Varda ended up being the only female director who worked during the cinematic movement and was later given the nickname, "the Godmother of the French New Wave." Unlike her peers, she didn't begin her

career as a film critic, instead studying photography, art history, literature, and psychology, and weaving these interests into her movies. Varda hadn't even watched many films before she started directing, which, as she said, enabled her to be "totally free and crazy and innocent." She also had a natural curiosity about the world and used her photographer's eye to discover the hidden delights of people, places, and objects that surrounded her.

Seeing, looking, and being looked at is another idea Agnès Varda explores in *Cléo from 5 to 7*—more specifically, what it is like to be a woman who is constantly observed, and the complicated feelings that arise when self-worth is tied to beauty. For that reason, film critic Molly

▲ Actress Corinne Marchand gives a searing performance as Cléo, playing with our emotions throughout the film.

Haskell wrote that this film "looks even more timely today in tackling the fashionable subject of female identity as a function of how women see and are seen by the world." She added that Varda "adroitly uses the camera's addiction to beautiful women's faces to subtly question the consequences of that fascination—on us, on them."

The movie is presented in real time, though it is slightly shorter than the title suggests; it joins Cléo at 5 p.m., as she visits a tarot card reader, and ends ninety minutes later, after Cléo has heard her test results. In between, she goes on a journey filled with self-discovery, slowly beginning to engage with the world around her. As she travels through the streets of Paris, she changes from being a woman who enjoys being looked at—gazing appreciatively at her own reflection in every mirror—to becoming someone who looks out at the world around her, enjoying the simple beauty of nature and the

lives of people in the streets. Or, as Agnès Varda succinctly explained, "From the object of the look, she becomes the subject who looks." Along the way, she overhears snippets of other people's stories, and news about the Algerian war. Life and death are always hovering close by—as is beauty—with Varda filming on the real streets of Paris in the summer of 1961. The city and its

inhabitants unknowingly became her set and extras, making *Cléo from 5 to 7* a fascinating time capsule of Paris in the early 1960s. We see the city as it was then, the fashions and the cars. There are several scenes where Varda's camera walks down a street, watching everyday people as they walk by. They have not been prewarned about this film and are not used to a camera being pointed at them, so they stare right back, with unvarnished glares that seem to tell a truth about who they are.

▲ "My unchanging doll's face, this ridiculous hat. I can't see my own fears." —Cléo

Throughout *Cléo from 5 to 7*, Agnès Varda's playfulness as a director and her innovative style is evident. Many real-time films re-create the look of a single take to further the reality of the time setting, as if there was no editing involved. But Varda gleefully edits with jump cuts and transitions suddenly from color to black and white, and also uses handheld cameras with unconventional framing. There's even a comedic silent film inserted into the middle of Cléo's story, starring three icons of the French New Wave: director Jean-Luc Godard, actress Anna Karina, and actor Jean-Claude Brialy. Blending these stylistic choices together could easily have had the effect of alienating the viewer, of being a case of style over substance, but instead, Agnès Varda uses her style to take us into the inner life of Cléo, to get to know her and to care as she faces her own mortality.

▲ "I always think everyone's looking at me, but I only look at myself. It wears me out." —Cléo

Documentaries by Agnès Varda

Uncle Yanco (1967)
Black Panthers (1968)
The Gleaners & I (2000)
Faces Places (2017), codirected with JR
Varda by Agnès (2019)

The same year she released *Cléo from 5 to 7*, Agnès Varda married director Jacques Demy, who was also a pioneer within the French New Wave. A few years later, Varda traveled with Demy to Hollywood when he was hired to direct *Model Shop* (1969) for Columbia Pictures. She could have sat idly by, but Varda loved to work, and took her camera out on the streets of Los Angeles. She created a playful short documentary about a distant relative (*Uncle Yanco*, 1967) and a more serious short documentary about the founder of the Black Panther Party (*Black Panthers*, 1968). And after returning to France, she alternated between directing narrative features and documentaries, with her creative work continuing to function as a vital part of her life.

Agnès Varda found inspiration all around her. When she gave birth to her son and needed to stay at home, she made a documentary about the people living on her street (*Daguerréotypes*, 1975), and after Jacques Demy died, she focused her grief into making three movies celebrating his life and work [*Jacquot of Nantes*

(1991), *The Young Girls Turn 25* (1993), and *The World of Jacques Demy* (1995)]. Even as she got older, Varda kept working, teaming up with the French artist JR in her late eighties for an inventive documentary that earned an Oscar nomination (*Faces Places*, 2017). At the age of eighty-nine, Agnès Varda became the first female director to be awarded an honorary Oscar and was a rare female director who lived long enough to see her forgotten work be rediscovered by a wider, more appreciative audience. When Varda gave her Oscar speech, she noted that the event was full of meaning and was very serious, but also that "between weight and lightness, I choose lightness. And I feel I'm dancing the dance of cinema," ending her speech with a graceful bow. Agnès Varda passed away at the age of ninety in 2019, leaving behind a wealth of innovative cinema and pure joy.

▲ Director Agnès Varda

▶ "As long as I'm beautiful, I'm even more alive than the others."—Cléo

It is only when Cléo refuses to see herself as the world sees her that she is truly capable of self-knowledge.

Sandy Flitterman-Lewis, professor

La Ciénaga

DIRECTED BY **Lucrecia Martel**

To watch when you . . . are feeling lethargic from the summer sun.

Argentina, 2001
Color, 101 minutes, Drama

Screenplay: Lucrecia Martel

Starring: Mercedes Morán (Tali), Graciela Borges (Mecha), Martín Adjemián (Gregorio), Andrea López (Isabel)

> "Why don't you shower? You haven't showered in four days. And that pool's filthy. You can't go in there. You'll catch something nasty."
>
> —Isabel

Watching *La Ciénaga* (2001), directed by Lucrecia Martel, can be a disorientating experience. Eschewing standard film language, Martel's editing is full of misdirection, and the relationship between her characters is left unclear. Scenes begin in the middle and end unexpectedly. Danger is always hovering nearby, and there is no clear narrative to hold on to. All of this is precisely what made Lucrecia Martel such an important part of the New Argentine Cinema in her native country—a time when, like the other cinematic new waves, a young generation of filmmakers threw out the rulebooks and made their mark on film history.

La Ciénaga was Lucrecia Martel's first feature, made after she gained critical notice for her short films and contributed to an anthology movie alongside several other notable Argentine directors. She had begun directing

in the 1980s, about a decade before the New Argentine Cinema movement exploded the late 1990s and early 2000s. This movement was the result of new film schools being established in Argentina, and a sustained period of political unrest. The country had endured about twenty years of continuous dictatorships, with endless censorship on the arts. This led, in the 1980s, to a series of overtly political films— most famously, the Best Foreign Film Oscar winner, *The Official Story* (1985), directed by Luis Puenzo. But the younger directors who graduated from these film schools didn't want to make message movies with traditional film-making methods. Instead, filmmakers such as Pablo Trapero, Martín Rejtman, and Lucrecia

▶▶ Sofia Bertolotto as Momi and Andrea López as Isabel

▶ The younger generation lies by the murky pool.

▲▲ Momi jumps into the pool and disappears . . .
▲ *La Ciénaga*

version was over two hundred pages long. That screenplay had been filled with intricate details about the characters and the story, but after creating a believable world and a backstory for each part, Martel stripped all that detail away, leaving a script that is sparse and uses realistic dialogue. The movie is set in Martel's home province of Salta, in Northern Argentina, at a run-down house where an extended family is on summer vacation. The nearby city is called La Ciénaga, which translates to "the swamp." It's a fictional place, but the name encapsulates the feeling of this film—it's swamp-like, with sweaty heat, constant bursts of rain, mud, a dirty pool, and languorous characters who are stuck in their lives.

The cast is a mixture of nonprofessional actors and established stars, and the film begins with a group of adults who lethargically drag their chairs to sit by the pool, ready to drink their way through a humid afternoon. The mother, Mecha (Graciela Borges) gathers up several wineglasses and then, suddenly, trips over and lands on the glasses. Her chest starts to bleed as she lies on the ground, but disturbingly, none of the other adults seem to notice or care. It is the children who come running out to help her, along with their housekeeper, Isabel (Andrea López). She tries to mop up the blood as a decision is made about which unlicensed child will illegally drive Mecha to the hospital—the adults being too drunk to participate.

This family aren't the sort of people you'd like to hang out with in real life. Isabel and the other housekeepers are native Argentinians and are treated like outcasts. The adults are constantly drinking and lying in bed, while the children always seem on the verge of seriously hurting themselves. The young boys go fishing with machetes, violently swinging them in the water. They take guns into the

Martel used experimentation as a way of being political—rebelling against the status quo and ruffling feathers in the process.

The script for *La Ciénaga* was also written by Lucrecia Martel, and reportedly, her initial

surrounding forest, where they find a cow stuck in the mud. In one scene, we see a young boy standing in front of another boy who is pointing his rifle directly at him. The scene then cuts to a view of the mountains, and a gunshot is heard. In a standard film, that series of events would indicate that the boy had been shot, but later, we see he is alive. There's another scene where the teenaged Momi (Sofia Bertolotto) jumps into a murky pool. The other kids gather around the edge, peering into the dirty water. Momi is nowhere to be seen. Again, this leads the audience to infer that Momi has drowned. But then, there's a cut, and all the kids are telling stories by the pool, Momi included.

Lucrecia Martel used these techniques to make her audience feel unsettled, and it is effective. She also designed her soundscape to focus the audience's attention, instead of relying purely on visuals. The clinking of ice in a glass of wine makes you realize that a worrying amount of alcohol is being consumed. The flickering noise of fluorescent lights in a hospital demonstrates how tenuous the connection to power is, and the general neglect of the facility. There's also the rumbling of thunder and the angry barking of a dog, which shows just how close danger lurks.

At the time when *La Ciénaga* was released, Argentina was in the middle of economic turmoil, and Martel's depiction of decadence and laziness hit hard in her home country.

▲ Director Lucrecia Martel

Elsewhere, critics were mixed on the film, some appreciating its innovative style, while others feeling it was a little too downbeat. Nowadays, film historians point to *La Ciénaga* as being a landmark film within the New Argentine Cinema movement, and the beginning of Martel's Salta Trilogy—three movies set in her home province of Salta—which also includes *The Holy Girl* (2004) and *The Headless Woman* (2008).

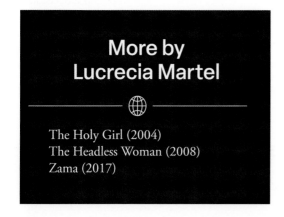

More by Lucrecia Martel

🌐

The Holy Girl (2004)
The Headless Woman (2008)
Zama (2017)

It's better to know going in that you're not expected to be able to fit everything together, that you may lose track of some members of the large cast, that it's like attending a family reunion when it's not your family and your hosts are too drunk to introduce you around.

Roger Ebert, film critic

Pierrot le Fou

DIRECTED BY **Jean-Luc Godard**

To watch when you . . . feel like breaking all the rules
and running away on a reckless summer adventure.

France, 1965
Color, 110 minutes, Crime

Screenplay: Jean-Luc Godard

Starring: Jean-Paul Belmondo (Ferdinand Griffon/Pierrot), Anna Karina (Marianne Renoir), Graziella Galvani (Maria Griffon)

"Film is like a battleground. There's love, hate, action, violence, death . . . in one word: emotion."

—Samuel Fuller

When the American filmmaker Samuel Fuller was asked by the French director Jean-Luc Godard to appear briefly in a film he was making, Fuller immediately said yes. Just five years after his debut, Godard was already an iconoclast. His debut film *Breathless* (1960), and the others he'd made in quick succession afterward, had shaken up cinema around the world—with Godard taking conventional genres (such as American film noir) and giving them new life by throwing out the cinematic rule book and improvising his own film language along the way.

Fuller had no idea what was expected of him when he showed up at a film studio in Paris, where Godard was shooting a scene for his tenth feature, *Pierrot le Fou* (1965). The set was made to look like a house, with the star, Jean-Paul Belmondo, playing a recently unemployed intellectual who becomes so bored at a party he decides to blow up his life and run

away with his former lover. Fuller was placed on the set with Belmondo and an actress playing a partygoer who spoke both French and English. "We never rehearsed the damn scene," Fuller wrote later in his memoir. "Belmondo turned and asked me, 'What is cinema?' I wasn't sure what Jean-Luc wanted, so I took a puff on my cigar and played myself, blurting out a line in my tough-guy vernacular, which a bilingual lady repeated in French as I spoke. 'Film is like a battleground,' I said. 'Love. Hate. Action. Violence. In one word: emotion.' One take, and that was that. Godard loved it. Believe me, I'd be rich if I had a nickel for every film magazine and festival program around the world who printed that goddamned line!"

Fuller's experience on *Pierrot le Fou* seems representative of Godard's process. Though Godard admired Alfred Hitchcock—a notoriously well-prepared director, who planned out every shot prior to filming—he could never

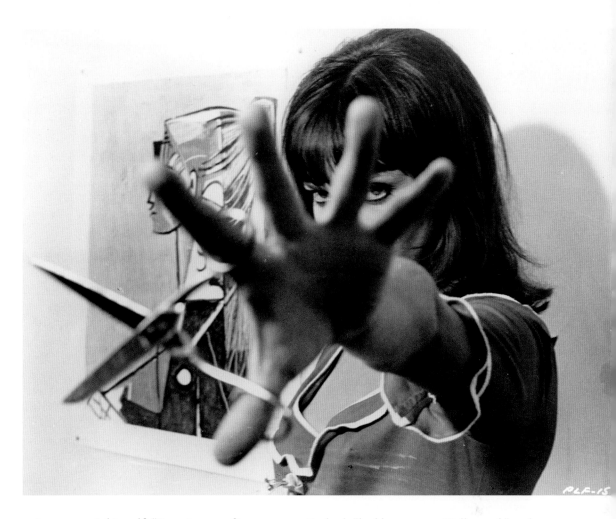

quite manage it himself. "Ever since my first film," Godard said, "I have always said I am going to prepare the script more carefully, and each time I see yet another chance to improvise, to do it all in the shooting, without applying the cinema to it or something." Godard had intended to carefully prepare *Pierrot le Fou*; while filming *Band of Outsiders* (1964), he announced that he was going to adapt a book by the American crime novelist Lionel White, called *Obsession*. Godard likened the book to *Lolita*, because it had a central relationship between an older man and much younger woman. Godard wanted to cast his wife (and frequent star of his movies), Anna Karina, with Richard Burton. But Burton, according

to Godard, "had become too Hollywood," and when he ended up asking Jean-Paul Belmondo to star with Karina at the last minute, he had to scrap all his plans. Instead of *Lolita*, Godard looked to the 1937 Hollywood crime movie *You Only Live Once* for inspiration, announcing that he'd decided to make a film about "the last romantic couple."

A week before shooting was due to begin, Jean-Luc Godard became panicked. "Based on the book," he said, "we had already established all the locations, we had hired the people . . . and I was wondering what we were going to do with it all." The character of Ferdinand (Jean-Paul

▲ Anna Karina as Marianne

◄◄ Director Jean-Luc Godard directs his then wife, Anna Karina, on the set of *Pierrot le Fou*.

◄ "I wonder what's keeping the cops; we should be in jail by now." —Ferdinand

Belmondo) was changed to be an aspiring novelist who gives up on his bourgeois married life and runs away with Marianne (Anna Karina). We first meet her as the babysitter to Ferdinand's daughter, but it is soon revealed that she and Ferdinand (whom she calls "Pierrot") used to be lovers and that she is on the run from dangerous gangsters. Not much is explained as they take off on a crime spree across France and out to the Mediterranean Sea, but the details don't really matter. Perhaps Godard didn't even know them, later saying about *Pierrot le Fou* that "I can't say I didn't work it out, but I didn't pre-think it." Instead, what is more interesting are the improvised diversions the couple takes—from singing songs to making up stories and performing a (problematic) play about the Vietnam War for American tourists.

Although *Breathless* would remain Jean-Luc Godard's ultimate defining film, *Pierrot le Fou* sums him up as an artist. If you wanted to watch just one movie to get an idea of what Godard was like as a filmmaker, this would be it. And in retrospect, *Pierrot le Fou* acts as a midpoint in his career. There are touches of his previous films—including *Breathless*, *Le Petit Soldat*, *Alphaville*, and *Contempt*—but also glimpses of where he would go to next, with *La Chinoise* and *Weekend*. Ever since he made *Breathless*, Godard had directed two or three movies a year, each experimenting with form and including the elements of Fuller's description of cinema: "Love. Hate. Action. Violence." The only one not as present in Godard's movies is "emotion." Godard was not a sentimental or an emotional director—despite being a romantic—with his unique visual style keeping emotions at bay. This was one criticism leveled at *Pierrot le Fou* when it was finally released.

▲ Jean-Paul Belmondo as Ferdinand

Pierrot le Fou premiered at the Venice Film Festival in 1965, and it was met with a chorus of loud boos. It didn't fare much better when it came out in France, becoming a box-office failure. But the film was not without its fans, including critics Michel Cournot (who said, "[It was] the most beautiful film I've seen in

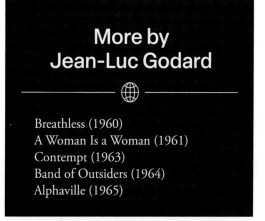

More by Jean-Luc Godard

🌐

Breathless (1960)
A Woman Is a Woman (1961)
Contempt (1963)
Band of Outsiders (1964)
Alphaville (1965)

throughout the years—and the announcement of Godard receiving an honorary Academy Award in 2010 sparked a debate about his worthiness. When he was asked what the Oscar meant to him, Godard replied, "Nothing."

Jean-Luc Godard was not an easy artist, but his contribution to cinema and his enduring legacy are undeniable. He always did it his way, even including his death in 2022, when he chose to end his life by assisted suicide after a lengthy struggle with illnesses. When his passing was announced, the French president, Emmanuel Macron, put out a statement that summed up his impact on film and art. "Jean-Luc Godard," he wrote, "the most iconoclastic of New Wave filmmakers, had invented a resolutely modern, intensely free art. We have lost a national treasure, one regarded as a genius."

my life") and Andrew Sarris (who called it "the kind of last film a director can make only once in his career"). And it was a last film of sorts, being the final professional collaboration between Anna Karina and Jean-Luc Godard, and marking the bitter end to their marriage, with the two getting divorced in 1965.

A few years later, following *Weekend*, Jean-Luc Godard became involved in the student protests that erupted in France during 1968. Alongside his peers from the French New Wave, Godard called for the cancellation of the Cannes Film Festival that year. This experience seemed to change him, and Godard made a radical shift in his filmmaking, turning even more experimental and political, and alienating more critics in the process. He also started to become something of a critic himself, lashing out at other filmmakers—including his former friend, François Truffaut. He made fun of Steven Spielberg in a movie and caused Anna Karina to walk out of a televised reunion when he was extremely cold toward her. Godard was also accused of antisemitism, thanks to several remarks he had made

The self-destructive romanticism, the artistic self-consciousness, the frenetically unhinged form, the blend of emotional extravagance and cool self-mocking, the vanished boundaries between irony and sincerity and between symbol and reality, the overt cinematic breakdown and breakup, were all of their moment. *Pierrot le Fou* was the last of Godard's first films, the herald of even more radical rejections and reconstructions to come—for Godard and for the world around him.

Richard Brody, film critic

Beau Travail

DIRECTED BY **Claire Denis**

To watch when you . . . feel like seeing a beautiful movie
that features a truly surprising ending.

France, 1999
Color, 93 minutes, Drama

Screenplay: Claire Denis, Jean-
Pol Fargeau, based on a novel by
Herman Melville

Starring: Denis Lavant (Galoup), Michel
Subor (Commandant Bruno Forestier),
Grégoire Colin (Gilles Sentain)

> "Now that I'm traveling this road through the past,
> I'm sorry I was that man, that narrow-minded legionnaire."
>
> —Galoup

Named the seventh "Greatest Film of All Time" in *Sight and Sound* magazine's 2022 poll, *Beau Travail* (1999) was originally funded by the French television station ARTE. They wanted director Claire Denis to make a film for a series of movies about "foreign lands." This was a perfect fit for Denis, who has spent her career investigating what it is like to be foreign. For *Beau Travail*, she expanded on the theme, looking at, as she explained, what it means to be "foreign to oneself."

Denis knows about foreignness intimately. She was born in France, but moved with her family to Africa when she was young. Her father worked as a colonial official, and the family was stationed in various countries across the continent. Young Claire stood out in that environment, and even became an urban legend of sorts in a region of Cameroon, after her family ran out of gas and their car was approached by a pride of lions. Her parents put Claire in the trunk of the car for safety, and the story of the white French girl hiding from lions was shared around—reportedly morphing into a version where she had survived for fifteen days in the middle of nowhere. In recalling this event, Denis remembers that she wasn't scared. Instead, she watched the lions with fascination, noting how their bodies moved against the landscape. Her time in Africa would be a formative one, and her future films would reflect the residual feelings of that experience—guilt over her colonial roots, a grappling with racial dynamics, and a continued interest in elegant bodies and natural landscapes.

Back in France, Claire Denis tried out a few different areas of study before going into filmmaking. In 1969, she attended the prestigious French film school, known as IDHEC, and

▲ Denis Lavant as Galoup

began her career as an assistant director. For over a decade, she worked as an assistant to the likes of Costa-Gavras, Jim Jarmusch, and Wim Wenders. She was the assistant director to Wenders on both *Paris, Texas* (1984) and *Wings of Desire* (1998), and it was during the production of the former that she began to think about directing her first feature. As she looked out at the American desert location of *Paris, Texas*, Denis considered which landscape she would most associate with the idea of "home." It wasn't her native France, but Cameroon that came to mind, and from that thought sprang her feature directorial debut, *Chocolat* (1988). This was a semi-autobiographical drama, set in Africa, about a young white French girl who strikes up a friendship with her family's

Black servant. As Denis later explained, she had "a desire to express a certain guilt I felt as a child raised in a colonial world." The film's thoughtful take on race earned Denis many accolades and legions of fans across the world, including American filmmaker Barry Jenkins, who calls himself a "student" of Denis' work.

In filming his Oscar-winning drama, *Moonlight* (2016), Jenkins took inspiration from *Beau Travail*. This was Denis's sixth feature as a director and is representative of her true artistry as a filmmaker—displaying the type of visual poetry she is particularly skilled at, being part of, as described by the French film critic Martine Beugnet, a "contemporary cinema of sensation." Beugnet pointed out how *Beau Travail* is textural rather than textual, meaning, the textures, bodies, movements, and landscapes

▲ Grégoire Colin as Sentain

tell the story more than any concrete dialogue. There is not much exposition to be found; Denis strips her story down to its bare minimum, allowing the viewer to come up with their own interpretation.

For inspiration in creating her script about "foreignness," Denis and her regular screenwriter, Jean-Pol Fargeau, looked at the Herman Melville short novel, *Billy Budd, Sailor*, and its subsequent opera adaptation composed by Benjamin Britten, *Billy Budd*. They took a few loose elements from Melville's story and gave it a contemporary and

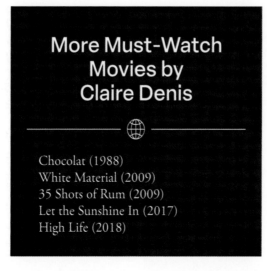

More Must-Watch Movies by Claire Denis

🌐

Chocolat (1988)
White Material (2009)
35 Shots of Rum (2009)
Let the Sunshine In (2017)
High Life (2018)

personal twist. Denis also saw her film as being an extension of the Jean-Luc Godard film *Le Petit Soldat* (1963). Set mainly in Djibouti, a former French colony in Africa, the story follows a group of French legionnaires who are training for no particular purpose under the command of the tough Galoup (Denis Lavant). Galoup strives to gain the approval of his commandant, Bruno Forestier (Michel Subor, who starred in *Le Petit Soldat* as a character with the same name). And Galoup begins to fall apart with the arrival of a young legionnaire named Gilles Sentain (Grégoire Colin), whom he becomes dangerously obsessed with. He is

▲ "Maybe freedom begins with remorse." —Galoup

It is impossible to write about *Beau Travail* without mentioning the ending, which has been called one of the best film endings of all time. But to mention it is not to give any type of spoiler, because, like most of the movie, Claire Denis purposely created it to be ambiguous. Galoup is in Marseilles, reflecting on his past behavior, and starts to make his bed in the manner he used to as a legionnaire. He lies down, a gun in his hand, as the camera shows his tattoo, which reads, "Serve the good cause and die." Suddenly, there's a cut, and Galoup is on a dance floor seen earlier in the film, alone and surrounded by mirrors. Watching his reflection, he begins to dance to the song "The Rhythm of the Night" by Corona. For the entire film, Galoup has been reserved, with straight-backed posture and almost robotic movements. Now, he is loose, carefree, and wild, writhing around, leaping on the floor and up again. Not feeling "foreign" to himself, he's finally free.

convinced that Sentain is hiding something and pushes him to his edge, hoping he will crack. Galoup's fixation on this young soldier infers either an infatuation with Sentain or a hatred of his natural innocence and talent—it's up to the viewer to decide which. All this brings about Galoup's downfall—the beginning and the ending of *Beau Travail* are set in present day, after Galoup has been discharged from the legion.

Galoup is played by Denis Lavant, an actor who had trained as a performer in the circus. He used this command of his body to record his dance scene in just two takes, with Denis's only instruction being that for Galoup this was "the dance between life and death." It was one of the few scenes not choreographed. *Beau Travail*'s choreographer Bernardo Montet said, "The final scene is 100% Denis [Lavant]. You cannot create this kind of dancing." Montet was hired by Claire Denis to help cast the group of legionnaires, and he also appears as one in the film. They chose nonprofessional dancers and a couple of real French legion soldiers. And Monet even choreographed the training scenes, mixing graceful balletic movements with macho exercises that required physical and psychological strength. To photograph those scenes, Denis and her longtime cinematographer, Agnès Godard,

◀ Director Claire Denis

▲ The Legionnaires in training . . .

used the camera in a way that seems to linger over the soldiers' bodies, with one memorable moment involving Galoup and Sentain. The two men are shirtless and appear to be part of the natural, rugged African landscape, the bright blue sea sparkling behind them. They circle each other, just like the lions Denis had witnessed as a child, sizing each other up, never touching.

Beau Travail became a critical hit when it was released in 1999 and has inspired many essays about Claire Denis's masterful use of movement and bodies. It has also influenced several young filmmakers—in addition to Barry Jenkins, Josh Safdie is a fan, as is Greta Gerwig. She told Criterion in an interview that *Beau Travail* was the film that made her understand cinema. "It snapped into focus for me," Gerwig said, "that things captured on film and put together through editing can create meaning beyond language . . . their whole bodies contain the story."

What Ms. Denis has made of *Billy Budd* is the visually spellbinding cinematic equivalent of a military ballet in which the legionnaires' rigorous drills and training rituals are depicted as ecstatic rites of purification, the embodiment of an impenetrable masculine mystique before which the director stands in awe. Where another filmmaker exploring the same material might emphasize its homoerotic subtext, Ms. Denis is in search of something deeper, more elemental and ultimately more elusive.

Stephen Holden, film critic

Parasite

DIRECTED BY **Bong Joon Ho**

To watch when you . . . are ready for an absorbing
and thoughtful thriller with a surprising twist.

South Korea, 2019
Color, 131 minutes, Thriller

Screenplay: Bong Joon Ho, Han Jin Won

Starring: Song Kang Ho (Kim Ki-taek), Lee Sun Kyun (Park Dong-ik), Cho Yeo Jeong (Yeon- kyo), Choi Woo Shik (Ki-woo), Park So Dam (Ki-jung), Chang Hyae Jin (Chung-sook), Jung Ziso (Da-hye), Jung Hyeon Jun (Da-song)

"You know what kind of plan never fails? No plan. No plan at all. You can't go wrong with no plans. It doesn't matter what will happen next. Even if the country gets destroyed or sold out, nobody cares. Got it?"

—Kim Ki-taek

Throughout cinema's history, the genre of science fiction has lent itself to addressing real-world problems via fantastical, and entertaining, means. In Hollywood, the mutant monster movies and alien invasion films of the 1950s spoke to America's fears about nuclear war and the threat of communism. In the 2000s, the mega blockbuster *Avatar* (2009) weaved messages about environmental destruction into a visual spectacle, and South Africa's *District 9* (2009) touched on xenophobia and apartheid while also being a thrilling action film. Over in South Korea, one director who knows all about the power of mixing allegory with excitement is Bong Joon Ho. And with *Parasite* (2019), he proved his true mastery by taking the story out of fantasy and placing it in reality, without squandering his message or a second of entertainment.

Bong Joon Ho was born in North Korea, but his family moved back to the South when he was three. His maternal grandfather was the esteemed writer Park Taewon, who had moved to North Korea during the Korean War of the 1950s. This move was controversial, and Park Taewon's work was banned from libraries, his name redacted when his writing appeared in other books or magazines. Bong Joon Ho discovered movies while at school, watching censored classic Hollywood films on South Korean television and catching the more risqué movies showing on the channel set up for the American

Forces. His family remembers him as being interested in social inequality from a young age, sometimes bringing home poorer friends for dinner. While studying sociology at university, he drew cartoons in support of student protests.

▲ Song Kang Ho, as Mr. Kim, looking out of the family's semibasement apartment.

He also helped to set up a filmmaking club and raised money to buy his own camera by selling donuts in the cafeteria.

Bong had to wait until he'd completed his two-year compulsory military service before he could study filmmaking, but as soon as he was able, he enrolled at the Korean Academy of Film Arts. He dove into complex social issues with his very first feature-length film, *Barking Dogs Never Bite* (2000), about a mild-mannered professor who is driven to violence and corruption by a barking dog. His directorial debut went under the radar, selling only ten thousand tickets in total, but Bong would have a big hit with his second feature, *Memories of Murder* (2003). The crime film was based on a real serial killer case in South Korea, and its success made Bong Joon Ho famous. He continued to impress with his next few movies, sci-fi hits that looked at a toxic chemical spill in Seoul (the monster movie *The Host*, 2006), the disparity between the wealthy and the poor (the dystopian *Snowpiercer*, 2013), and dangers to the environment (the fantasy *Okja*, 2017).

Bong Joon Ho writes or cowrites all the scripts for his movies, and while working on *Snowpiercer*, he began to consider writing a play set in two very different houses. Inspired by *Snowpiercer*'s focus on wealth inequality, he started to write about a rich family living in a fancy house, and a poor family living in a small apartment. Bong also wanted to do something with the idea of the poor family infiltrating the house of the rich, later saying, "I was fascinated with this idea of infiltration. When I was in college, I tutored for a rich family, and I got this feeling that I was infiltrating the private lives of complete strangers. Every week I would go into their house, and I thought how fun it would be if I could get all my friends to infiltrate the house one by one."

Quickly, his play turned into a screenplay, for a film named *Parasite*. That title is apt for this story about the poor Kim family, who manage to squirm their way into the house of the rich Park family, infecting all of their lives in the process. Frequent Bong Joon Ho star Song Kang Ho plays Kim Ki-taek, the father of the Kim family. They are struggling to make ends meet in their semibasement apartment, but while they don't have money, they are smart and have amassed enough skills from their various jobs to be able to shape-shift as needed to survive. When the son,

Ki-woo (Choi Woo Shik), is offered a job as an English tutor to the daughter of the Park family, Da-hye (Jung Ziso), he realizes an opportunity to get his whole family hired. The mother of the Park family, Yeon-kyo (Cho Yeo Jeong), needs an art teacher for her rambunctious son, Da-song (Jung Hyeon Jun), so Ki-woo (who the Parks call "Kevin") suggests a great teacher named Jessica, who is actually his sister Ki-jung (Park So Dam), a master of forgery and con artistry. "Jessica" then suggests a new chauffeur for the family, a veteran driver named Mr. Kim (really her father) and he in turn suggests a high-end company for Park Dong-ik (Lee Sun Kyun) to find a new housekeeper, which turns out to be his wife, Chung-sook (Chang Hyae Jin).

Though set in the real world, and not science-fiction, *Parasite* is still something of a genre movie. Call it a ghost story, or a haunted house picture, the film is full of symbolism and allegory, with sharp messages about the widening gap between the wealthy and the poor—not only in Korea, but also around the world. Even the way the houses look are symbolic. The Parks' architectural home is full of private areas, with the house itself shielded from the outside world by a fence. Meanwhile, the Kims' semibasement apartment is cramped, with the family living on top of one another, and a big window where people on the street can see straight in (even drunk young men, who frequently choose that spot to urinate). Bong Joon Ho explained that he wanted to show the difference between rich and poor in terms of access to privacy, and that the semibasement apartment also symbolizes the financial state of the Kim family. "Semibasement means you're half above the ground, half beneath it. They still want to believe that they're over ground but carry this fear that they could fall completely below. It's that limbo state that reflects their economic status."

There are many more examples of symbolism within *Parasite*, which—as well as being genuinely funny—made the film like catnip for

▲▲ Park So Dam as Ki-jung and Choi Woo Shik as Ki-woo

▲ Lee Sun Kyun as Mr. Park and Cho Yeo Jeong as Mrs. Park

▲ Director Bong Joon Ho poses with his Palme d'Or award for *Parasite*.

critics and audiences alike. Bong Joon Ho has been compared to Steven Spielberg, and to Alfred Hitchcock, for the way he makes popular movies that critics appreciate, too. The Hitchcock comparison is easy to spot in *Parasite* in terms of the psychological nature of the thriller and a shocking twist that happens three-quarters into the movie. This had *Parasite*'s publicity team begging critics to not spoil the twist in their reviews, much like Hitchcock had implored audiences to do the same with *Psycho* (1960). Bong is a longtime fan of Hitchcock's work and rewatched *Psycho* for inspiration while making *Parasite*, saying, "[Hitchcock] always gives me very strange inspiration. I rewatched *Psycho* because the Bates house, not the motel, it had a very interesting structure."

Parasite seems poised to become a classic in its own right. It premiered at the Cannes Film Festival in 2019, where it picked up positive reviews and Oscar buzz, and also received a lengthy standing ovation from the premiere crowd. At the end of all that applause, Bong Joon Ho simply said, "Let's all go home," later explaining that he and his cast were very hungry. *Parasite* took home the major award from Cannes, the Palme d'Or, and went on to sweep multiple award shows, ending up with

six Academy Award nominations—a rare feat for a South Korean film. It won four of those awards: Best Foreign Film, Best Director, Best Screenplay, and Best Picture. With that, *Parasite* broke a record as the first film not in English to win the Academy Award for Best Picture in the Oscars' ninety-two-year history. Bong Joon Ho looked shocked as he made his way to the stage with his cast and producers to collect his Best Picture statuette, and the *Parasite* team received another standing ovation, this time from a crowd of famous faces. Now, instead of looking up to his filmmaker heroes, like Martin Scorsese and Quentin Tarantino, they were in the audience, clapping and literally looking up at Bong Joon Ho, on the Oscars stage.

More Sensational Cinema from South Korea

🌐

The Housemaid (1960)
Memories of Murder (2003)
Oldboy (2003)
Train to Busan (2016)
Burning (2018)

Parasite is clear-eyed about the illusions that inequality needs in order to perpetuate itself, and about the many systems that shield one-percenters like the Parks from having to get their own hands dirty while engaged in the project of oppression. But it also reveals the Kims, as sympathetic and unfairly treated as they are, as utterly capable of the banality of evil, in part because of their own overidentification with underdogs, and the inherent goodness they assume they can lay claim to. The layers of self-deception build on top of one another until, finally, it all comes crashing down.

Inkoo Kang, film critic

Monsieur Hulot's Holiday

DIRECTED BY **Jacques Tati**

To watch when you . . . want a gentle laugh at human behavior, and to marvel at a master of intricate comedy.

France, 1953
B&W, 87 minutes, Comedy

Screenplay: Jacques Tati, Henri Marquet, Pierre Aubert, Jacques Lagrange

Starring: Jacques Tati (Monsieur Hulot), Nathalie Pascaud (Martine), Louis Perrault (Fred)

"Mr Hulot is off for a week by the sea. Take a seat behind the camera, and you can spend it with him. Don't look for a plot, for a holiday is meant purely for fun, and if you look for it, you will find more fun in ordinary life than in fiction."

—Opening Titles

It's quite remarkable for a filmmaker who only directed five feature films to be called a genius who changed cinema. Yet, that is exactly what French director-writer-comedian Jacques Tati did—elevating cinema comedy to a high art form and winning over tough critics (such as Pauline Kael and André Bazin) and cantankerous filmmakers (like Jean-Luc Godard) in the process.

Jacques Tati's birth name was Jacques Tatischeff. He was born in Paris to a family with Russian noble ancestry but refused to enter the family business of picture framing. Instead, he became a semiprofessional rugby player. In the 1930s, he brought this athleticism into vaudeville

music halls, performing a mime act where he "played" various sports, and he shortened his last name so it would fit on a marquee. In 1936, the famed French author Colette saw Tati's act and wrote a review, saying that Tati had "the suggestive power of all great artists." Tati was encouraged by her words and reportedly carried that review with him everywhere he went, which included film sets, as he began to act in small roles in films directed by the likes of René Clément and Claude Autant-Lara.

Tati also started directing his own short films during the latter half of the 1930s and began to experiment with his visual style and use of sound

▲ Jacques Tati as Monsieur Hulot

▲ Monsieur Hulot tries kayaking. . . .

effects. Then came World War II, where he served in the army, and then the postwar years—a time when he truly flourished as a filmmaker. Tati's 1947 short film, *School for Postmen*, was a pivotal moment in his early directing career, and it inspired his first feature, *Jour de Fête* ("The Big Day," 1948). With this feature, Tati established what would become his signature film structure: There was not much of a narrative and barely any dialogue, but the central character (played by himself) was the connective tissue between a series of sketches that involved complex visual gags. Interestingly, he combined the physical comedy and choreography of silent films from the past, with a present-day interest in modernization. This was how Tati was unique; he combined the old

and the new to come up with movies that still feel both timeless and fresh.

His second feature, *Monsieur Hulot's Holiday* (1953), is an example of this. Deciding against reprising his role as the postman from *Jour de Fête*, Tati created the sweet, shy, and bumbling Hulot, who would become his alter ego. Hulot is a well-meaning character, an everyman, with a posture and gait that has been compared to that of an ostrich—his head protrudes forward, with his pipe in his mouth and too-long legs poking out of too-short pants. Hulot is stuck in the past, at odds with modern-day France. We see this right from the beginning of *Monsieur Hulot's Holiday*, as Hulot slowly makes his way to the beach in a tiny vintage car that is not even threatening enough for a dog to move out the way. This contrast between Hulot and the modern

world was the source of much of the humor in the four films Tati played him in and highlighted the point that Tati was making about what (and who) gets left behind amid the rapid pace of technological change.

In *Monsieur Hulot's Holiday*, Hulot is one of a group of vacationers who travel to a beach to stay in a seaside hotel for the summer. As the opening titles warn, there is not much of a plot, but this structure (of a loose group of vignettes) seems fitting for the pace of a real summer holiday. Not much goes right for these vacationers, but also, not much goes horribly wrong. Jacques Tati's humor is subtle, and unlike some of the broader comedic actors, his setups involve realistic scenarios—with most of the laughs coming from the other characters' lack of reaction to what has just happened. For

example, during one scene in *Monsieur Hulot's Holiday*, Hulot's spare car tire falls off his car at a church where a funeral is taking place. As it rolls onto the ground, the tire picks up leaves and is mistaken for one of the funeral wreaths. A mourner notices how it deflates once it has been hung up to be displayed, but does not say anything, and can only look at Hulot with confusion as Hulot delightedly joins the grieving line—simply because he likes shaking hands with the attendees.

The sweetness and innocence of Hulot makes him a charming character to follow, even as he causes chaos without realizing it. Jacques Tati masterfully built long scenes with a series of complex gags, mostly filmed in a wide shot, as if

▲ Monsieur Hulot tries tennis. . . .

more complicated visual gags and biting satire, using bigger budgets and costly production design. For *Playtime*, Tati built a huge set, and the production ended up costing so much that he was never able to recoup his losses, despite the film being another critical success. Following *Playtime*'s financial disaster, Tati directed *Trafic* for television, and made one more TV movie and a short film before retiring from the film business. His filmography was short, but his influence continues to be immense. The work of Jacques Tati has inspired filmmakers as diverse as Robert Altman, Wes Anderson, Steven Spielberg, and David Lynch, who once said, "When you watch his films, you realize how much he knew about—and loved—human nature. And it can only be an inspiration to do the same."

you were (as the opening titles state) "taking a seat behind the camera," or, on the beach itself, watching from the sideline. The comedy appears effortless, but it took a great deal of effort to achieve. Tati worked on *Monsieur Hulot's Holiday* for four years, and even though it is essentially a silent film—using sound effects, music, and the occasional line of dialogue—Tati carefully crafted the script alongside three writers. He planned on a short shoot, but production on *Monsieur Hulot's Holiday* stretched into multiple months, partly due to the intricacy of the physical comedy (which took numerous takes to get right), partly because of a colder than normal summer on the location, and partly due to the sand that kept getting into the camera, ruining the film. Tati even continued to work on it after the release date, doing more edits, some reshoots, and changing the soundtrack, releasing two more versions in 1962 and 1978.

Monsieur Hulot's Holiday has been called a masterpiece by several film critics and historians, and a few years after its French release, the movie made its way to the United States, where it was nominated for Best Screenplay at the 1956 Academy Awards. More accolades followed for Jacques Tati, who played Hulot again in the Best Foreign Film Oscar-winning *Mon Oncle* (1958), as well as *Playtime* (1967) and *Trafic* (1971). As he continued to direct, Tati's artistry as a filmmaker grew, and he came up with ever

---

Tati's penchant for realism, combined with his taste and restraint, make *M. Hulot's Holiday* the sort of comedy that one can enjoy again and again. A first viewing will have you laughing at the classic comedy scenes like Hulot's tennis game, or the uproarious scene in which the hapless Hulot finds himself mistaken for a mourner at a country funeral—and that's not to mention the bits with the muddy footprints, the raucous jazz record, or the runaway car. But later viewings reveal something else, for Tati is the antithesis of the laughs-at-any-price gagman. He wants us to laugh, but he also wants something more.

David Ehrenstein, film critic

▲ Monsieur Hulot tries driving. . . .

Swept Away

DIRECTED BY Lina Wertmüller

To watch when you . . . feel like seeing a challenging and dark comedy made by a pioneering female director who refused to fit into a box.

Italy, 1974
Color, 114 minutes, Comedy/Drama

Screenplay: Lina Wertmüller

Starring: Mariangela Melato (Raffaella Pavone Lanzetti), Giancarlo Giannini (Gennario Carunchio)

"Every dog has his day; every servant gets his pay."

—Gennario

Throughout her directing career, Lina Wertmüller proved she was not afraid of controversy. Both she, and her movies, consistently pushed buttons. She wrote and directed dark comedies filled with provocative dialogue about gender equality and politics, though she made it impossible to know which side she was on, or what point she was trying to make. Her characters were usually unlikable, making it hard to figure out who the viewer is supposed to be rooting for. And she was a trailblazing female filmmaker—being the first to ever be nominated for a Best Director Academy Award—but her work was not feminist, she repeatedly mistreated her female characters, and sometimes she upheld misogynistic ideas.

Overall, Lina Wertmüller had the spirit of an anarchist, which began at a young age. She was born in Rome in 1928, to a family from Swiss noble ancestry and a father who could be controlling. The two fought constantly, and Lina's rebellious streak caused her to be expelled from fifteen different schools—she often snuck out of class to watch movies. Her father wanted her to follow in his footsteps and become a lawyer, but Lina dreamed of being involved with theater or film. Much to her father's chagrin, she enrolled in a drama academy, and then started a career in the theater, spending the 1950s working on experimental productions and puppeteering, using puppets to tell stories by Franz Kafka.

As a teenager, Wertmüller had befriended the actress Flora Carabella, who was older and instrumental in shaping her love for the arts. Carabella also aided Wertmüller in getting her first break into the film industry. In 1950, Carabella had married the actor Marcello Mastroianni, and at the start of the 1960s, Mastroianni had introduced Wertmüller to director Federico Fellini. Fellini hired

▶▶ Mariangela Melato as Raffaella
▶ Giancarlo Giannini as Gennarino

Wertmüller to be an assistant director on his landmark film, *8½* (1963), which gave her invaluable experience, and the inspiration to start directing. Her first few films—*The Basilisks* (1963) and *Let's Talk About Men* (1965) were well regarded, but she struggled throughout the rest of the decade to raise financing to make more movies. She turned to working in television, but her fortune changed when she cast the actor Giancarlo Giannini in *Rita the Mosquito* (1966),

a TV movie that Wertmüller directed under the pseudonym of "George H. Brown." These two struck up a friendship, with Giannini becoming her muse, and his good reputation as a stage actor helped with financing feature films.

The Seduction of Mimi (1972) marked Lina Wertmüller's comeback to big-screen cinema, and she switched back to using her real name. This political satire (starring Giancarlo Giannini) won Wertmüller the Best Director award at the Cannes Film Festival. Her next three movies cemented her reputation as a provocateur and earned her a cult following throughout the 1970s: *Love and Anarchy* (1973), *Swept Away* (1974), and *Seven Beauties* (1975). It was *Seven Beauties* that took Wertmüller to the Oscars, where she was the first female director in the Academy Awards' forty-nine-year-history

▲ Mariangela Melato and Giancarlo Giannini in *Swept Away*

to earn a Best Director nomination. But throughout her triumphs, she had a fair share of detractors, particularly over her treatment of female characters, with respected critics such as Pauline Kael, Molly Haskell, and Ellen Willis objecting to her films. (Willis once called Wertmüller "a woman-hater who pretends to be a feminist.") Male critics also challenged Wertmüller's beliefs. Anthony Kaufman from the *Village Voice* called *Swept Away* "possibly the most outrageously misogynist film ever made by a woman."

Lina Wertmüller wrote all the films she directed, and her screenplay for *Swept Away* follows a wealthy woman, Raffaella (Mariangela Melato), who has chartered a yacht for her husband and friends. She doesn't hide her disdain for the boat's employees, especially the scruffy Gennarino (Giancarlo Giannini), whom she dismisses for being a communist. Gennarino doesn't think much of Raffaella, either, and

is not happy when he's told to take her out on a boat to meet her friends for swimming. Gennarino points out that it's about to get dark, but Raffaella won't hear it, and during their journey, the boat's motor dies. By the time Gennarino gets it working, they've drifted so much that they are lost, and they soon end up shipwrecked on a deserted island. Once on the island, the balance of power is tipped on its head, as the resourceful Gennarino finds shelter and food, while the spoiled Raffaella flounders hopelessly. Gennarino revels in his new position and dominates Raffaella, abusing her physically and sexually. And in the most controversial part of the film, Raffaella falls in love with Gennarino.

Swept Away caused much debate, but audiences flocked to see it. Lina Wertmüller cast her political net so wide that viewers from all

sides—liberals and conservatives, feminists and antifeminists—could all find something to love and something to hate in the film. Wertmüller herself defended her choices for the character

More Must-See Movies by Female Filmmakers

The House Is Black (1963, Iran)
Fish Tank (2009, UK)
Stories We Tell (2012, Canada)
Toni Erdmann (2016, Germany)
Anatomy of a Fall (2023, France)

▲ "This is a desert island and wild." —Gennarino

▲ Director Lina Wertmüller

of Raffaella, calling her a feminist character for the way she represents the privileged in society; "therefore," she said, "she represents the man." Her male characters (such as Gennarino) were equally objectionable, only saved by the sleepy-eyed charm and acting talent of Giancarlo Giannini.

Following *Seven Beauties*, Wertmüller struggled to make another critical hit. She was invited to direct an American film, *A Night Full of Rain* (1978), but it failed at the box office. She continued to work in Italy, directing whenever she could get money together, right up until her death in 2021—and in 2020, she was given an honorary Academy Award. Throughout her impressive career, Lina Wertmüller made movies that were called both "essential" and "grotesque"; she had fierce fans and fierce critics, and her divisive body of work built her an unrivaled reputation as one of the most daring and controversial directors in Italian film history.

> Although Wertmüller is a leftist, she is not, apparently, a feminist. She seems to be trying to tell us . . . that woman is an essentially masochistic and submissive creature who likes nothing better than being swept off her feet by a strong and lustful male. This is a notion the feminists have spent the last 10 years trying to erase from our collective fantasies, and it must be unsettling, to say the least, to find the foremost woman director making a whole movie out of it.
>
> Roger Ebert, film critic

Picnic at Hanging Rock

DIRECTED BY **Peter Weir**

To watch when you . . . want to see a movie that is as beautiful as it is haunting.

Australia, 1975
Color, 107 minutes, Drama

Screenplay: Cliff Green, based on a novel by Joan Lindsay

Starring: Rachel Roberts (Mrs. Appleyard), Helen Morse (Mademoiselle de Poitiers), Anne Lambert (Miranda), Margaret Nelson (Sara), Karen Robson (Irma), Jacki Weaver (Minnie), Dominic Guard (Michael Fitzhubert), John Jarratt (Albert Crundall)

> "What we see, and what we seem, are but a dream.
> A dream within a dream."
>
> —Miranda

When director Peter Weir made *Picnic at Hanging Rock* (1975), the Australian film industry was experiencing a revival after decades of lying dormant. That dormancy hadn't been due to any lack of enthusiasm from local filmmakers; instead, their work had been drowned out by an overdominance of American product.

For a while, it had seemed like Australia might just be the leaders of motion picture making, alongside America. There was certainly a lot of excitement in 1884, when Edison's Kinetoscope went on display in Sydney and an estimated twenty-five thousand Australians visited the exhibition over five months. Ten years later, in 1896, came Australia's first film, *Passengers Leaving the SS Brighton at Manly*, which captured exactly what the title states, filmed by Frenchman Marius Sestier. The first film studio in the country had been established just before this, in 1891, created by the Salvation Army to film religious movies. And in 1900, they released their most famous production, *Soldiers of the Cross*. Australia's first feature-length film came six years later—a crime movie called *The Story of the Kelly Gang* (1906)—which was not only the first narrative feature to come out of Australia, but some claim it was also the first narrative feature film ever made in the world.

Production on Australian movies continued into the early 1910s, and the film industry grew. But around the middle of that decade, during World War I, American films started

▲ Anne Lambert as Miranda

to dominate. Prior to 1914, less than half of the films screened in Australian movie theaters came from America. By 1923, that number had grown exponentially, with Hollywood movies making up around 94 percent of all films shown in Australia. The local film industry suffered, and although movies were still being produced, the numbers were small. This remained true for several decades, right up until 1967. That year, the prime minister of Australia established the Australian Council of the Arts, including a

Film and Television Committee. They recommended the opening of a national film school, a film development corporation, and a film fund designed to give grants to new filmmakers.

Peter Weir had worked in a government-funded film unit as a cameraman and director, making short films of his own on the side. He took the leap into features in 1974, directing the comic-dystopian punk movie *The Cars That Ate Paris.* This now cult classic gained him attention, but he was still surprised when he got a call from an established and respected film producer named Patricia Lovell. The South

▲ Miranda, Irma, Edith, and Marion explore the rock.

Australian Film Corporation was financing an adaptation of the Joan Lindsay novel *Picnic at Hanging Rock*, and Lovell wanted Weir to direct it, despite it being drastically different in tone from his previous film. The book by Joan Lindsay had been a bestseller. Reportedly, she had feverishly written it in just two weeks. Her story about a group of schoolgirls going missing during a summer picnic captured the imagination of readers, who wanted to know whether it was based on fact or if it was pure fiction. Lindsay had been purposely ambiguous, adding a foreword that stated that readers would have to decide for themselves, and her ending left them without any concrete resolution about what happened to the missing girls.

At this stage in Australian film history, the idea of adapting a book was a foreign one—as Weir later said, it was thought of as "the big time, what they do overseas." He sat down and read the novel cover to cover, and as he did, he became more determined to direct the adaptation. Before they could begin, however,

Top Picks from the Australian New Wave

Wake in Fright (1971)
The Cars That Ate Paris (1974)
The Chant of Jimmie Blacksmith (1978)
Breaker Morant (1980)
The Year of Living Dangerously (1982)

▲ "Everything begins and ends at the exactly right time and place." —Miranda

Weir and Patricia Lovell were summoned to meet with Lady Joan Lindsay at the farm she shared with her husband, Sir Ernest Lindsay. Weir described his lunch as an audition, and Lindsay as "a woman from a world as vanished as the world in *Hanging Rock*." He had been told by the book's publisher to not—under any circumstances—ask Lindsay whether her book was fact or fiction, but he couldn't help himself. She refused to answer and told Weir to never ask that question again. His curiosity remained, so he tried a different tactic, asking her what she thought happened to the schoolgirls. "Did they fall down a hole?" he asked. "Were they abducted by aliens?" Lady Lindsay just smiled and said, "Any of the above."

In creating his adaptation, with a screenplay by Cliff Green, Peter Weir wanted to capture that same feeling of haunting ambiguity. The story is set on Saint Valentine's Day in 1900, at Appleyard's College for young women in Victoria, Australia. As it begins, the girls are reading love poems to each other, excited by their romantic notions of everlasting love. They're also getting ready for a summer picnic, taking place at the foot of Hanging Rock. During the picnic, four of the girls go to explore the rock formation: Miranda (Anne Lambert), Irma (Karen Robson), Edith (Christine Schuler), and Marion (Jane Vallis). But only one girl returns, and by the time the group leaves to go back to the school, a teacher has also gone missing.

New York Times film critic Vincent Canby noted in his review that "instead of exposition, Mr. Weir and his screenwriter, Cliff Green, deal in moods." Indeed, the entire movie is a mood, as if stepping into a gorgeous yet disturbing dream, complete with an otherworldly soundtrack: an eerie theme played on a pan flute by the infamous Zamfir, and a spooky, low-toned hum that seems to emanate from the rock. The cinematography is also striking, with Russell Boyd at the lens. He captures the wild and specific beauty of Australia's landscape—the dry grass, the rugged rock formation, the colorful parrots, the harshness of the sun—fluffing out the edges to make it seem as if we're viewing it all through a pair of stockings. The soft light lends a strange sensuality to the visuals, and an uncomfortable contrast between the girls in their restrictive, modest clothing, and the untamed landscape. This highlights a theme that Peter Weir wanted to explore in *Picnic at Hanging Rock*—that of colonialism, and how the repressed English ways brought over by the colonials did not fit with the savage, natural land. Like the girls, this land cannot be tamed, and it seems both silly (and a shame) to try and do so.

Like Joan Lindsay's book, Peter Weir's *Picnic at Hanging Rock* is a film that is full of questions but no answers. The lack of resolution left many audience members and film critics frustrated when the movie was released in 1975. Ultimately, though, it became a huge success around the world and launched Peter Weir as a director of note. With this movie, plus his previous film, *The Cars That Ate Paris* (1974), and future movies like *The Last Wave* (1977), *Gallipoli* (1981), and *The Year of Living Dangerously* (1982), Weir established himself as a vital voice in what would become known as the Australian New Wave of the 1970s and early '80s. Weir would also go on to establish himself in Hollywood, directing big-budget movies like *Witness* (1985), *Dead Poet's Society* (1989), *The Truman Show* (1998), and *Master and Commander: The Far Side of the World* (2003). In 2020, Peter Weir

▲ Director Peter Weir works on the set of *The Mosquito Coast* (1986).

retired from filmmaking, stating that at the age of seventy-five, "quite simply, I have no more energy."

> Horror need not always be a long-fanged gentleman in evening clothes or a dismembered corpse or a doctor who keeps a brain in his goldfish bowl. It may be a warm sunny day, the innocence of girlhood and hints of unexplored sexuality that combine to produce a euphoria so intense it becomes transporting, a state beyond life or death.
>
> Vincent Canby, film critic

L'Avventura

DIRECTED BY **Michelangelo Antonioni**

To watch when you . . . feel as if summer is slipping away.

Italy, 1960
B&W, 143 minutes, Mystery

Starring: Monica Vitti (Claudia), Gabriele Ferzetti (Sandro), Lea Massari (Anna)

Screenplay: Michelangelo Antonioni, Elio Bartolini, Tonino Guerra

---

"Sometimes I wonder what I could have done to prevent all of this from happening."

—Claudia

The premiere screening of *L'Avventura* (1960) at the Cannes Film Festival was a complete disaster. The audience hissed, whistled, and stomped their feet throughout most of the film—even yelling "cut" when they felt the movie was dragging—and the ending was met with a chorus of loud boos. It was an extreme reaction to a movie that would end up winning both the Special Jury Prize and the Critic's Prize at the festival and go on to become an undeniable classic; but it spoke to the uniqueness of Michelangelo Antonioni's direction. And while the audience might not have understood what they were seeing, critics had recognized that they were witnessing something new. Slowly, as *L'Avventura* began to be released around the world, the moviegoing public caught on.

Michelangelo Antonioni was forty-six at this time and had directed five previous features, but *L'Avventura* was the first of his movies to gain international attention. He had started his filmmaking career in Italy in the 1940s—though, he was not part of the Italian Neorealism cinematic movement that was flourishing at the time. Instead, Antonioni found his stride after the trend for realism had died down, and his minimalist, lyrical style contrasted sharply with the neorealist movies of the past. As did his content, especially in the case of *L'Avventura*. Because rather than focusing on the struggles of the working class during the war, Antonioni was exploring the existential ennui of the bourgeoisie in the wake of the war. As the famed American critic Pauline Kael wrote, this was "upper-class neorealism—the poetry of moral and spiritual poverty." But while *L'Avventura* had diverged from the style of Italian Neorealism, one of the pioneers of that movement was a big fan of the film—following the disastrous Cannes premiere, thirty-five filmmakers and critics had written a statement

▲ Monica Vitti as Claudia

in support of *L'Avventura*, with a notable name being Roberto Rossellini.

L'Avventura translates to "The Adventure," and when the film opens, a young woman named Anna (Lea Massari) is getting ready to go on a boat trip with her friend Claudia (Monica Vitti) and her lover Sandro (Gabriele Ferzetti). He is just one of Anna's lovers, and on the boat, she seems bored with him. She also treats Claudia like a third wheel, but Claudia cares for Anna. The boat stops to explore a rocky island where the group of friends enjoy the sunshine, and Sandro dozes off next to Anna. When it's time to depart, Claudia realizes that Anna is nowhere to be found. This is a third of the way into the story, and suddenly, the film switches protagonists—Anna is gone, and it's Claudia who is the main character. She and Sandro search the surrounding areas for her, but as time wears on, Claudia and Sandro

▲ Lea Massari as Anna

fall for each other, and it's Anna who starts to fade into the background.

Despite Anna's mysterious disappearance and the sudden switch of protagonist, there's not a lot of action (or "adventure") to be found in *L'Avventura*. The long scenes of dialogue plus the melancholic listlessness of the characters and the absence of a neat conclusion frustrated those initial viewers. They had also struggled to understand the lack of morality the characters seem to possess—the missing Anna is quickly forgotten during the pursuit of erotic desires. But with *L'Avventura*, Antonioni was creating a new kind of cinematic language, using a free-form structure and an open (or unresolved) ending.

The same year that *L'Avventura* had premiered in Cannes, Alfred Hitchcock released *Psycho* (1960), which had also featured a change of protagonist. But unlike Hitchcock's carefully planned and controlled direction, Antonioni was experimenting with form, later saying that with his style, he never knew exactly how the film would turn out. This was the beginning of the era of the "art movie," with a growing number of art house theaters being built around the world, and the importation of European movies into America increasing.

As *L'Avventura* started to find success, Monica Vitti became a star. Claudia was her breakout role and would be the most enduring part of her entire career. Filming *L'Avventura* wasn't always easy—Vitti's drama school study hadn't quite prepared her for the rocky island or for the scarce direction from Michelangelo Antonioni. He had refused to explain the film to her, and Vitti later said, "Michelangelo treats his

▲ Gabriele Ferzetti as Sandro

actors as objects, and it is useless to ask him the meaning of a scene or a line of dialogue." But she did believe in his talent and, in turn, she became his so-called muse of incommunicability. The two would go on to work together several more times, including on Antonioni's two follow-up films, *La Notte* (1961) and *L'Eclisse* (1962).

Because of their similar themes, film historians now view Antonioni's *L'Avventura*, *La Notte*, and *L'Eclisse* as an unofficial trilogy. Each of these movies capture a feeling of contemporary ennui, exploring what critic William S. Pechter called "the death of feeling." A few years later, Antonioni changed course, traveling to England to make the murder mystery *Blow-Up*

More from Michelangelo Antonioni

La Notte (1961)
L'Eclisse (1962)
Red Desert (1964)
Blow-Up (1966)
Zabriskie Point (1970)

▲ "I've never felt so shaken in my whole life."
—Claudia

(1966). Set in London during the swinging sixties, *Blow-Up* would be Antonioni's most commercially successful film, and influential in a different way from *L'Avventura*—examining, as photography expert Philippe Garner said, "the very insubstantial, unsatisfying nature of the collective dream [of the swinging sixties] that people were buying into."

Later, Antonioni flew to Hollywood to make the drama *Zabriskie Point* (1970), which was not a success, and then *The Passenger* (1975), starring Jack Nicholson, who was a big supporter of Antonioni's work. *Blow-Up* and *L'Avventura* would remain Antonioni's most influential films, and in 1995, the director was awarded with an honorary Oscar for his lifetime of work. Jack Nicholson presented the award, summing up Michelangelo Antonioni's

difference as a director, saying, "Most movies celebrate the ways we connect with one another. The films of this master mourn the failures to connect. In the empty, silent spaces of the world, he has found metaphors that illuminate the silent places of our hearts, and found in them too, a strange and terrible beauty."

L'Avventura is a study of the human condition at the higher social and economic levels, a study of adjusted, compromising man— afflicted by short memory, thin remorse, easy betrayal.

Pauline Kael, film critic

▲ Director Michelangelo Antonioni

FALL

Metropolis

DIRECTED BY **Fritz Lang**

To watch when you . . . are ready to fight for equality
at work and need some inspiration.

Germany, 1927
B&W, 153 minutes, Science Fiction

Screenplay: Fritz Lang, Thea von Harbou,
based on a novel by Thea von Harbou

Starring: Gustav Fröhlich (Freder), Alfred
Abel (Joh Frederson), Brigitte Helm (Maria),
Rudolph Klein-Rogge (Rotwang)

"Head and hands want to join together,
but they don't have the heart to do it."

—Maria

Metropolis (1927) was one of the first feature-length science fiction movies to become internationally famous. Now considered a truly essential film, it offered a prescient look at a future where the wealth of the 1 percent is made by the struggling masses, and where technology is a weapon used to influence them.

The director was the Austrian-born Fritz Lang, who started in the film industry in Germany, writing scripts during the silent era. Not long into his career, Lang decided he'd like to direct and made his directorial debut in 1919 with *The Halfbreed*. His reputation as a director of note grew throughout the 1920s, particularly after his four-hour, critically acclaimed movie *Dr Mabuse, the Gambler* in 1922. This so-called super-film used the visual style of German Expressionism, and Fritz Lang became one of the pivotal filmmakers within that cinematic movement.

German Expressionism in cinema grew out of a wider trend across all mediums of art in Germany. Following World War I, poetry, theater, paintings, and, eventually, movies became darker and stranger as they channeled the collective anxieties, nightmares, and pessimism of the country. *The Cabinet of Dr Caligari* (1920) was one of the first to display the style on film—director Robert Wiene used chiaroscuro lighting with deep shadows, created sets with distorted angles, placed his actors in dramatic makeup, and set his camera shots at an extreme tilt. All of this was designed to throw the audience off balance, reflecting the tumultuous experiences of the war and the distorted view of the character telling the story. *Nosferatu: A Symphony of Horror* (1922) was another landmark German Expressionist film, with director F. W. Murnau applying the style to amplify the horror in his vampire film.

With *Metropolis*, Fritz Lang conceived an expressionistic dystopian future, complete with huge Art Deco sets that dwarf the actors. In the city of Metropolis, the privileged ("the head") live in tall skyscrapers, with the workers (the "hands") toiling away below—charged with operating the "heart machine" that powers the city. One day, a beautiful woman named Maria (Brigitte Helm), ventures up to the top with a group of children, where she is seen by Freder (Gustav Fröhlich). He is the son of a wealthy industrialist, and he follows Maria from his world in the upper echelons of the city to hers in the subterranean depths, where he witnesses the true inequality that exists below. And Maria, after seeing the immense wealth up top, becomes an activist who rallies the workers for equality. As Maria starts to gather a following,

▲ Alfred Abel and Rudolf Klein-Rogge

▲▲ Brigitte Helm on the set of *Metropolis*　　　▲ Gustav Fröhlich

Freder's father, Joh Frederson (Alfred Abel), fears a revolution is imminent, so he hires a scientist (Rudolph Klein-Rogge) to create an evil robot version of Maria to throw off the workers.

Fritz Lang often claimed that he got the idea for *Metropolis* during a trip to the United States with producer Erich Pommer. According to Lang, the image of the New York City skyline, as seen from his ship, inspired him to create a futuristic city, with Lang later saying, "The buildings seemed like a vertical curtain, shimmering and weightless—an opulent staged backdrop set against a sinister sky—in order to dazzle, divert and hypnotize." However, newspaper articles and memos from his film studio UFA tell a different story, proving that the script was already in production before Lang and Pommer took that trip, with the story being based on a novel by Thea von Harbou (who also happened to be Fritz Lang's wife).

Right from the start, Lang envisioned *Metropolis* to be an epic film. It was hugely ambitious for the time—production stretched over a year as enormous sets, miniature models, and matte paintings were created. Groundbreaking special effects were achieved using a variety of ingenious tricks, such as mirrors, double exposure captured in camera, and stop-motion animation. To create traffic flowing through the city, over three hundred miniature cars were photographed, each moving in tiny increments

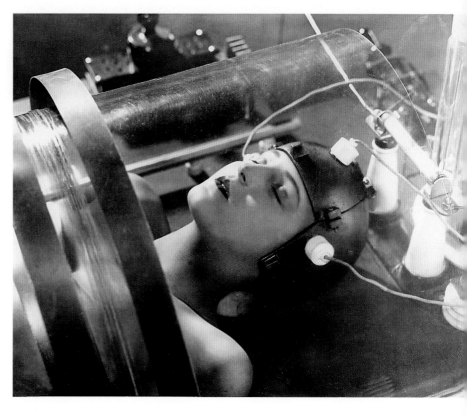

▲ The evil robot

from frame to frame to simulate driving. It took several days to film mere seconds of screen time, and all of this increased the budget, which ended up at about four times its initial amount. Reportedly, by the end of the shoot, the crew had used nearly two million feet of film.

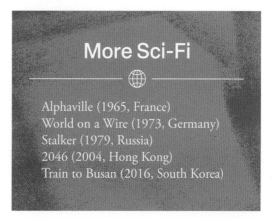

More Sci-Fi

Alphaville (1965, France)
World on a Wire (1973, Germany)
Stalker (1979, Russia)
2046 (2004, Hong Kong)
Train to Busan (2016, South Korea)

▲ "Look! These are your brothers!" —Maria

Metropolis preaches equality among workers and those in power, but ironically, Fritz Lang himself was a hard taskmaster, pushing his actors to the breaking point and slapping his ever-present riding whip against his thigh when annoyed. Brigette Helm, who played Maria in her film debut, said, "I can't forget the incredible strain they put us under. The work wasn't easy . . . Once I even fainted, during the [robot] transformation scene . . . the shot took so long, I didn't get enough air." Helm was also forced to stand in cold water for hours during the filming of a climactic flooding scene, alongside the five hundred children Lang had found in the poor areas of Berlin. And he instructed extras to throw themselves at powerful jets of water, instead of using dummies or stunt doubles. As Gustav Fröhlich, who played Freder, said, "Working under the directing hand of Fritz Lang wasn't a picnic for anyone."

The film premiered in Berlin in 1927 and wasn't an immediate success. Shortly after the premiere, UFA took it out of circulation and cut the length by about an hour. The American version was also changed, with the distributor, Paramount Pictures, cutting the film down to 115 minutes and removing some of the backstories of the characters. Because of all those changes, for about eighty years—as the reputation of the film grew in esteem—it wasn't known if an original print still existed. But remarkably, in 2008, a film archivist found a full-length copy in Argentina, which was able to be restored.

It's now been nearly one hundred years since its initial release, and the DNA of *Metropolis* can be seen in a variety of movies, such as *Frankenstein* (1931), *Blade Runner* (1982), *Brazil* (1985), and *The Fifth Element* (1997). It helped to popularize the style of Art Deco around the world, and in 2002, *Metropolis* became the first film admitted by UNESCO to their "Memory of the World Register"— an archive of the most important historical artifacts—where it sits alongside the Gutenberg Bible and Beethoven's Ninth Symphony.

▲ Director Fritz Lang

Unrivalled for beauty and visual imagination, this film is the passage between 19th century folklore and fairytale on the one hand, and a future full of multiple genre possibilities and iffy political questions on the other.

Meaghan Morris, film critic

The Rules of the Game

DIRECTED BY **Jean Renoir**

To watch when you . . . are ready to laugh at a comedy of manners directed by a true master of cinema.

France, 1939
B&W, 106 minutes, Comedy

Screenplay: Jean Renoir, Carl Koch

Starring: Nora Grégor (Christine de la Cheyniest), Jean Renoir (Octave), Marcel Dalio (Marquis Robert de la Cheyniest), Paulette Dubost (Lisette), Roland Toutain (André Jurieux), Gaston Modot (Schumacher), Julien Carette (Marceau), Mila Parély (Geneviève de Marras)

> "You see, in this world, there is one awful thing, and that is that everyone has his reasons."
>
> —Octave

One interesting aspect of film studies is how a movie can change from being reviled upon release to being revered years later. *The Rules of the Game* (1939), directed by Jean Renoir, is an example of this. Met with a chorus of boos by its first audiences, it is now called one of the greatest movies ever made. Ironically, on those "greatest movie" lists, *The Rules of the Game* sits alongside two films that also weren't appreciated until years after they were released: Orson Welles's *Citizen Kane* (1941) and Alfred Hitchcock's *Vertigo* (1958).

The main issue for *The Rules of the Game* was its timing. Jean Renoir set out to create a biting comedy about French society, poking fun at the intersecting lives of aristocrats and their servants, complete with many adulterous love affairs. He was inspired by the satirical

romantic plays of the eighteenth century, but by 1939, France was about to go to war with Germany, and moviegoers were in no mood to see a frivolous film about the rich behaving badly. Renoir attempted to salvage his movie by editing it, but it was no use. *The Rules of the Game* was taken off the screen after just a few weeks, and banned from further viewings under the advisement that it was "demoralizing." The original film print was placed into storage, and Renoir escaped the Nazis by traveling to America. Then, during the bombings of World War II, the warehouse that was storing the negatives of *The Rules of the Game* was destroyed.

This seemed to spell the end for the movie, but in 1956, two film lab technicians

▶ Julien Carette as Marceau

(Jean Gaborit and Jacques Marechal) uncovered boxes from the bombed-out warehouse, which contained most of the movie, in bits. Under the watchful eye of Jean Renoir, they began a painstaking process of piecing *The Rules of the Game* back together, stitching the usable parts of the negatives, and restoring the film to 106 minutes. This was shorter than the original length, but according to Renoir, there was only one scene that was lost, and as he claimed, it wasn't "very important" to the story.

Renoir also stars in the film, playing Octave, one of the characters mixed up in a complicated romance. The movie begins with Octave's friend, a pilot named André Jurieux

(Roland Toutain) touching down after a dangerous trip across the Atlantic, following in the famous footsteps of Charles Lindbergh. The flight was successful, but Jurieux does not celebrate, because he notices that the married woman he is in love with, Christine (Nora Grégor), isn't there to greet him, as she had promised. He says as much to a radio reporter, and the broadcast is overheard by Christine's husband, Marquis Robert de la Cheyniest (Marcel Dalio). However, he doesn't mind that his wife is having an affair, because he is having one of his own, with Geneviève (Mila Parély).

▲ Gaston Modot as Schumacher

Robert invites Jurieux to join himself and
Christine—with their friends and their personal staff—at his country estate for a weekend
of hunting.

    The Rules of the Game can be seen as the
grandfather of the domestic upstairs-downstairs
drama—a direct predecessor to films such as
Gosford Park (2001) and TV series like *Downton
Abbey* (2010)—though with slightly more bite.
This film came over a decade after Jean Renoir
had started writing and directing and followed
two of his critically acclaimed films: *The Grand
Illusion* (1937) and *La Bête Humaine* (1938).
Their success had allowed him to set up his own
production company. *The Rules of the Game* was

▲ Paulette Dubost as Lisette

More Essential Jean Renoir

The Lower Depths (1936)
The Grand Illusion (1937)
La Bête Humaine (1938)
A Day in the Country (1946)
The River (1951)

▲ Paulette Dubost as Lisette

Renoir was awarded an honorary Academy Award for his remarkable filmography. He was too ill to attend the ceremony, so Ingrid Bergman accepted on his behalf, with the award summing up his immense contribution to world cinema by stating that Renoir was: "A genius who, with grace, responsibility and enviable devotion through silent film, sound film, feature, documentary and television has won the world's admiration."

The restored version of *The Rules of the Game* was screened in 1959 at the Venice Film Festival, and the reception to it was vastly different this second time around. The film was hailed by critics, and in 1962 it made an appearance in the "Greatest Films of All Time" poll conducted by *Sight and Sound* magazine, voted by critics as the third-best movie in film history. It has remained in the top ten ever since.

its first project and would be one of the most expensive French movies of the time.

Jean Renoir was born with art in his blood, as the son of the renowned French impressionist painter, Pierre-Auguste Renoir. His father died in 1919, and the younger Renoir financed his early film career using money from the sale of some of his paintings. With that, his film career began, starting during the silent film era and transitioning to sound pictures. Slowly, Renoir developed the visual style and cinema language that he would become famous for and use to great effect in *The Rules of the Game*—namely, deep-focus photography and complex camera shots that follow the characters as they move through a space.

Renoir made films in various genres throughout his career—as a writer, director, and (sometimes) actor. His body of work spanned fifty years, making over thirty feature films, two of which are considered true masterpieces: *The Grand Illusion* and *The Rules of the Game*. A solid argument could also be made for a few of his others, such as *La Bête Humaine* and *The River* (1951). In 1975, Jean

The centerpiece of Renoir's intricate structure, the pivot on which the action turns, the symbolic core of his critique of French society, is the hunt, the scene that most clearly reveals the volcano that seethes beneath the dancers. In a film whose shots often run for a minute or more, here fifty-one shots appear in less than four minutes, in a mounting rhythm of cutting and movement that culminates in an awesome barrage of gunfire as, in twenty-two shots—fifty-three seconds—twelve animals die. Surely one of the most powerful scenes in all of cinema.

Alexander Sesonske, film studies professor

▲ Director Jean Renoir as Octave

The Double Life of Véronique

DIRECTED BY Krzysztof Kieślowski

To watch when you . . . feel like getting lost in a beautiful, autumnal dream.

Poland/France, 1991
Color, 97 minutes, Drama

Screenplay: Krzysztof Kieślowski,
Krzysztof Piesiewicz

Starring: Irène Jacob (Weronika/
Véronique), Philippe Volter (Alexandre
Fabbri), Claude Duneton (Véronique's
Father), Wladyslaw Kowalski
(Weronika's Father)

> "Not long ago, I had a strange sensation. I felt that I was alone.
> All of a sudden. Yet nothing had changed."
>
> —Véronique

It's difficult to describe exactly what happens in *The Double Life of Véronique* (1991) or to articulate why the film is so captivating. The story begins with Irène Jacob as Weronika, a singer in Poland who glimpses a woman who looks exactly like herself. Suddenly, she has a feeling that she is not alone in the world, but unexpectedly, Weronika dies. The woman she had seen is Véronique (also played by Irène Jacob), who lives in France, and after Weronika's death she has a feeling that she *is* alone in the world. Polish director Krzysztof Kieślowski enjoyed playing with themes about second chances and missed opportunities, and this feature—made a few years before his own death—has confounded and intrigued audiences for over thirty years.

Krzysztof Kieślowski was part of a new generation of Polish directors that came to prominence in the 1970s and '80s, including Agnieszka Holland, Wojciech Marczewski, and Krzysztof Zanussi. They were following in the footsteps of the previous wave of filmmakers who had revived the industry in the country during the 1950s and '60s and had brought the attention of the world to Polish cinema—directors like Andrzej Wajda, Jerzy Kawalerowicz, and, most famously, Roman Polanski. Poland had started making films in the early 1900s, but two World Wars had wiped out the industry, and following the immense destruction of World War II, Polish cinema had to start from scratch. The subsequent Soviet occupation of the country meant that all films made in the postwar years were heavily censored and had to fit in with Stalin's socialist realism doctrine. But in 1948, the Łódź film school was established, and after the

▲▲ Irène Jacob as the Polish Weronika   ▲ "Why two? Why did you make two?"—Véronique

cultural thaw of 1956, young filmmakers who had graduated from the school emerged—with a fresh perspective and a desire to confront tough political issues.

Kieślowski had applied to study at the Łódź film school twice and was twice rejected. He was about to give up completely when his mother encouraged him to try once more—and that third time was a charm. He started making documentaries while at Łódź, and following graduation he stayed within that genre, directing a couple of state-commissioned short documentary films, and two industrial movies, *Between Wroclaw and Zielona Góra* (1972) and *The Principles of Safety and Hygiene in a Copper Mine* (1972). Those films required little creativity, but Kieślowski later said that it wasn't a shameful thing to do. "It's a profession—film director. Sometimes you just have to render some services. It was boring, far more boring than anything else I've done, but I could live because of it."

Kieślowski intended to remain a nonfiction filmmaker, but at the end of the 1970s he started to branch out to make narrative films, such as his breakout feature—the sharp satire *Camera Buff* (1979), about a factory worker who buys a camera and starts to film his corrupt workplace. *Camera Buff* won awards at various film festivals, and more acclaim came with Kieślowski's next two narrative features— *No End* (1985), a supernatural drama about the show trials of political prisoners in Poland; and *Blind Chance* (1987), which followed three different versions of one man's life, all depending on whether he caught or missed a train. In one scenario, he catches the train and ends up joining the Communist Party. In another,

More Must-Sees by Krzysztof Kieślowski

Camera Buff (1979)
No End (1985)
Blind Chance (1988)
The Decalogue (1989)
Three Colors Trilogy: Blue,
    White, Red (1993–1994)

he misses it and becomes an anti-communist. And in the third, he still misses the train, and chooses to stay politically neutral but dies in the end. *Blind Chance* was completed in 1981, and it was banned from being screened until 1987. The success of its eventual release built Kieślowski's growing international reputation as an intelligent filmmaker concerned with ethics, morality, politics, and philosophy.

While researching show trials for *No End*, Krzysztof Kieślowski met Krzysztof Piesiewicz, a criminal defense lawyer who had dealt with many political cases. Piesiewicz convinced Kieślowski to make a narrative feature on the subject, rather than the documentary he'd been planning, and Kieślowski invited Piesiewicz to cowrite the script with him. This kicked off a collaboration that would last through the rest of Kieślowski's filmography. And following the banning of *Blind Chance*, Kieślowski decided to stop making overtly political films. His next feature, *The Double Life of Véronique*, he focused on more universal humanistic issues. A few film critics have pointed out that when Weronika sees Véronique, the character is walking in the opposite direction of a civil protest—a statement, perhaps, by the filmmaker about abandoning the political side of his movies. To make *The Double Life of Véronique*, Kieślowski traveled outside of Poland and collaborated with a French production company. He had wanted to stay in his own country to continue to make movies, but the tough economic climate of the postcommunist era meant that financing was hard to come by.

Kieślowski doesn't give any straight answers in *The Double Life of Véronique*; instead, he

▲ Irène Jacob as the French Véronique

prompts questions around identity and fate. You could read the film as being literal—Weronika and Véronique are doppelgängers of each other, or long-lost twins, somehow. Or you could think about it more obscurely—is it about the parts of ourselves that we never really know? Is it about loneliness and the human desire for connection? At one point, Véronique watches a marionette show but finds herself more intrigued by the reflection of the puppeteer she can see

▲▲ Irène Jacob on the set of *The Double Life of Véronique*

▲ Krzysztof Kieslowski directs Irène Jacob

in a mirror. He is Alexandre (Philippe Volter), who leads her on a mysterious scavenger hunt, where he appears to know more about her than he lets on. Is he manipulating Véronique, like his puppets? (He also creates a puppet of Véronique, making two. He claims the second is just a backup, but does he know about Weronika?)

There are many unexplained symbols and coincidences, and very little dialogue, but for a film that is purposely vague, *The Double Life of Véronique* is not frustrating to watch. All the questions come after the viewing, because during it, Krzysztof Kieślowski lulls you into a dreamlike state with the autumnal-tinged cinematography (by Slawomir Idziak), the haunting score (by Zbigniew Preisner), and close-ups lingering on the beautiful face of Irène Jacob. She is a Swiss-French actress whom Kieślowski had spotted in her debut role, playing a piano teacher in *Au Revoir les Enfants* (1987), directed by Louis Malle. She starred in several French

▲ Director Krzysztof Kieslowski

films in between her debut and *The Double Life of Véronique*, but it was Kieślowski's movie that would introduce her to a wider audience. *The Double Life of Véronique* premiered at the 1991 Cannes Film Festival, where it received an overwhelmingly positive response. It won the Fipresci Award at the festival, decided by the International Federation of Film Critics, as well as the Ecumenical Jury Award, a Christian prize given to films that best "touch the spiritual dimension of our existence," and Irène Jacob won Best Actress.

Irène Jacob would work with Krzysztof Kieślowski just one more time, for his final feature film, *Three Colors: Red* (1994). After almost thirty years of directing movies, Kieślowski retired from filmmaking in 1994, aged fifty-three. Just two years later, he died after undergoing heart bypass surgery. Two months after his death, Irène Jacob appeared at the Cannes Film Festival to help pay tribute to him, where she spoke about how important he was to her and her career, with tears in her eyes.

[Kieślowski's] films can be mystical experiences. He trusts us to follow him, to sense his purpose, to leave the theater having shared his openness to a moment. The last thing you want to do after a Kieślowski film is "unravel" the plot. It can't be done. If you try it, you will turn clouds into rain. If there seem to be inconsistencies, it is because life and time itself sometimes try again and take an unexpected turn.

Roger Ebert, film critic

Day for Night

DIRECTED BY **François Truffaut**

To watch when you . . . want to experience life on a movie set.

France, 1973
Color, 116 minutes, Drama

Screenplay: François Truffaut, Jean-Louis Richard, Suzanne Schiffman

Starring: Jacqueline Bisset (Julie Baker), Jean-Pierre Léaud (Alphonse), Valentina Cortese (Séverine), Jean-Pierre Aumont (Alexandre), François Truffaut (Ferrand)

> "Making a film is like a stagecoach ride in the old West. When you start, you're hoping for a pleasant trip. By the halfway point, you just hope to survive."
>
> —Ferrand

There's a common argument among cinephiles that centers around "movies about movies." Namely, which is the best film about the film industry? For admirers of classic Hollywood, there are many answers, from *The Bad and the Beautiful* (1952) to *Singin' in the Rain* (1952), *Sullivan's Travels* (1941), *Sunset Boulevard* (1950), or *A Star Is Born* (1937, 1954, 1976, 2018—take your pick). Modern Hollywood lovers might say *The Player* (1992), *Ed Wood* (1994), *Mulholland Drive* (2001), *La La Land* (2016), or *Once Upon a Time . . . in Hollywood* (2019). For foreign film fans, it's similarly divided, usually split between Federico Fellini's *8½* (1963), Jean-Luc Godard's *Contempt* (1963), and François Truffaut's *Day for Night* (1973).

It's interesting that both Godard and Truffaut made a movie about the movies. They had been pivotal directors during the French

New Wave of the early 1960s, right from the start of the cinematic movement, with Godard's *Breathless* (1960) and Truffaut's *The 400 Blows* (1960). At that time, Godard and Truffaut were close friends and coworkers at the movie magazine *Cahiers du Cinéma*, where they shared an admiration for the films of classic Hollywood and had a desire to change the French film industry. But by the late 1960s, the French New Wave was over, and each director took their careers into different territory. Jean-Luc Godard's films became more political and experimental, while François Truffaut experienced commercial success with mainstream movies. "He is engaged in another kind of cinema," Truffaut explained about Godard, pointing out how after 1968 (a period of civil unrest in France), they seemed to have opposite goals for their work. Truffaut said that Godard felt that

"since May '68, it's impossible to make the same kinds of movies and he resents people who still do." But for Truffaut, as he said, "I've made a choice, my thoughts are perfectly clear, I want to make normal films, it's my life." With this divergence, their friendship suffered, and after the release of *Day for Night*, it was severed for good.

The French title for *Day for Night* is *La nuit Americaine*. It refers to the technical filmmaking term "shooting day for night," which means filming during the day, but adding a filter to the camera to make it appear as though it's night. This was a method more commonly used during the Golden Age of Hollywood, and by using the term—and inferring to American

▲ François Truffaut as the director of the movie within the movie, *Meet Pamela*

▲ Jean-Pierre Léaud, Jean-Pierre Aumont, Jacqueline Bisset, and Valentina Cortese

films in the French title—François Truffaut was evoking the fantasy aspect of Hollywood moviemaking. And Truffaut had long wanted to make a movie about both the fantasy and the reality of directing films. The idea for *Day for Night* came together during the postproduction process for his 1971 drama *Two English Girls*. He was editing that film at a movie studio in Nice,

and Truffaut became fascinated with the remains of an exterior set on the lot. There were building facades, an entrance for a Metro station, a town square, roads, and a café, originally built for the American production of *The Madwoman of Chaillot* (1969), starring Katharine Hepburn, but left behind after that film had wrapped.

This set is shown as *Day for Night* begins. It's a busy town square, with adults, children, dogs, and cars bustling about. A young man walks out of the subway station, and through the square. He stops in front of an older man, swings his arm back, and slaps him in the face. Suddenly, François Truffaut calls cut. He is not playing himself, but a version of himself, a film director named Ferrand, who is making a movie called *Meet Pamela*, a melodrama about a man who introduces his father to his fiancée, and then they fall in love. The cast of the fictional film includes the movie-obsessed Alphonse (Jean-Pierre Léaud), the former romantic lead Alexandre (Jean-Pierre Aumont), the aging diva Séverine (Valentina Cortese), and the emotionally fragile English actress Julie (Jacqueline Bisset), who struggles with past demons.

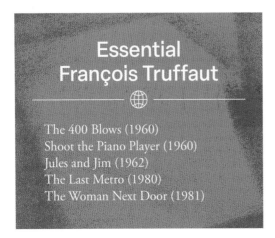

Essential François Truffaut

🌐

The 400 Blows (1960)
Shoot the Piano Player (1960)
Jules and Jim (1962)
The Last Metro (1980)
The Woman Next Door (1981)

There's a lot of drama on and off the fictional set of *Meet Pamela*, as Ferrand is bombarded with problems and questions: A drunk Séverine struggles to shoot a scene, Alphonse mistakes Julie's concern for love, a kitten causes trouble—there's even a death in the cast. But throughout it all, François Truffaut's love of the madness, magic, and messiness of moviemaking shines through.

For the final screenplay, Truffaut hired his former assistant director Suzanne Schiffman to ensure that all the technical aspects of filmmaking were correct. He cowrote the script with Jean-Louis Richard, mixing in many of his own experiences.

▲ François Truffaut accepts the Oscar for Best Foreign Film for *Day for Night*.

▲ Director François Truffaut

And Truffaut decided that he didn't want to "tell the whole truth about filming," instead saying that he just wanted to include "some real things that happened in my past movies or in other movies." His bigger goal was to capture his own love and belief in the power of cinema. Ironically, it wasn't easy to find a movie distributor who believed in this idea. United Artists turned *Day for Night* down, claiming it was "too intellectual," but eventually, Warner-Columbia came on board for the French release.

Day For Night screened at the 1973 Cannes Film Festival, and among the glowing reviews, the film had one vocal detractor: Jean-Luc Godard. He wrote Truffaut a letter where he called him a liar for showing filmmaking through rose-colored glasses. Cheekily, Godard had ended his letter by asking Truffaut to finance his next film: "After *Day for Night*," Godard wrote, "you ought to help me, so that audiences don't think that the only kinds of movies being made are your kind." In response, Truffaut wrote a twenty-page letter to Godard, defending his film and his direction of Jean-Pierre Léaud. (Godard had written a separate letter to Léaud, reproaching him for working with a director who had, in his opinion, sold out.) "I'm sending back your letter to Jean-Pierre," Truffaut wrote. "I've read it and I find it disgusting. Because of that letter I feel it's finally time to tell you, at length, that in my opinion you've been behaving like a shit." Truffaut went on to say that he thought Godard's recent political stance was merely an act, writing, "You need to play a role and the role has to be prestigious . . . you make a four-minute appearance, just enough time for the cameras to flash, for you to make two or three startling pronouncements, and then you disappear, shrouded in appealing mystery . . . The idea that all men are equal is theoretical to you, not sincerely felt." With that, their friendship was forever damaged.

Ultimately, François Truffaut's intent with *Day for Night* was to "make the audience happy on seeing a film in the making, to infuse joy and lightheartedness from all the sprocket holes of the film." His satirical love letter to cinema was embraced by audiences and won the Best Foreign Language Film Oscar at the 1974 Academy Awards, before being nominated for a further three Oscars (Best Screenplay, Best Director, and Best Supporting Actress for Valentina Cortese) the following year, after the film was released in the United States.

Nothing in it feels like the product of meticulous design, even as the craft behind the simplest moments of a feature film is exposed. Depicting the shoot, from first day to last, of a movie called *Meet Pamela*, *Day for Night* seems effortless, as if this was the movie Truffaut had been preparing for all his life.

David Cairns, film critic

Devi

DIRECTED BY **Satyajit Ray**

To watch when you . . . feel like getting lost in a lyrical poem
about the dangers of blind faith.

India, 1960
B&W, 99 minutes, Drama

Screenplay: Satyajit Ray, based
on the short story by Prabhat
Kumar Mukhopadhyay

Starring: Sharmila Tagore (Doyamoyee),
Soumitra Chatterjee (Umaprasad), Chhabi
Biswas (Kalikinkar Roy), Karuna Banerjee
(Harasundari), Purnendu Mukherjee
(Taraprasad), Arpan Chowdhury (Khoka)

"Kneel before her son. I've had a dream.
She is the incarnation of the Goddess, Kali."

—Kalikinkar Roy

Devi (1960) was the sixth feature film directed by Indian filmmaker Satyajit Ray. He was a master—right out of the gate—winning worldwide acclaim and a special jury prize at the Cannes Film Festival for his directorial debut, *Pather Panchali* (1955). He followed that film with two more that continued the story of the same lead character: *Aparajito* (1956) and *The World of Apu* (1959). With *Devi*, Ray made a more overtly political film, delving into the destructive nature of blind faith and the rights of women.

Satyajit Ray had been born in Calcutta to a Bengali family who had been involved in the arts and literature for generations. Ray first studied economics and physics, graduating from the University of Calcutta with honors, and then became an art student at Visva-Bharati University in Tagore. That experience opened

his mind, with the university being run by the poet and philosopher Rabindranath Tagore. It was also during this time when Ray discovered a love of cinema, reading about and watching Hollywood movies whenever he could, later saying that he learned everything he needed to know about directing films by watching American movies. He also wrote letters to Hollywood figures, including Deanna Durbin, Ginger Rogers, and director Billy Wilder. After seeing Wilder's film noir *Double Indemnity* (1944), Ray had written a twelve-page letter to him, but Wilder never replied. Ray took a job as an art director in advertising, and his most formative film-watching experience came while on a business trip in London in 1950. He saw *Bicycle Thieves* (1948), directed by Vittorio De Sica, a pivotal movie made during the Italian Neorealism cinematic wave, using first-time

actors and real locations to tell a heartbreaking story about an everyday working man in Rome. This film encouraged Ray that he could make a movie, and he decided to start directing.

Ray wrote the first draft of his screenplay for *Pather Panchali* on the ship home to India, adapting it from a book by Bibhutibhushan Bandyopadhyay. The film took him a long time to complete; he needed to shoot on weekends as he found money, and he finished it with funds donated by the Museum of Modern Art in New York. In the meantime, Ray received some advice on his script from one of the best directors in cinema history—Jean Renoir. Ray had bumped into Renoir at a hotel where Renoir was staying while scouting locations for his Indian-set film *The River* (1951). Renoir noticed how enthusiastic

Ray was about movies, and asked if he was planning on becoming a filmmaker. Ray gave Renoir a copy of his script, and Renoir later invited Ray to be part of his film unit, but Ray had to say no because of his day job.

He was able to give up his job in advertising after *Pather Panchali* was released and he quickly gained a reputation for making simple, lyrical, and poetic films using his native Bengali language. These contrasted with the Hindi-language movies made by Bollywood, which were full of music, dance, and romance.

For *Devi*, Satyajit Ray adapted a script from a short story by Prabhat Kumar Mukhopadhyay. Set in the last half of the nineteenth century, the

▲ Sharmila Tagore as Doya

film begins in a Bengali village, where the annual Durga Puja, a Hindu festival, is taking place. This celebrates the victory of the goddess Durga over a demon king, and there's music and fireworks as a statue of the goddess is adorned and later is carried to the ocean and sunk into the sea. We then meet the family at the center of the story: a traditional father, Kalikinkar Roy (Chhabi Biswas), who is dedicated to worshipping the goddess Kali; his son Umaprasad (Soumitra Chatterjee), who is about to leave for Calcutta to study at university; and Uma's young wife, Doyamoyee (Sharmila Tagore), who has to stay behind. Also in the house is Uma's brother, Taraprasad (Purnendu Mukherjee); his wife, Harasundari (Karuna Banerjee); and their son, Khoka (Arpan Chowdhury), who is infatuated with his auntie Doya. One night, Kalikinkar Roy has a dream, which makes him believe that Doya is an incarnation of the goddess Kali. In the morning, Roy bows at Doya's feet, instructing Taraprasad to do the same. Soon, Doya is being worshipped by local villagers who want her to heal them. Being a teenager and a woman, Doya has no say in the matter, and when her shocked husband comes home and urges her to leave with him to Calcutta, Doya starts to question herself—if she is the goddess, shouldn't she stay and help?

▲▲ Doya and Umaprasad
▲ "No medicine has the power of the Goddess."
—Kalikinkar Roy

Doya is seen as an object and an ideal—one who is literally put up on a pedestal—yet she has no power herself, and the deification of such a young woman is incredibly damaging. Her experience has been likened to that of becoming a celebrity, with a similar destruction of her mental health as we've witnessed with countless child stars. Doya's husband doesn't believe his father's vision and realizes how dangerous it is to follow superstition rather than science. These clashes between Uma and his father are representative of the changes and conversations that were happening in India at the time, when formal education brought traditional beliefs into question. This wasn't Satyajit Ray's first film

to explore the modernization of his country or the rights of women, but because of how critical it was of a Hindu belief, *Devi* was temporarily

▲ Chhabi Biswas as Kalikinkar Roy

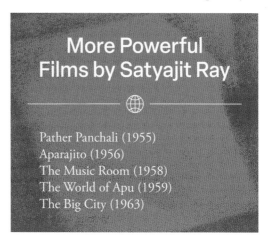

More Powerful Films by Satyajit Ray

Pather Panchali (1955)
Aparajito (1956)
The Music Room (1958)
The World of Apu (1959)
The Big City (1963)

banned from being released overseas, finally being distributed outside of India in 1962.

Satyajit Ray had more of a following internationally than in his own country. The tiny local audiences meant he could get financing only for small budgets, and he often did the bulk of the work himself—including composing the music and designing the sets. As he explained it, the international audience kept him working. "I have survived because of my foreign market," he said. "Without that I wouldn't have survived at all. I would have stopped making films and gone back to my old profession, advertising." Among those international admirers have been some powerful fans. Ray's films have influenced the likes of Martin Scorsese and Wes Anderson, and the Japanese filmmaker Akira Kurosawa once said about his work, "Never having seen a Satyajit Ray film is like never having seen the sun or the moon."

In 1992, Satyajit Ray received an honorary Academy Award in recognition of "his rare mastery of the art of motion pictures and for his profound humanitarian outlook, which has had an indelible influence on filmmakers and audiences throughout the world." Ray was unwell at this time, suffering from a heart condition that meant he couldn't travel to the ceremony, so delegates from the Academy visited him in hospital in Calcutta to deliver his award. Ray gave an acceptance speech from his hospital bed, calling the Oscar "the best achievement of my movie-making career." About a month later, Satyajit Ray died, just short of his seventy-first birthday, leaving behind a remarkable body of work that continues to influence and inspire today.

Doya's unsure eyes offer a wordless answer, bringing into focus the real object of critique in *Devi*: the denial of self-knowledge, a gaping void that neither religion nor rationalism can fill. Shockingly young, unworldly, and uneducated, Doya is a cipher to her own self, caught between the certainties of her father-in-law and her husband—a dynamic that emerges organically from Ray's pitch-perfect casting of a fourteen-year-old Sharmila Tagore.

Devika Girish, film critic

Cure

DIRECTED BY Kiyoshi Kurosawa

To watch when you . . . feel up to watching an intelligent psychological horror that will haunt you long after the credits have ended.

Japan, 1997
Color, 111 minutes, Horror

Screenplay: Kiyoshi Kurosawa

Starring: Kōji Yakusho (Detective Takabe), Masato Hagiwara (Mamiya), Anna Nakagawa (Fumie Takabe)

> "Lunatics like you have it easy,
> while citizens like me go through hell."
>
> —Takabe

Given the tradition of horror within Japanese culture, it's surprising that horror films came to Japanese cinema quite late. Ghost stories have long been woven into Japanese folktales, where mythologies combined with moral messages. In the late nineteenth century, Irish folklorist Lafcadio Hearn began to record the scary fairytales he had been told, compiling them in his book, *Kwaidan: Stories and Studies of Strange Things*, published in 1904. It would be around fifty years before supernatural horror films started to be made at a regular rate, such as Kenzi Mizoguchi's *Ugetsu* (1953) and *The Ghost of Yotsuya* (1959), directed by Nobuo Nakagawa. In the 1960s came Kaneto Shindo's *Onibaba* (1964), and Masaki Kobayashi's anthology horror *Kwaidan* (1964), which used Lafcadio Hearn's book as its basis.

The late 1990s saw a huge increase in the popularity of Japanese horror films around the world, with one British distributor of the movies nicknaming the genre "J-Horror." *Ringu* from 1998, directed by Hideo Nakata, become a huge international hit, spawning a Hollywood remake in 2002 called *The Ring*. Takashi Shimizu's horror *Ju-on: The Grudge* (2002) was also a phenomenon, leading to an American version, *The Grudge*, in 2004. And among all of this, director Kiyoshi Kurosawa (no relation to Akira Kurosawa), quietly established himself as a skilled artist of psychological horror— using J-Horror hallmarks like vengeful spirits and modern-day media but mixing them with an exploration of deeper societal issues. His film, *Pulse* (2001) was a particularly prescient horror, with a supernatural story that analyzed the isolation caused by the internet. And *Cure* (1997), Kurosawa's most famous horror, takes a traditional serial-killer police procedural and blends it with contemporary, existential feelings of dread, alienation, and loneliness within a big city.

▲ Detective Takabe interrogates Mamiya.

Kōji Yakusho stars as Detective Takabe, who is put in charge of an investigation involving a series of gruesome murders. All the victims are brutally killed and found with the same mark—an "X" slashed into the chest with a knife—but the victims are unconnected to one another. The perpetrators, too, are all different people, with no connection, and they are schoolteachers, doctors, policemen—upstanding citizens who don't fit the profile of a murderer. Takabe's investigation leads him to a psychology student named Mamiya (Masato Hagiwara), and he starts to suspect that Mamiya is behind it all.

This intriguing premise was dreamed up by director Kiyoshi Kurosawa, who also wrote the screenplay. He had been inspired to write the film ten years earlier, after watching news coverage about the arrest of a murderer. The killer's

neighbors were in disbelief over how such a nice man could be capable of dark deeds, and Kurosawa was interested in the way the reporter had described the killer—that under the guise of a normal person, a murderer had been lurking all along. As Kurosawa told Criterion, "I thought that wasn't the case. Maybe he wasn't this dangerous murderer in the beginning, who had been pretending to be a normal person. Rather, he was a nice, normal person to begin with, but something got triggered in him and he committed murder."

Kiyoshi Kurosawa had been directing feature films since the early 1980s and quickly became a prolific filmmaker, averaging around three films a year during the 1990s. Most of his movies went straight to home video in

▲ "All the things that used to be inside of me . . . now they're outside." —Mamiya

Japan, but *Cure* gave Kurosawa his first taste of international success, making waves at film festivals all over the world and finding its way to American theaters in 2001. Following *Cure*, Kiyoshi Kurosawa decided to move away from

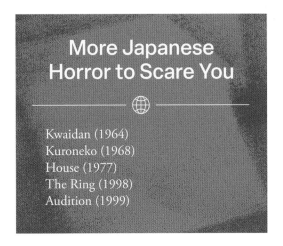

More Japanese Horror to Scare You

🌐

Kwaidan (1964)
Kuroneko (1968)
House (1977)
The Ring (1998)
Audition (1999)

horror and into drama, gaining more accolades in the process. *Tokyo Sonata* (2008) again starred Kōji Yakusho and focused on a disintegrating family, winning Kurosawa the Jury Prize at the Cannes Film Festival. He was back at the festival for his supernatural drama *Journey to the Shore* (2015), winning Best Director, and again for *Before We Vanish* (2017), a science-fiction film about an alien invasion.

Cure was not Kiyoshi Kurosawa's only hit, but in the twenty years since its release, this film has gained a host of passionate fans, including South Korean director Bong Joon Ho. He placed *Cure* among his ten choices for *Sight and Sound* magazine's once-in-a-decade poll of the "greatest movies of all time." You can see the influence of *Cure* in Bong Joon Ho's murder mystery *Memories of Murder* (2003), as well as his psychological horror-comedy, the Academy Award–winning *Parasite* (2019).

Discarding the reassurances typically associated with the police in such films, [Kurosawa] widens the social, political, psychological, and metaphysical issues surrounding random violent death and, in so doing, brings out the full irony and ambiguity of his deceptively simple title.

Chris Fujiwara, author

▲ Director Kiyoshi Kurosawa works on the set of *Creepy* (2016).

The Vanishing

DIRECTED BY **George Sluizer**

To watch when you . . . can handle a psychological horror
that will not be easily forgotten.

Netherlands, 1988
Color, 107 minutes, Crime/Horror

Screenplay: Tim Krabbé, George Sluizer

Starring: Bernard-Pierre Donnadieu
(Raymond), Gene Bervoets (Rex), Johanna
ter Steege (Saskia)

"I logically conceived the most horrible deed
that I could envision right at that moment. But I want
you to know, for me, killing is not the worst thing."

—Raymond

Some movies have a way of crawling into your brain and refusing to leave. *The Vanishing* (1988) is one of those, featuring an ending that shocked and titillated audiences around the world.

The premise is simple, a Dutch couple, Rex (Gene Bervoets) and Saskia (Johanna ter Steege) are traveling through the south of France. They pause at a crowded rest area; Saskia goes inside the gas station to buy some cold drinks . . . and never returns. Rex does everything he can to find her, without any luck. The film then cuts to the character of Raymond (Bernard-Pierre Donnadieu), a French chemistry professor whose benign looks mean he can easily disappear into a crowd. But Raymond is not an average man—he keeps a fake arm cast in his car, and practices using a chloroform-like substance on himself to note how long he remains

unconscious for. A flashback shows Raymond saving the life of a drowning child, and after his family hails him as a hero, he starts to wonder— if he can commit such an act of good, is he also capable of doing evil?

The script was adapted from a novel written by journalist, author, and avid chess player Tim Krabbé, who cowrote the screenplay alongside director George Sluizer. By this time, Sluizer was a veteran director, starting his career in the Netherlands in the 1960s by making documentaries and TV specials. His first feature film was a rock documentary called Stamping Ground (1971); prior to *The Vanishing*, his best-known movie had been *Twice a Woman* (1979) starring Bibi Andersson and Anthony Perkins. Sluizer had gotten to know Tim Krabbé after reading a series of articles he'd written about his travels through America. The director was particularly

interested in Krabbé's take on filmmaking in the United States. Krabbé turned his experiences into a short book, called *Red Desert Penitentiary,* which Sluizer adapted into a film in 1985. Krabbé then started working on an original novel called *The Golden Egg* and asked Sluizer (who had been born in France) for names of small towns in the south of France to use for his story. The author was only up to his third chapter when Sluizer decided to buy the film rights.

The Vanishing was completely different in tone from Sluizer's prior films, and he wasn't interested in the idea of "whodunit," revealing Raymond to be the villain early in the story. Instead, he plays with the audience's curiosity about how Raymond pulled it off, building suspense slowly over the film's runtime. Sluizer adds in plenty of misdirection along

▲ Johanna ter Steege as Saskia and Gene Bervoets as Rex

the way, focusing on objects that may (or may not) be clues; even casting extras who looked like Johanna ter Steege, placing them in the background to tease viewers. The tension is added with an impressive amount of precision, and Rex's later choice feels both plausible and inevitable. This makes the ending even scarier, forcing the viewer to confront their own morbid curiosity by asking themselves what they might do in that situation.

Vital to George Sluizer pulling off his shocking twist was the casting of the three main roles of Saskia, Rex, and Raymond. As Saskia, this was Johanna ter Steege's first feature film,

and her charm in this small (but unforgettable) role catapulted her to relative stardom, gaining her work with international directors like Robert Altman for *Vincent & Theo* (1990), Bruce Beresford for *Paradise Road* (1997), and Stanley Kubrick for *Aryan Papers*, a Holocaust project that he scrapped in the wake of Steven Spielberg's *Schindler's List*. Dutch actor Gene Bervoets was also relatively new to the screen, making just six films before this, and he was chosen by Sluizer to play Rex for his ability to

▲ Bernard-Pierre Donnadieu as Raymond

speak both Dutch and French. Sluizer hadn't been completely convinced that Bervoets was the right choice when they started filming, and Bervoets knew this, leading to a performance filled with anxiety—perfect for his role.

As for Raymond, George Sluizer said this casting was crucial, because everything is built upon the character. Originally, he wanted to hire the legendary French actor, Jean-Louis Trintignant, but when he wasn't available, Sluizer widened his search. In thinking about who he could cast, the director remembered an extra who had only a line or two in his film *Twice a Woman*, and although it had been ten years since Sluizer

had made that movie, he could distinctly recall the way the actor had thrown away his cigarette. "That's someone," Sluizer remembered, "who put—in throwing a cigarette away—a whole character." His name was Bernard-Pierre Donnadieu, and within the decade since he had worked with Sluizer, he had built up a sizable body of work, playing small roles in movies and TV shows. Donnadieu agreed to take on the challenging part and felt that he understood how to play the character—in particular, how Raymond's high intelligence had led him to morbid conclusions.

Bernard-Pierre Donnadieu's chilling performance was singled out in reviews of the film, which screened to a positive reception at film festivals. But George Sluizer struggled to find a distributor who was willing to release the movie, talking to every movie studio imaginable for over a year. Finally, the Sydney Film Festival called Sluizer to ask whether they could screen *The Vanishing*, and Sluizer traveled to Australia for the event. *The Vanishing* won the sole award given at the Sydney Film Festival—the audience award—and from there, the movie began to catch on. Buoyed by strong reviews and the tantalizing promise of a twist ending, *The*

▲ "You start with an idea in your head, and you take a step . . . Soon, you realize you're up to your neck in something intense." —Raymond

amped up the scares, adding plenty of gore and, inexplicably, a happy ending that was derided by critics. The original version of *The Vanishing* doesn't feature an ounce of blood and remains a truly disturbing film boasting legions of fans. Among those fans was Stanley Kubrick, who called George Sluizer to talk about the movie, dissecting it shot by shot and reportedly saying that *The Vanishing* was the most terrifying film he'd ever seen. Jokingly, Sluizer asked Kubrick if he'd ever seen *The Shining* (1980), the iconic horror film directed by Kubrick. *The Shining*, Kubrick replied, was "child's play" in comparison to *The Vanishing*.

> The influence of Claude Chabrol, for whose work Mr. Sluizer has expressed admiration, is especially noticeable in the film's later stages as quiet malice and fatal curiosity become intertwined.
>
> Janet Maslin, film critic

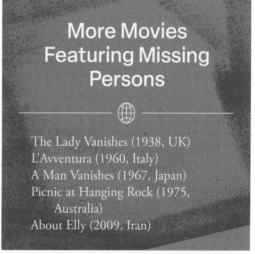

More Movies Featuring Missing Persons

The Lady Vanishes (1938, UK)
L'Avventura (1960, Italy)
A Man Vanishes (1967, Japan)
Picnic at Hanging Rock (1975, Australia)
About Elly (2009, Iran)

Vanishing started to screen in art house theaters in the United States two years after its initial European release.

Hollywood took notice, and in 1993, George Sluizer was hired to direct an American version of *The Vanishing*, with Sandra Bullock as the vanished woman, Kiefer Sutherland as her tormented partner, and Jeff Bridges as the sadistic killer. Being Hollywood, this version

Peeping Tom

DIRECTED BY **Michael Powell**

To watch when you . . . want to meet a truly disturbing (and unique) movie villain.

UK, 1960
Color, 101 minutes, Horror

Screenplay: Leo Marks

Starring: Carl Boehm (Mark Lewis), Anna Massey (Helen Stephens), Shirley Ann Field (Diane), Moira Shearer (Viv), Pamela Green (Milly)

"Whatever I photograph I always lose."

—Mark

Peeping Tom (1960) is now considered a masterpiece of horror, but when it was released, it just about ruined director Michael Powell's career. The film was savaged by British critics. They were disgusted by the violence depicted in the movie and the perversity of the lead character, who enjoys filming women as he kills them. A reviewer for the *Daily Express* compared the "nausea and depression" he felt watching the film with visiting slums in poverty-stricken areas of the world. While another reviewer in the *Tribune* said, "The only really satisfactory way to dispose of *Peeping Tom* would be to shovel it up and flush it down the nearest sewer."

Up until that point, Michael Powell had been something of a revered figure in British cinema. He had worked at the famed Elstree studios with the likes of Alfred Hitchcock in the late 1920s, and started directing in the 1930s, making a series of low-budget pictures, known as "quota quickies" for the way they filled the quota of British-made films that local cinemas

were required to show. Powell's breakthrough came when he teamed up with a German screenwriter named Emeric Pressburger in 1939 for *U-Boat 29*, where Powell directed and Pressburger wrote the screenplay. After directing two more solo films, Powell decided to cement a formal working partnership with Pressburger, and they formed the production company The Archers. As cowriters and codirectors, Powell and Pressburger made a series of remarkable films in the 1940s—dramas with style and substance—such as the lush, color-soaked *Black Narcissus* (1947) and *The Red Shoes* (1948). The passionate story and gorgeous dreamlike visuals in *The Red Shoes* have made the film a particular favorite for many cinephiles and filmmakers (and dance professionals) and landed it a spot on several lists of the greatest films of all time.

Michael Powell had been especially focused on the visual style of The Archers' productions, though he and Emeric Pressburger split duties during filming. They made a great team, but in 1956 Powell and Pressburger amicably dissolved

their partnership. As Powell started to look for material to direct solo, he was introduced to screenwriter Leo Marks. They began working on a film about the life of Freud but had to abandon it when John Huston acquired the film rights to Freud's story. So, Powell asked Marks if he had any other ideas, and Marks told him that he'd always wanted to do a film about "scopophilia." That term is defined as the "pleasure derived by looking," and is most used to describe a man watching a woman—or, colloquially, a "Peeping Tom." In cinema studies, it is also used to describe the "male gaze" of the camera. That is, the way a movie (usually directed by a man) peers at a woman on film, essentially making the audience complicit in the looking—as if the viewer is also appraising the actress as a sexual object, regardless of their own sexual orientation.

Leo Marks had also wanted to write a story about a cameraman whose camera is his murder weapon, and he told Powell all of this. Powell, Marks said, "listened in silence—and he has a habit of looking into the middle distance when he's interested—I didn't know it at the time, I thought it meant he was bored, but . . . he stared into the middle distance and then he said, 'that's mine, go and write it.'" The final script centers on a camera focus puller named Mark—the character's name was a nod to Leo Marks. Mark Lewis is a quiet, unassuming young man, who keeps to himself and always carries a camera with him. But Mark's dark secret is revealed at the beginning of the film—he hires a sex worker and then kills her, while filming her reaction. Mark goes back to his apartment to view his work on-screen, getting pleasure from seeing how frightened she was. His peculiar predilection is tied to the abuse he suffered as a child, where his scientist father used him as a test

▲ Carl Boehm as Mark

been impressed with his performance in a popular German film trilogy. His impassive face is perfect for this character, who only really shows pleasure when he is watching the footage of his murders. In this way, Mark is not unlike Anthony Perkins's character in *Psycho* (1960), who peers at Janet Leigh through a peephole. Director Alfred Hitchcock liked to use voyeurism in his films (such as in *Psycho* and *Rear Window*, 1954) to make the audience feel uncomfortable, as if they are enjoying what they're seeing, too. *Peeping Tom* and *Psycho* were released at the same time, both made by British directors, but while *Psycho* would help Hitchcock's career, *Peeping Tom* would seriously hurt Powell's. One theory for this is that *Peeping Tom* more directly spoke to the complicity of audiences who enjoy watching horror films and women being murdered, and that was a little too close to comfort for the critics.

Michael Powell would direct a few more movies after *Peeping Tom*, though he never again reached the heights he'd experienced with Emeric Pressburger at The Archers. But *Peeping Tom* and the work of Powell and Pressburger has had its champions over the years, most especially in filmmaker Martin Scorsese and his longtime editor, Thelma Schoonmaker. Both Scorsese and Schoonmaker had seen a Powell and Pressburger film in their youth and it had made a huge impression on them. For Scorsese, it was *The Red Shoes*, and Schoonmaker had seen *The Life and Death of Colonel Blimp* (1943). They became fans of the directors' work, a fact they realized when they started working together on Scorsese's *Raging Bull* (1980). Also during that production, the film studio that owned *Peeping Tom* approached Scorsese to ask if he would support a rerelease.

subject. Interestingly, the father is played (in an uncredited role) by Michael Powell.

Originally, Powell had wanted to cast British actor Laurence Harvey as Mark, but Harvey had recently starred in the successful British New Wave film *Room at the Top* (1959) and was getting offers from Hollywood that he found hard to turn down. Instead, Powell cast a German-born actor named Karlheinz Böhm, credited here as Carl Boehm. He was the son of famed composer Karl Böhm, and Powell had

▲ "Do you know what the most frightening thing in the world is? It's fear." —Mark

The film had been little seen over the two decades since its release, because, as Michael Powell explained, the original distributors had "canceled the British distribution" following the poor reviews and box office, and "sold the negative as soon as they could to an obscure black marketer of films, who tried to forget it, and forgotten it was, along with its director, for 20 years."

Scorsese agreed to lend his name to a release of *Peeping Tom* at the New York Film Festival in 1979 and also put up the money to fund the screenings. Nineteen years after its original release, *Peeping Tom* was much more enthusiastically received, and since then, Scorsese, along with Schoonmaker, have become the custodians of Powell's work—overseeing restorations to keep this movie (and his others) alive. Scorsese also introduced Schoonmaker to Powell, and the two fell in love, marrying in 1984 and staying together until Powell's death in 1990. "My relationship with Michael was the happiest years of my life," Schoonmaker said in an interview. "When he died, he left a little furnace burning inside me." That furnace continues to burn, with Thelma Schoonmaker championing Michael Powell's movies, though she's quick to give credit to Martin Scorsese. After the controversy that surrounded *Peeping Tom* in 1960, Michael Powell "lived

▲ Director Michael Powell

in oblivion," she said, until Scorsese stepped in. "No one has done more for Powell and Pressburger than Marty."

Martin Scorsese once said that this movie, and Federico Fellini's 8½ contain all that can be said about directing. The Fellini film is about the world of deals and show biz, and the Powell is about the deep psychological process at work when a filmmaker tells his actors to do as he commands, while he stands in the shadows and watches.

Roger Ebert, film critic

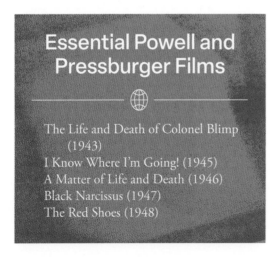

Essential Powell and Pressburger Films

🌐

The Life and Death of Colonel Blimp (1943)
I Know Where I'm Going! (1945)
A Matter of Life and Death (1946)
Black Narcissus (1947)
The Red Shoes (1948)

The Orphanage

DIRECTED BY **J. A. Bayona**

To watch when you . . . feel ready to handle jump scares and creepy children.

Spain, 2007
Color, 105 minutes, Horror

Screenplay: Sergio G. Sánchez

Starring: Belén Reuda (Laura), Fernando Cayo (Carlos), Roger Príncep (Simón), Geraldine Chaplin (Aurora)

"Seeing is not believing. It's the other way around.
Believe, and you will see."

—Aurora

The *Orphanage* (2007) was an impressive feature debut from Spanish director Juan Antonio "J. A." Bayona, who uses plenty of tried-and-true horror elements (jump scares, creepy kids, sound design, a Gothic-horror setting) but also mixes in moments that are genuinely surprising. He wanted to allow the viewer to have their own interpretation on the events in the film, essentially directing two versions in his mind—making *The Orphanage* either a scary supernatural horror or an emotional domestic drama, depending on your reading.

J. A. Bayona had started his career as a film journalist at a young age. When he interviewed Mexican director Guillermo del Toro at the 1993 Stiges Film Festival, del Toro thought Bayona was ten years old and was impressed with his questions and his depth of film knowledge. Really, Bayona was eighteen, but his cinema knowledge was still impressive, fostered as it was since early childhood, where he received a film education by watching classic movies on the one television station that was available. "When I was a child," Bayona explained, "we used to watch movies from Alfred Hitchcock, François Truffaut, Federico Fellini, [Pier Paolo] Pasolini . . . The storytelling in my movies is as a result of watching all these movies. I saw Jack Clayton movies, Jack Arnold movies, Jacques Tourneur [movies], I saw Steven Spielberg [movies] and I saw Francis Ford Coppola [movies]. I think my generation was lucky to have that sort of education."

J. A. Bayona also took on formal study, learning directing at a film school, and after graduation, he started his career by directing commercials, short films, and music videos. One person who was championing his every move, even during this early stage, was Guillermo del Toro. The two had struck up a friendship after their film festival interview, and del Toro became Bayona's mentor. All the while, Bayona continued to travel to film festivals to watch as many movies as he could.

▲▲ Belén Rueda as Laura

▲ Simón, just before he disappears

▲ Geraldine Chaplin as Aurora

written. Sánchez had been trying to get it financed for many years but kept being told by Spanish studios that the script would need to change. "They all kept complaining about the same things," Sánchez later explained. "They said, 'You know, this is a mixture of drama and horror, and those two elements cannot mix. They're like oil and water, you can't do that.' 'You don't have a main villain.' 'You have two different endings . . .' Basically, all the things that made the script unique they didn't like. They wanted to go for a formula."

This uniqueness in Sánchez's script was exactly what drew J. A. Bayona to it. He did a deal with Sánchez that if he managed to get it financed, Sánchez would give the script to Bayona to make as his feature film directorial debut. Bayona then turned to his friend Guillermo del Toro for help. Del Toro was excited by the script, which was similar to his own film *The Devil's Backbone* (2001), and classic horror movies like director Jack Clayton's *The Innocents* (1961). The Henry James novel *The Turn of the Screw*—which had formed the basis of *The Innocents*—had been a big influence on Sergio G. Sánchez while he was writing the script.

At one festival, he saw a short film titled *7337*, directed by Sergio G. Sánchez. Bayona, impressed, contacted Sánchez to ask him if he had any other projects he was working on, and Sánchez told him about a horror script he had

Guillermo del Toro came on as the producer of *The Orphanage*, also lending his name as the "presenter" of the film, which enabled J. A. Bayona to raise double the amount of

budget he had originally wanted. Bayona and Sánchez then set the story in 1970s Spain, allowing Bayona to evoke the visual look and mood of the Spanish films of that era he admired—especially *Cría Cuervos* (1976), directed by Carlos Saura. That film had starred Geraldine Chaplin, who was the daughter of Charlie Chaplin and Oona O'Neill, and the granddaughter of playwright Eugene O'Neill. She had memorably appeared in the epic *Doctor*

▲ Tomás (Óscar Casas) appears. . . .

Spanish director Carlos Saura, moved to Spain, stayed with him for seventeen years, and starred in several of his movies. In a nice nod to *Cría Cuervos* (in which Chaplin played a ghost), J. A. Bayona cast her in *The Orphanage* in a small role as a medium named Aurora.

Aurora is hired by Laura (Belén Reuda), who is living in the orphanage where she grew up. Laura and her husband, Carlos (Fernando Cayo), have bought the old building, planning to open it up to house disabled orphans. They are also hopeful that their adopted son, Simón (Roger Príncep), will find some real friends to play with, instead of his group of imaginary ones. Simón is HIV positive and needs medication to survive, but on the day that Laura and Carlos hold a welcome party for the new kids, Simón disappears. Laura is desperate to find him, and worries he has

Zhivago (1965), directed by David Lean, but in the late 1960s she had fallen in love with

▲ Director Juan Antonio Bayona on the set of *The Orphanage*

followed his new imaginary friend, Tomás, into a cave on the beach.

Bayona's direction is full of unexpected shocks—including the gruesome discovery of the house's dark past and the sudden death of

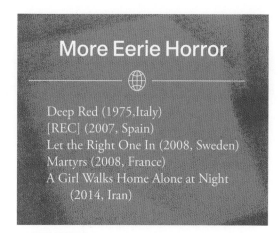

an important character. As Laura frantically searches for her son, she starts to hear noises and have visions. Whether what she is seeing is happening or not is left purposely ambiguous; Bayona and Sánchez want the audience to bring their own interpretation to the story. They also weaved in real emotion, including the fears and anxieties of being a parent to a missing child, and Laura's own mysterious past as an orphan. As the film progresses, Laura is left to face the demons (real or imagined) alone, with Bayona saying that he "stripped the movie of all the classic Gothic elements until finally the movie is bare: there's just one character in the house, there's no dialogue." He also added an extra ending, explaining, "The audience doesn't know where to go, because after the mystery is solved, they think the movie is ending, but the whole point of the movie comes after that."

All of this was a real challenge during the rewriting stage, with Bayona and Sánchez trying to balance the supernatural horror with the emotional drama. "It was crazy to try to set a perfect puzzle with pieces that fit perfectly with two different readings at the same time. For example, in the séance sequence [with Aurora] we couldn't use cheap tricks or digital effects, because at the end you couldn't have justified one of the readings. What we had to do was work with the sound design and the idea of point of view so that it makes the results more interesting."

Their hard work paid off. *The Orphanage* premiered at the Cannes Film Festival in 2007, where it received a rapturous response and a ten-minute standing ovation. The applause for the horror film continued as it made its way around the world, winning seven Goya awards in Spain and rave reviews in the United States. It also attracted the attention of Hollywood: New Line Cinema put an American version into production, produced by Guillermo del Toro—though that project has not come to fruition at the time of writing. Meanwhile, J. A. Bayona has forged his own successful career in Hollywood. Following *The Orphanage*, he attracted more critical acclaim with *The Impossible* (2012), a drama about the deadly 2004 tsunami in Thailand, starring Naomi Watts, Ewan McGregor, and Tom Holland in his debut credited role. Then came the children's fantasy *A Monster Calls* (2016); the fifth *Jurassic Park* film, *Jurassic World: Fallen Kingdom* (2018), and the survival drama *Society of the Snow* (2023), which was nominated for two Academy Awards.

Even though *The Orphanage* is Juan Antonio Bayona's first feature film, there is no doubting his skill. But like his patron Guillermo del Toro (who is both producer and "presenter" of this movie), Mr. Bayona is interested in using the horror genre to explore emotions beyond mere fright. Though there are plenty of sudden jolts and eerie atmospherics, *The Orphanage* is ultimately concerned with grief, remorse, and maternal longing.

A. O. Scott, film critic

Death of a Cyclist

DIRECTED BY **Juan Antonio Bardem**

To watch when you . . . feel like a moody noir with a moralistic edge.

Spain, 1955
B&W, 87 minutes, Film Noir

Screenplay: Juan Antonio Bardem, Luis
Fernando de Igoa

Starring: Lucia Bosé (María José de
Castro), Alberto Closas (Juan Fernández
Solar), Otello Toso (Miguel Castro), Carlos
Casaravilla (Rafa Sandoval)

"The war is very convenient. You can blame everything on it.
All the death and destruction, all the guys like me left hollow
inside—who never believe in anything ever again. Not even the
sweetheart who doesn't wait and marries a rich man. Now
I'm talking nonsense. I sound like a dime store novel."

—Juan

At the beginning of *Death of a Cyclist* (1955), a lone bicyclist makes his way up a deserted road. Suddenly, a car appears over the hill, swerving and coming to a stop. Inside the car is María José (Lucia Bosé) and Juan (Alberto Closas), with María José at the wheel. We don't see their car hit the cyclist, but when Juan gets out, the bike is on the road, and the cyclist is down. María José convinces Juan to leave him lying there on the road, and they drive off. It's a brutal opening to a film that does not shy away from exposing the ugly side of privilege, made by a director who wasn't afraid of speaking truth to Spain's dictatorial power.

The filmmaker, Juan Antonio Bardem, had been born into a family of performers with both of his parents working as actors. He had studied

agricultural engineering but couldn't seem to escape the arts; he was assigned to the cinema section of Spain's agriculture ministry after graduation. This was during the time when, following the Spanish Civil War, the local film industry had been placed in the hands of Francisco Franco's government. The Franco regime lasted from the start of the civil war, in 1936, until Franco's death in 1975, and during that time, Spain was under his strict and oppressive rule. The arts had suffered, with Spanish films from the 1940s reflecting the political repression of the era. But in the 1950s, a new generation of filmmakers entered the industry with brave energy, ready to make films that challenged the government. They were willing to face any consequences from their actions, and after

his stint in the agriculture ministry, Juan Antonio Bardem became one of these filmmakers. He studied film at the Spanish Institute of Cinema Research, though his political views prevented him from receiving a diploma.

One of his classmates at film school was Luis García Berlanga, who shared Bardem's left-wing views and his desire to confront Franco's regime through cinema. After a few years of working as a film critic and directing documentaries, Bardem teamed up with Berlanga to codirect their first feature together, *That Happy Couple* (1953). Bardem and Berlanga

had been inspired by Italian Neorealism, for the way the cinematic movement focused on the struggles of everyday, working-class Italians. In *That Happy Couple*, Bardem and Berlanga used humor to criticize Spanish society, sneaking their film past government censors by disguising their opinions with satire. It worked, and the two cowrote their next feature, *Welcome, Mr Marshall!* (1953), with Berlanga directing. This was another sharp look at Spain, with a story about a poor village

▲ Alberto Closas as Juan and Lucia Bosé as María

▲ The site of the bicycle crash

trying to make a good impression on visiting Americans so they can receive aid from the postwar Marshall Plan. *Welcome, Mr Marshall!* was a hit, though Hollywood actor Edward G. Robinson (who was on the jury at the Cannes Film Festival) spoke out against the film, calling it anti-American.

Also in 1953, Juan Antonio Bardem took further action against the fascist Franco government by publishing a film criticism magazine, with the aim of informing readers about movies that had been banned from screening in Spain. The magazine, called *Objetivo*, was stopped by the government after just nine issues, but before that, Bardem used the platform to speak his mind. *Objetivo* organized a conference in 1955, where Bardem delivered a scathing speech called *Report on the Current State of Our Cinema*. He laid bare his frank views on the Spanish film industry, saying, "After 60 years, Spanish cinema is politically futile, socially false, intellectually worthless, aesthetically valueless, and industrially paralytic. Spanish cinema has turned its back on reality and is

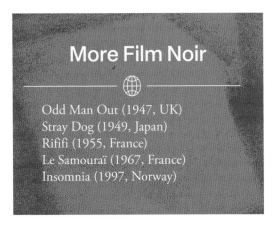

More Film Noir

🌐

Odd Man Out (1947, UK)
Stray Dog (1949, Japan)
Rififi (1955, France)
Le Samouraï (1967, France)
Insomnia (1997, Norway)

▲▲ "We have to find out what we did." —María

▲ Juan and Maria rush over to see if the cyclist is hurt.

totally removed from Spanish realistic traditions as found in paintings and novels."

Death of a Cyclist was released in the United States under the flimsy title of *Age of Infidelity*, but it represents Juan Antonio Bardem's endeavor to make films that were critical of Franco's regime. This was his third solo movie as a director, and he cleverly disguised his views with a compelling crime thriller plot. Bardem adapted the script from a short story by Luis Fernando de Igoa and mixed the cinematic styles of Italian Neorealism and American film noir. The film examines the gap between rich and poor in Spain and how the privilege of wealth makes the rich feel like they are above the law—when really they should look at their own ethical choices.

Soon after the opening scene, it is revealed that María José and Juan are having an affair. The two were childhood sweethearts, but while Juan was away at war, María José married the wealthy Miguel (Otello Toso) to have a comfortable life—though she still loves Juan. Following the accident, Juan and María José deal with their actions in different ways. María José is primarily concerned about their affair being made public and becomes fearful when an art critic named Rafa (Carlos Casaravilla) threatens to blackmail her, with vague comments about "her secret." Juan, a university professor, is racked with guilt and visits the cyclist's home to see the fallout. The cyclist is much poorer than Juan or María José, and Juan wants to right their wrong by going to the police, but María does not feel the same way.

There was one concession that Juan Antonio Bardem had to make to appease the censors, and that was to change the ending. Even with that, the final film was deemed anti-Francoist by the government, and while filming his next movie, *Main Street* (1956), Juan Antonio Bardem was arrested on political grounds. He was still in jail when *Death of a Cyclist* screened at the 1955 Cannes Film Festival, where it won the critics' prize. Bardem was released after much public uproar, but he

would be put back seven more times during the reign of Francisco Franco, though this never stopped him from speaking out.

In 1958, Bardem set up a production company alongside other Spanish filmmakers like Luis García Berlanga and Carlos Saura. Through this company, called UNINCI, they brought the acclaimed Spanish filmmaker Luis Buñuel back from exile to direct a film, *Viridiana* (1961). Buñuel's movie was quickly banned and UNINCI was shut down, but they had made their point, and Bardem continued to release films that ruffled feathers. His artistry as a filmmaker also helped to create a new Spanish cinema, and when Franco died in 1975, Bardem and his colleagues were finally able to experience a creative freedom in their country.

Juan Antonio Bardem kept working until 1993 and passed away at the age of eighty in 2002. His work reflects his bravery in using art to fight against fascism, and his legacy in Spanish cinema also lives on with his nephew, the Oscar-winning actor Javier Bardem.

Death of a Cyclist borrows the language of classical Hollywood melodrama, specifically the Hitchcock thriller—its strategies of emotional identification, its glossy surface, and its glamorous close-ups that emphasize the star. Yet by exaggerating these conventions the film exposes their implicit endorsement of the destructive egotism of the bourgeoisie.

Marsha Kinder, film scholar

Elevator to the Gallows

DIRECTED BY **Louis Malle**

To watch when you . . . want to be surprised by a tense thriller, set to a cool Miles Davis jazz soundtrack.

France, 1958
B&W, 92 minutes, Film Noir

Screenplay: Louis Malle, Roger Nimier, based on a novel by Noël Calef

Starring: Jeanne Moreau (Florence Carala), Maurice Ronet (Julien Tavernier), Yori Bertin (Véronique), Georges Poujouly (Louis)

"I lost you in the night, Julien. I should have left you alone.
I shouldn't have kissed you or caressed your face."

—Florence

Louis Malle was only twenty-four when he directed *Elevator to the Gallows* (1958), and he couldn't possibly have known the influence it would end up having. He was a fan of Hollywood film noir and filmmakers like Robert Bresson (known for his sparse style) and Alfred Hitchcock (the master of suspense), and he mixed all of that together for *Elevator to the Gallows*—creating a sparse and suspenseful film noir.

This was his narrative feature debut as a director, though Malle had recently experienced success in the documentary genre, teaming up with the underwater explorer and filmmaker Jacques Cousteau for *The Silent World* (1956). That film won the major award at the Cannes Film Festival, as well as Best Documentary at the Academy Awards, turning Louis Malle into

a new director who would be taken seriously. He didn't have much luck getting his first narrative feature script financed, receiving a series of nos to a romantic script he had based on his own life. But then, according to Malle, his friend gave him a book he'd bought from a train station newsstand called *Elevator to the Gallows* written by Noël Calef. This friend told Malle that the book was interesting and could possibly make a good film noir. Malle read the book and agreed, then took it to screenwriter and author Roger Nimier. Nimier, however, thought the book was silly. "Yes," Malle replied, "but the plot is good." Eventually, they both agreed to throw out much of the book's substance and start again, adding more characters and tension to their adaptation.

▲ Jeanne Moreau as Florence

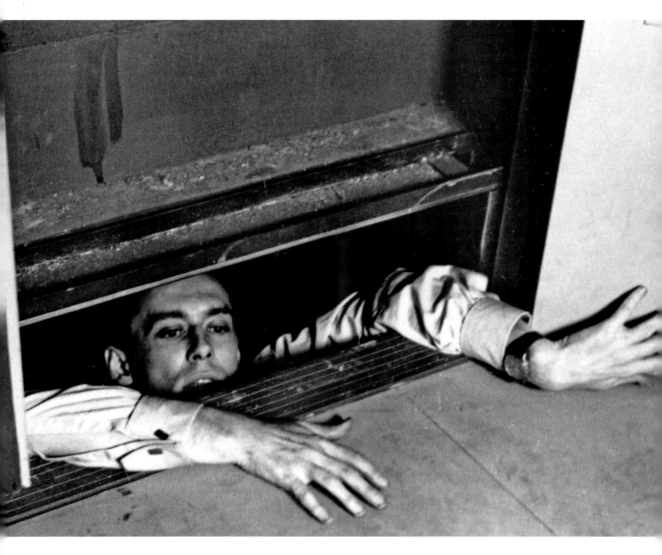

▲ Julien (Maurice Ronet) gets into a sticky situation.

The plot is simple, but its brilliance lies in the execution. As the film opens, we hear a conversation between two lovers, Florence Carala (Jeanne Moreau) and Julien Tavernier (Maurice Ronet). They appear to be in the same room, but as the scene continues, we see they're in different locations and talking to each other on the phone. Florence is in a phone booth, and she promises Julien that she'll meet him at a cafe at 7 p.m. And Julien is in an office, where he hangs up the phone and

quietly goes about his business. He tells the office assistant not to disturb him. He enters his office and shuts the door. Then he goes out the window. Julien moves with the ease of a professional criminal as he climbs one floor up and enters the office of his boss, and Florence's husband, Simon Carala (Jean Wall). The planned crime goes off without a hitch, and Julien calmly leaves the office building, his colleagues none the wiser. Just as he's about to drive away, he notices he's left a rope hanging on the outside of the building—a big mistake that could give him away. He runs back inside

the office, gets into the elevator, and as it is making its way upstairs, the power is turned off and Julien is stuck inside.

It's a classic "crime gone wrong" thriller, but Malle and Nimier tie up all the loose ends so perfectly, it's hard to imagine how Julien will ever make it out. His car is stolen by two young lovers, and Florence, waiting at the café, sees Julien's car drive past with another woman in the passenger seat. Believing he has left her, she walks around the streets, panicking, searching for him, not knowing what to do. Much of Jeanne Moreau's performance is internal, with the camera focusing on her face as she flicks through a range of emotions—from

▲ Jeanne Moreau and Miles Davis during the recording of the score for *Elevator to the Gallows*.

sadness, to fear to despair. With this performance, Jeanne Moreau became a star. She was thirty years old and had been working in movies for almost a decade, but she'd mostly been cast in small roles in B pictures. Moreau's

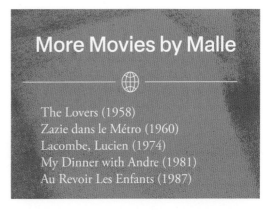

More Movies by Malle

The Lovers (1958)
Zazie dans le Métro (1960)
Lacombe, Lucien (1974)
My Dinner with Andre (1981)
Au Revoir Les Enfants (1987)

▲ Director Louis Malle

performance in *Elevator to the Gallows* gained her notice, and she worked with Louis Malle again for *The Lovers* (1958).

In 1960, Jeanne Moreau appeared in *The 400 Blows*, directed by François Truffaut. Both *The 400 Blows* and Jean-Luc Godard's *Breathless*, also released in 1960, became landmark films, part of the French New Wave, the cinematic movement that ushered in a newly experimental style of filmmaking. *Breathless* came two years after *Elevator to the Gallows* and shares a few similarities with it—both films were inspired by American crime movies, both tapped into the alienation felt by young French men of the time (who were affected by the Indochina and Algerian wars), and both were filmed on the real streets of Paris by cinematographer Henri Decaë.

The standout moments in *Elevator to the Gallows* happen when Jeanne Moreau is walking through the dark Parisian streets, lost in her thoughts about Julien. These scenes were filmed guerilla-style, with real Parisians unaware that they were being filmed. Henri Decaë used streetlights and the light from store windows to illuminate Moreau's face and placed his camera in a baby stroller to follow her walk. The laboratory processing these negatives was reportedly alarmed at how dark the film was and told the producer that Malle was going to "destroy" Jeanne Moreau. But this was truly innovative cinematography by Decaë, who would go on to shape much of the look of the French New Wave. And in this way, *Elevator to the Gallows* can be seen as a precursor to the cinematic movement, paving the way for what was to come.

The sparseness of the dialogue allows Decaë and Malle's visual style to shine and leaves room for a musical score. Louis Malle was a fan of jazz music, and when he'd heard that Miles Davis was visiting Paris to perform, he went to the airport to meet him. Malle made his case to Davis to compose the film score for *Elevator to the Gallows*, and although Davis hadn't scored a film before, he agreed. The composition was almost entirely improvised; Miles Davis watched the film as he played, working with his French quintet. Over one night in December 1957, Davis created a series of tracks of original jazz music, and the resulting score is beautiful and a little haunting—highlighting the desperation that Florence feels as she walks the lonely streets.

Meanwhile, the young couple who stole Julien's car end up at a modern motel, where they spend time with German tourists who own a flashy sports car. This speaks to the economic prosperity Germany was experiencing at the time, and in showing the streets of Paris, the motel, and the cars, Louis Malle also wanted to comment on what was being lost as France rapidly changed. "I showed a Paris," he said, "not of the future but at least a modern city, a world already dehumanized." This is a world that is weary from endless wars, and angry at the businessmen who prosper from them.

Louis Malle never made another film noir after *Elevator to the Gallows*; he simply wasn't interested in remaking the same movie. Instead, he went on to show his versatile talents with films like the romantic drama *The Lovers*, the quirky comedy *Zazie dans le Métro* (1960), and much later, the painfully personal *Au Revoir les Enfants* (1987).

Titled *Anscenseur Pour l'Échafaud* (literally *Elevator to the Scaffold*) it has both the brisk craftsmanship and efficiency of class French cinema and a breathless hint of the energy of the New Wave that was only a few years away.

Kenneth Turan, film critic

Pale Flower

DIRECTED BY **Masahiro Shinoda**

To watch when you . . . are feeling particularly hopeless about the state of the world.

Japan, 1964
B&W, 96 minutes, Film Noir

Starring: Ryō Ikebe (Muraki), Mariko Kaga (Saeko), Takashi Fujiki (Yoh)

Screenplay: Ataru Baba, Masahiro Shinoda, based on a story by Shintaro Ishihara

> "Ask anyone, I'm no good. Even I think so. I'm the scum of the earth. I have nothing in common with ordinary society. But still, I forgive myself."
>
> —Muraki

Ten years after the release of *Pale Flower* (1964), director Masahiro Shinoda talked about the film in an interview, saying "When I finished shooting it, I realized that my youth was over." Shinoda was thirty-three at the time, and in *Pale Flower*, he captured the certain feeling of nihilism that the youth of Japan were feeling at that time.

Masahiro Shinoda was one of the leading filmmakers of the Japanese New Wave. This was a loose cinematic movement, called "taiyo-zoku," or "Sun Tribe," that began around 1960. The term "Sun Tribe" refers to the characters within the author (and future governor of Tokyo) Shintaro Ishihara's books, particularly *Season of the Sun* and *Crazed Fruit*, which depicted a youth that were bored, rich, and violent. The late 1950s

and early 1960s was a period of rapid change in Japan, when students were protesting the continuing military presence of the United States, and the popularity of television had decimated local cinema attendance. Established movie studios were going bankrupt and adult audiences were choosing to see erotic "pink" films in independent theaters over mainstream offerings. It was clear that the Japanese film industry needed to adapt to survive and tap into the energy of the youth of the country.

Young filmmakers like Masahiro Shinoda, Nagisa Ōshima, Seijun Suzuki, and Shōhei Imamura were waiting in the wings to take over. Many of these directors had been working as assistants at Nikkatsu and Shochiku studios and were hungry for the opportunity to start making

▲ Muraki and Saeko in *Pale Flower*

▲ Ryō Ikebe as Muraki

their own films. Shinoda worked at Shochiku, where he had assisted their star directors, including Yasujirō Ozu on *Tokyo Twilight* (1957). While he undoubtedly learned a lot from that experience, in Shinoda's words, the main thing he took from it was: "If I become a director myself, under no circumstances would I use the kind of scripts Shochiku was then using." In much the same way as the French New Wave and the Italian Neorealism movement before it, these young directors brought with them a new style, experimenting with their cameras and editing techniques, and abandoning old storytelling conventions. Their taiyozoku films were explosive, modern, and often controversial, exploring the taboo subjects of race, sexuality, youth alienation, and crime. They were lucrative, too, with the old established studios turning a profit on this new use of violence and sex.

Shinoda's first film as a director was *One Way Ticket to Love* (1960), where his assignment had been to build a film around Neil Sedaka's hit song "One Way Ticket." He wrote the script quickly, coming up with a story about three nightclub performers, and while its box-office failure didn't help Shinoda's fledgling directing career, it did allow him to start experimenting with a striking visual style, one that he'd hone over his next few movies.

Pale Flower was Shinoda's ninth film, and for it, he and writer Ataru Baba adapted a novel by Sun Tribe author Shintaro Ishihara. Shinoda was also inspired by American film noir, and particularly a heist noir directed by Robert Wise called *Odds Against Tomorrow* (1959). As Shinoda explained in an interview, "The daily life of an assassin interests me more than the assassin. The routine of coming home and daydreaming or sitting still and thinking about what you'll do next is what I wanted to capture in *Pale Flower*. The American movie, *Odds Against Tomorrow*, by Robert Wise has a scene with gangsters gathered before their big heist. They have time to kill until that appointed hour, and they're doing nothing but hanging out at a place by the riverside. I was very moved by that scene. I think

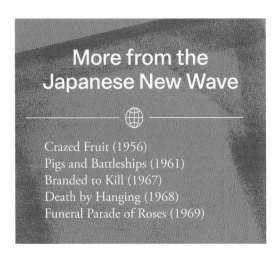

More from the Japanese New Wave

🌐

Crazed Fruit (1956)
Pigs and Battleships (1961)
Branded to Kill (1967)
Death by Hanging (1968)
Funeral Parade of Roses (1969)

maybe that feeling was one of the big motivations for doing *Pale Flower*."

In *Pale Flower*, the assassin kills time in between his killings by gambling. Muraki (Ryō Ikebe) has just been released after a stint in jail for a gang-related killing. His murder seems pointless once Muraki returns to his gang and hears that his boss has formed a partnership with the gang Muraki was sent to avenge. He retreats to gambling dens, which give Muraki a sense of order and ceremony—as well as being a way to rebel against that order, gambling his money in risky bets. "My subject," Shinoda explained, "is a man in traditional yakuza society who finds himself hopelessly out of place in the modern social structure and learns something about himself through this discovery."

Muraki doesn't see much point to life, and the people in modern Tokyo are meaningless to him. "People, such strange animals," Muraki says in a voice-over. "What are they living for? Their faces are lifeless, dead. They're desperately pretending to be alive. Why make such a big deal about slaughtering one of these dumb beasts?" He meets his nihilistic match in Saeko (Mariko Kaga), a young woman who stands out in the male-dominated gambling dens. She is also reckless with her bets, but unlike Muraki, she is searching for ways to feel alive, getting her thrills by drag-racing her car in the middle of the night, or considering what it would be like to shoot up hard drugs, and asking Muraki to set her up in a high-stakes game.

Ryō Ikebe was forty-five when he starred as Muraki in *Pale Flower*, and he brought the same world-weary toughness to this role as he had to the parts that made him a star. Throughout the 1940s and '50s, his was a familiar face in Japanese cinema, playing a series of tough guys and cops and featuring in films like *Early Spring* by Yasujirō Ozu. At the time when he was cast in *Pale Flower*, Ikebe was at a low point in his career and had recently been fired from a play for freezing onstage. When Mashiro Shinoda approached him with this offer, Ryō Ikebe reportedly said

to him, "Why do you want me? I'm just a ham actor." In contrast, Mariko Kaga was nineteen and had only joined Shochiku studios the year before she was cast to play Saeko. Her beautifully bored face and anarchic giggle turned this role into her most famous.

When screenwriter Ataru Baba saw Shinoda's version of his script, he was reportedly so incensed that he tried to delay the film's release. *Pale Flower* was put on hold for almost a year, partly due to Baba's reaction but also because Japanese censors had objected to the film, with its focus on gambling. When *Pale Flower* was finally released in 1964, it captured the imaginations of audiences not only in Japan but also around the world, who were enthralled by its restless energy, its driving heartbeat, and the constant feeling that at any moment, violence could explode on-screen. Masahiro Shinoda increased the tension by adding heavy breathing into the soundtrack, and amping up the sound of the hard Hanafuda gambling cards as they are flicked between the hands of sweating gamblers. He mixed the visual style of American film noir with the traditions of a Japanese yakuza film to create a truly stylish thriller, filled with stark black-and-white cinematography (filmed by Masao Kosugi), an erratic jazz score (by Tōru Takemitsu), and gangsters who wear sharp suits as they commit dark deeds.

Pale Flower is one of the most haunting noirs I've seen, and something more; in 1964 it was an important work in an emerging Japanese New Wave of independent filmmakers, an exercise in existential cool. It involves a plot, but it is all about attitude.

Roger Ebert, film critic

Babette's Feast

DIRECTED BY **Gabriel Axel**

To watch when you . . . want to be reminded of the joy of eating and gathering.

Denmark, 1987
Color, 104 minutes, Drama

Screenplay: Gabriel Axel, based on a short story by Karen Blixen (Isak Dinesen)

Starring: Stéphane Audran (Babette), Bodil Kjer (Filippa), Birgitte Federspiel (Martine)

"An artist is never poor."

—Babette

When director Gabriel Axel was asked about the religious backdrop of *Babette's Feast* (1987), he answered in a way that perfectly spoke to the paradoxical nature of his film. "All I can say," Axel explained, "is that in *Babette's Feast* there's a minister, but it's not a film about religion. There's a general, but it's not a film about the army. There's a cook, but it's not a film about cooking. It's a fairy tale, and if you try to overexplain it, you destroy it." That is true, because like all good fables, *Babette's Feast* means different things to different people. For some, it's a paean to the work of an artist. For others, a religious tale about faith and how not all pleasures need to be sinful. And for others, it's simply a good movie about good food.

Babette's Feast was also the first Danish film to win an Academy Award, taking home the Oscar for Best Foreign Language Film for the year of 1987. Director Gabriel Axel was delighted when he took to the stage, with this award being the culmination of many years of hard work. Axel had wanted to adapt the short story by Danish author Karen Blixen for a long time, writing the adapted script himself. Blixen's original piece was reportedly written after she made a bet with a friend that she could write an entire story about food and get it published in the *Saturday Evening Post*. Her idea was about two devout sisters living in a remote village, whose lives change when a French housekeeper is sent to them and they get to experience a multi-course, authentic French dinner. The *Saturday Evening Post* wasn't interested, but the *Ladies Home Journal* was, and Blixen's story was published in 1950 under her pen name of Isak Dinesen.

Gabriel Axel was a fan of Blixen's work, but he had struggled to get financiers interested in funding his film adaptation of *Babette's Feast*. At this time, Blixen was not as popular as she'd once been—even in her home country—and a movie based on her writing

▲ The younger versions of Martine and Filippa and their father

didn't seem like it would have commercial appeal. That all changed in 1985, with the international success of *Out of Africa*, directed by Sydney Pollack and based on Karen Blixen's memoir—with Meryl Streep playing Karen Blixen. Suddenly, Blixen came back into fashion, and Axel was able to make his movie.

Axel was already an established director, having started to direct in 1955, and he was also an actor and a writer—acting and directing the well-received *The Goldencabbage Family* in 1975. But it was *Babette's Feast* that would become his masterpiece, and the film he was best known for when he passed away in 2014.

Axel's mastery of the camera and light are evident in *Babette's Feast*, from how the rough Scandinavian coastal setting looks almost

▲ Birgitte Federspiel as Martine, Stéphane Audran as Babette, and Bodil Kjer as Filippa

Feast on More Food Films

—— ⊕ ——

Tampopo (1985, Japan)
Like Water for Chocolate
    (1992, Mexico)
Eat Drink Man Woman
    (1994, Taiwan/USA)
Chocolat (2000, UK)
The Trip (2010, UK)

bucolic through his lens, to the way the camera lingers on the sensuous preparation of the titular feast. It's enough to make your mouth water, even if you can't stomach the idea of having turtle soup or eating quail.

The story is set in the 1800s, where two sisters are raised in a small village by their devout father, who serves as the local Lutheran priest. The sisters are Martine and Filippa—named after the German Martin Luther and his friend, Philipp Melanchthon. As the sisters grow up, their natural beauty is undeniable, and they each catch the eye of a potential suitor. A Swedish soldier falls for Martine and starts to attend their religious

▶ "I'd like to prepare the celebration dinner for the pastor's birthday by myself . . ." —Babette

▲ The feast begins. . . .

gatherings in earnest. Meanwhile, an opera
singer sees potential in Filippa, offering to give
her singing lessons and promising to make her
a star. Both men are soon turned away, with
the sisters choosing faith and service over love.
Many years later, their father has passed away,

and Martine and Filippa are still living in
their village, cooking food for their neighbors,
when Babette arrives. She is a French refugee
who has escaped the Franco-Prussian war and
wants to cook for the two sisters. Her help
changes the lives of Martine and Filippa in
numerous ways, and when Babette approaches
them with an offer—to create a special meal

for an upcoming celebration—Martine and Filippa reluctantly agree. They worry that an extravagant dinner will be sinful and warn their pious guests to restrict their enjoyment over the food. "It will be as if we never had the sense of taste," one of the disciples agrees.

For this climactic dinner scene, Gabriel Axel wanted to ensure that the lavish French dinner looked, and felt, real. "We ordered everything from Paris," Axel explained. "So, all the porcelain and silver were completely authentic. The food included real caviar, real cailles en sarcophage (stuffed quails), with truffles and authentic sauces. We did absolutely everything to ensure that the feast was truly 'grandiose.'" Axel was also determined to cast an authentic French actress in the role of the French Babette, choosing Stéphane Audran for this crucial role. "She opens a door differently from a Danish woman," he said. "She even moves differently. Now this is very important. It wouldn't have been the same with a Danish actress." Audran was already famous in France, having starred in many films made by her ex-husband, the director Claude Chabrol, and appearing in Luis Buñuel's *The Discreet Charm of the Bourgeoisie* (1972). Audran spoke no Danish, but Gabriel Axel had lived in France and was able to direct her in fluent French. Audran also brought with her an important contact—the famed French fashion designer Karl Lagerfeld. He had designed many of Audran's costumes for her films, and agreed to design the cape that Babette wears.

Babette's Feast was selected to play at the Cannes Film Festival in 1987 and had a limited release in the United States to qualify for the Academy Awards. Following its

▲ Director Gabriel Axel on set

Best Foreign Film Oscar win in 1988, the movie was given a wider release in America and slowly gained notice, with *Babette's Feast* picking up more fans who watched it at home. Over the years, *Babette's Feast* has truly become a favorite from Danish cinema and a favorite film about food.

A great meal is, Blixen argues, not a mere fleshy indulgence; like a love affair, it offers a mystical fusion of bodily and spiritual delight.

Sheila Johnston, film critic

WINTER

(YEAR END)

Fanny and Alexander

DIRECTED BY Ingmar Bergman

To watch when you . . . are not looking for an overly happy Christmas movie.

Sweden, 1982
Color, 188 minutes, Drama

Screenplay: Ingmar Bergman

Starring: Bertil Guve (Alexander Ekdahl), Pernilla Allwin (Fanny Ekdahl), Ewa Fröling (Emilie Ekdahl), Jan Malmsjö (Bishop Edvard Vergérus)

> "Let us be happy while we are happy. Let us be kind, generous, affectionate, and good. It is necessary and not at all shameful to take pleasure in the little world."
>
> —Gustav Adolf Ekdahl

In the 1980s, the legendary Swedish director Ingmar Bergman decided to make his final feature film. The physical toll of directing movies had become too much, and his final film, he said, would be "the sum total of my life as a filmmaker." That was *Fanny and Alexander* (1982), a film that would also end up being something of the sum of Bergman's entire life—or at least, his childhood—using his abusive upbringing for inspiration. He had coped with his trauma as a child by escaping into fantasy, and the paradox of such torture was that it gave Bergman the ability to hone an imagination that would see him become an important figure in world cinema, one who would consistently explore the human condition with both darkness and light.

Ingmar Bergman's father was a Lutheran minister who became the chaplin to the Swedish king, but he was far from a benevolent soul. Erik Bergman was a severe disciplinarian who tormented his son, abusing him both physically and psychologically. Young Ingmar had a deep love for his mother, but she was caught in a broken marriage and felt unable to help, so Ingmar retreated into himself. Later, he talked about how this childhood trauma followed him throughout his life and seeped into his films, saying, "The demons are unnumerable, appear at the most inconvenient of times and create panic and terror. But I have learnt that if I can master the negative forces and harness them to my chariot, then they can work to my advantage."

Bergman started writing and directing films in Sweden in the 1940s but wouldn't become widely known outside his home country until a decade later, when his comedy *Smiles of a Summer Night* (1955) won a special prize at the Cannes Film Festival for "Best

Poetic Humor." Bergman abruptly switched to dark drama for his next movie, the now legendary *The Seventh Seal* (1957), where a knight plays chess against the Grim Reaper during the Black Plague. He continued to adroitly change from comedy to drama throughout his career, directing around fifty films over four decades, as well as many stage productions and made-for-TV movies. He would return to themes of religion, death, dreams, memories, the redemptive power of love, and family in all its dysfunctions, time and time again—including in his milestone films, such as *Wild Strawberries* (1957), *The Virgin Spring* (1960),

▲ The titular Fanny and Alexander

▲ Bertil Guve as Alexander

Winter Light (1963), *Persona* (1966), *Hour of the Wolf* (1968), and *Scenes from a Marriage* (1973). Bergman's willingness to embrace existentialism, plus his expertise with writing scripts and directing actors (many of whom became part of his troupe) turned him into a master filmmaker.

He was also often thought of as only being a dark director, but even his dramas contained humor. That's true of *Fanny and Alexander*, but Bergman had another purpose: "I want at last to show the joy that I carry within me in spite of everything, joy that I have so seldom and so poorly given life to in my work. Being able to portray energy and drive, capability for living, kindness. That wouldn't be so bad, for once." The film certainly begins with joy, as the Ekdahl family gather for a rowdy Christmas feast. They live in Sweden at the beginning of the twentieth century, and they are dysfunctional, but full of love and laughter. At the center of it all are Oscar (Allan Edwall) and Emilie (Ewa Fröling), who are parents to two kids, Fanny (Pernilla Allwin) and Alexander (Bertil Guve), and owners of a theater, where they act in the troupe.

Not long into the story, the Ekdahl family suffers a tragedy when Oscar dies, and Emilie remarries a local bishop, Bishop Vergérus (Jan Malmsjö). Suddenly, Fanny and Alexander are taken from a loving, warm home to the bishop's austere residence, where he lives with his stern mother, sister, and aunt, and presides over the house with an authoritarian presence. The bishop takes a particular dislike to Alexander, who tries to fight his rules and becomes the subject of harsh punishment. As a survival mechanism, Alexander invents stories and has fantasies about his stepfather dying. He also starts to see ghosts and has conversations with his late father.

Fanny and Alexander is all about imagination, fantasies, dreams, nightmares, and the resilience of children. By filming the story through the child's eyes of Alexander, Ingmar Bergman felt free to let his creativity run wild. It was an ambitious project, with a large budget and over 250 filming days. Bergman had publicly announced that this would be his last feature, so there was a lot of press interest. Unusually for Bergman, he allowed media onto the set. He even tasked one of his crew members

▲ Jan Malmsjö as Bishop Vergérus and Ewa Fröling as Emilie

to film the behind-the-scenes of the production, which he directed and edited into a documentary feature, called *The Making of "Fanny and Alexander"* (1984).

Bergman had initially made *Fanny and Alexander* as a feature film, and it premiered at Christmastime in 1982 as a three-hour movie. But following that, it was screened as a four-episode TV miniseries, which added two extra hours of footage. With all the anticipation of Bergman's final theatrical film, critics

▲ "You have a weakness in your character."
—Bishop Vergerus

were chomping at the bit to review it. *Fanny and Alexander* seemed to divide them, with reviewers separating into those who loved it and those who hated it. Vincent Canby in the *New York Times* said it was "another triumph in the career of one of our greatest living filmmakers," while John Simon in *National Review* wrote that "few things are sadder than the attempt of a great artist, hither-to fully appreciated only by a minority, to reach the masses." In any case, the masses responded well, with *Fanny and Alexander* being one of the most accessible films of all of Ingmar Bergman's work, reaching a wide audience who

made it a festive favorite. *Fanny and Alexander* also won four Oscars, including Best Foreign Film. It was Ingmar Bergman's final theatrical film, but he kept on working—directing TV movies and writing scripts, novels, and plays at his home on the quiet Swedish island of Fårö—right up until his death in 2007.

▲ Director Ingmar Bergman works on the set of *Fanny and Alexander*.

Fanny and Alexander is a brilliant—in fact maybe unique—fusion of Shakespeare and Dickens, with some Chekov in an uncle's morose musings on his own failure and mediocracy and also some Strindberg—"that nasty misogynist" as the grandmother sharply calls him when asked by her daughter to produce his *A Dream Play* at the family theater.

Peter Bradshaw, film critic

Even More to Explore by Bergman

🌐

Summer with Monika (1953)
Wild Strawberries (1957)
All These Women (1964)
Cries and Whispers (1972)
Autumn Sonata (1978)

Paris Pick-Up

DIRECTED BY **Marcel Bluwal**

To watch when you . . . want to give yourself the Christmas gift of discovering a new favorite film noir.

France, 1962
B&W, 90 minutes, Film Noir

Screenplay: Marcel Bluwal, based on a novel by Frédéric Dard

Starring: Robert Hossein (Robert Herbin), Lea Massari (Marthe Dravet), Robert Dalban (The Inspector), Maurice Biraud (Adolphe Ferry)

"Christmas comes once a year; I don't want to spoil it."

—Robert

One of the most exciting parts about being a cinephile is how there is never an end to your education. There's always more to learn, and always more films to discover. This is especially true with international cinema, and there's nothing quite like finding a previously unseen movie that becomes a new favorite. *Paris Pick-Up* (1962) is one of those—a compelling French film noir that would likely have been wider known if not for the timing of its release.

Paris Pick-Up was directed by Marcel Bluwal, a French filmmaker who primarily worked in television, making TV movies across various genres. He also directed two feature films of note: *Paris Pick-Up* and the comedy *Carambolages* (1963), starring Jean-Claude Brialy. For *Paris Pick-Up*, Bluwal cowrote the script alongside author Frédéric Dard, adapting the story from Dard's novel *Bird in a Cage*. Frédéric Dard was a prolific crime writer whose work was popular in France, but the majority of his works were translated to English only in 2016. He wrote hundreds of novels starring a detective named San Antonio, and though his books were beloved by fans, he struggled to gain any appreciation from critics. One of his supporters, and personal friends, was the actor Robert Hossein, who stars in *Paris Pick-Up*.

Hossein plays Robert Herbin, an ex-criminal back in his hometown for Christmas. He is spending Christmas Eve alone, buying a tree ornament of a bird from a store, before going to eat dinner by himself. At the restaurant, he meets a beautiful woman named Marthe Dravert (Lea Massari), who is eating with her young daughter. Marthe is Italian and reveals to Robert that her French husband is having an affair. She invites Robert back to her place for a drink—an apartment housed inside the industrial printing factory that her husband owns. While she puts her daughter to bed, Robert

takes out his bird ornament and adds it to her tree. Later, they leave the apartment for a walk, and when they return, Robert and Marthe are shocked to find her husband dead on the couch from an apparent suicide. Curiously, the bird ornament is gone, and Robert rushes out, scared to have another encounter with the police.

The script is tightly constructed and cleverly written, featuring a twist that is genuinely surprising. There are only a few characters, and the whole story takes place over just one night. This time frame increases the tension, as Robert desperately runs through the shadowy darkness of the town, trying to uncover what Marthe's secret is before morning comes. And the setting of Christmas also adds an element of loneliness.

Both Robert and Marthe seem separate from the groups of merry revelers that surround them, two people who need each other. The classic film noir cinematography—shot on highly contrasting black-and-white film—is by a veteran cinematographer of film and TV, André Bac, and the tautness of the mystery is further heightened by the music score composed by Georges Delerue, who would go on to create scores for Hollywood films such as *A Little Romance* (1979) and *Platoon* (1986).

The complex crime and compelling story are anchored by the excellent performances of the two lead actors. Lea Massari is an Italian actress and singer who is best known for her roles in Michelangelo Antonioni's *L'Avventura* (1960) and Louis Malle's *Murmur of the Heart* (1971). Meanwhile Robert Hossein was an actor, a writer, and a director, whose face will be familiar to those who enjoy Jules Dassin's *Rififi* (1955). He who never quite broke through to audiences outside of France, despite his extensive body of film work and his stellar reputation in the theater. It was in the theater where Hossein started a

◄ *Paris Pick-Up*
▼ Lea Massari as Marthe

More One-Night Movies

🌐

That Night's Wife (1930, Japan)
All Night Long (1962, UK)
Attack the Block (2011, UK)
Victoria (2015, Germany)
Down Under (2016, Australia)

friendship with the novelist Frédéric Dard. In 1958, Hossein adapted a book by Dard, *Toi . . . le venin*, which Hossein wrote, directed, and starred in. Hossein lived to ninety-three, passing away a week after his birthday in 2020, after contracting COVID-19.

His performances live on in films such as *Paris Pick-Up*, which was released in France in 1962 under the title *Le Monte Charge*. This was at the height of the French New Wave, and this fascinating film noir would likely have been a hit if not for all the focus and excitement that surrounded the cinematic movement. Films that were released around this time got lost among the influx of experimental pictures by the likes of François Truffaut, Jean-Luc Godard, and Claude Chabrol, but movies like *Paris Pick-Up* and Robert Hossein's *Toi...le venin* have since been rediscovered by movie buffs and reconsidered by critics.

A stylistic tour de force brushed aside by the rush to laud the Nouvelle Vague. Put it on your aspirational list.

Paul Schrader, filmmaker

Black Christmas

DIRECTED BY **Bob Clark**

To watch when you . . . want a Christmas movie that's
served with a twist of slasher.

Canada, 1974
Color, 98 minutes, Horror

Screenplay: Roy Moore

Starring: Olivia Hussey (Jess), Keir Dullea
(Peter), Margot Kidder (Barb), Andrea
Martin (Phyl)

"Filthy Billy!"

—The Moaner

If you watch *Black Christmas* (1974) today, the Canadian festive slasher film seems as if it's replaying tired horror tropes. A group of scared sorority girls are being picked off in a series of violent deaths. The "final girl" receives harassing phone calls from the killer that are coming from . . . inside the house. Her boyfriend is devoted to her, but is he a little too intense? Another girl's boyfriend wears a hockey mask. We've seen these ideas used in several horror films, from *Halloween* (1978) to *Scream* (1996), but it pretty much all started with *Black Christmas*. This certainly wasn't the first slasher film, with director Bob Clark drawing on inspiration from classic horrors such as Alfred Hitchcock's *Psycho* (1960) and Michael Powell's *Peeping Tom* (1960); but unlike the films it would end up influencing, *Black Christmas* stands out because it doesn't stick to any rules. It's surprising, weird, and over-the-top, and the Christmas setting adds an extra creepy twist.

John Carpenter's landmark horror *Halloween* would be released four years later, and its immense popularity ensured the slasher film subgenre would endure. He and Bob Clark were friends and, prior to *Halloween*, had worked together on a film that didn't end up happening. In a later interview, Clark recalled that Carpenter had enjoyed *Black Christmas* and had asked him if he was planning a sequel. Clark told him an idea for one, involving the killer escaping from a mental institution and returning to terrorize the same sorority house. He'd even thought of another seasonal name: *Halloween*. But, Clark clarified, "John didn't copy *Black Christmas*; he wrote a script, directed the script, did the casting. *Halloween* is his movie. He liked *Black Christmas* and may have been influenced by it, but in no way did John Carpenter copy the idea."

Both movies begin the same way, with a camera showing the perspective of the killer walking up to a house. In *Black Christmas*, it's a

▲ Olivia Hussey as Jess receives a distressing phone call from "The Moaner."

▶ "Little baby bunting, Daddy's gone a-hunting . . ."
—Billy

Canadian sorority house, where a festive party is happening inside, and the unseen killer climbs up into the attic. When *Black Christmas* was filmed, the Steadicam rig—which allows a camera operator to wear the camera on their body—was two years away from hitting the market, so this camera operator had to get crafty to achieve the POV shot. He designed a special setup that allowed him to attach the camera to his head and use his own limbs for those of the killer's. It's a chilling start to the film, and inside the Pi Kappa Sig sorority house we meet Jess Bradford (Olivia Hussey), and her housemates, Barb (Margot Kidder) and Phyl (Andrea Martin). Everyone is excited about leaving college for the holidays, but soon, Jess is fielding a series of obscene phone calls made to the house, one

of their housemates has gone missing, and Jess also has to deal with her increasingly intense boyfriend, Peter (Keir Dullea).

The script for *Black Christmas* started in the early 1970s with writers Roy Moore and Timothy Bond, who had been inspired by the story of "the babysitter and the man upstairs." This was an urban legend made popular during

the 1960s, about a teenage babysitter who receives phone calls from a stalker telling her to "check on the children," and the police trace the calls to the same house. Moore and Bond's script was originally titled *The Babysitter*, but that changed when producers Harvey Sherman and Richard Schouten became involved. The urban legend would eventually be made into the 1979 horror *When a Stranger Calls*, but for *Black Christmas* the setting was switched to a university.

Bob Clark was brought in to direct. He was an American expatriate who would go on to make another festive favorite, albeit very different in tone—*A Christmas Story* (1983). Clark reportedly had big plans for the cast of *Black Christmas*, including hiring Bette Davis to

▲ John Saxon as Lt. Ken Fuller

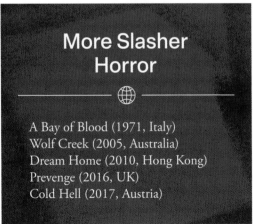

More Slasher Horror

A Bay of Blood (1971, Italy)
Wolf Creek (2005, Australia)
Dream Home (2010, Hong Kong)
Prevenge (2016, UK)
Cold Hell (2017, Austria)

play the sorority den mother. Her salary was out of their budget range, so Mrs. Mac was eventually played by Marian Waldman. Gilda Radner was also attached to play Phyl, but dropped out when she got a job on *Saturday Night Live* and

◄ Keir Dullea as Peter

helped to shape the modern slasher movie. But *Black Christmas* stands apart from other slashers in a few important ways—one being the involvement of Christmas, taking a holiday that is supposed to be cozy and comforting and making it terrifying. The normally busy sorority house is empty. And while everyone else is at home, safe with their families, for the few left behind it's not Santa who is creeping around the house. Another unique take for *Black Christmas* is its depiction of the young women. Bob Clark said he wanted to portray the college girls the way he knew college students to be—smart and interested in the world. Margot Kidder's Barb is brash and foul-mouthed, even toward the police and the father of her missing friend. And Jess refuses to fit into the life society tells her to have. When she discovers she is pregnant by Peter, he wants to get married

was replaced by Andrea Martin. This was early in Martin's long career, which has seen her flex her comedic talent onstage and in films such as *My Big Fat Greek Wedding* (2002). And Clark secured a few other young stars on the rise— Olivia Hussey was just six years from her break-out hit *Romeo and Juliet* (1968), Margot Kidder was about to make her star turn in *Superman* (1978), and Keir Dullea was also experiencing success from his role in Stanley Kubrick's *2001: A Space Odyssey* (1968).

Reviews of *Black Christmas* were mixed, and the initial release in the United States— where it was retitled *Silent Night, Evil Night*— failed. Once the original title was restored, the movie slowly started to pick up a cult audience, and over the years, horror aficionados began to note how this strange Canadian film had

and have her drop out of college, but she wants to stay at college, not get married, and have an abortion. *Black Christmas* is also a horror film that ends on an ominously ambiguous note. The presumed killer is dead, the final girl is sleeping . . . but the phone keeps on ringing.

Made at a time where there were as yet no fixed rules for the slash subgenre, here anything goes, and the survival of neither virgin nor even final girl comes guaranteed.

Anton Bitel, film critic

My Night at Maud's

DIRECTED BY **Éric Rohmer**

To watch when you . . . are considering what fate, destiny, and miracles mean in your life.

France, 1969
B&W, 111 minutes, Drama

Screenplay: Éric Rohmer

Starring: Jean-Louis Trintignant (Jean-Louis), Françoise Fabian (Maud), Marie-Christine Barrault (Françoise), Antoine Vitez (Vidal)

"I'm happy around you. If I'm happy with you, it's because we'll never meet again. The thought of the future needn't depress us since we have none."

—Jean-Louis

Between 1963 and 1972, French director Éric Rohmer made a series of loosely connected films. Now collectively called Rohmer's *Six Moral Tales*, each of these movies explore a moral quandary for a man who is faced with the temptation of a new woman, and each are filmed on location and set during a particular season.

Éric Rohmer had been one of the founding members of the film critic magazine *Cahiers du Cinéma*, alongside other future icons of the French New Wave, such as François Truffaut and Jean-Luc Godard. Unlike Truffaut and Godard, who would direct fast-paced, experimental movies, Rohmer's films were quieter and more contemplative, featuring long scenes of dialogue and beautiful landscapes. But they were no less groundbreaking—pushing boundaries with their dialogue about sex, philosophy, and religion. And Rohmer's influence continues into today, present in the work of writer-directors such as Woody Allen and Whit Stillman.

The films of Éric Rohmer have often been criticized as being overly talky or cold, but his interest in showing adults having intelligent conversations about their passions demonstrates his warmth and fascination for the everyday people who surrounded him. The use of the word "moral" in the title of his series of six films may lead people to believe there will be a preachiness or definitive message in his work; but Rohmer was more interested in the gray areas of life and the magic of missed (or made) connections. He explores the idea of fate and destiny in *My Night at Maud's* (1969), the third film of his *Six Moral Tales*. Rohmer released the fourth film first, but it makes more sense in the official order he later placed them, with *My Night at*

▲ Françoise Fabian as Maud

Maud's representing a turning point halfway through the series, and a change from black-and-white photography (in *My Night at Maud's*) to color (in *La Collectionneuse*, 1967).

Each of the moral tales is set within a particular season. *My Night at Maud's* is a Christmas movie, taking place on and around the holiday in a snowy town in the French provinces. Jean-Louis Trintignant plays the central character, called Jean-Louis—he is an engineer for Michelin who has recently been transferred to the small town of Clermont-Ferrand. Jean-Louis is a serious young man who is religious

but prefers mathematics to faith. He enjoys the logic behind math and the philosophy of Blaise Pascal—who was both a scientist and religious, and once said, "It is not possible to have reasonable grounds for not believing in miracles."

Miracles, or coincidences, seem to happen to Jean-Louis—first, he bumps into an old friend, Vidal (played by Antoine Vitez) at a bar that neither of them usually goes to. But he disagrees with Vidal that their meeting is fate. Vidal points out how unlikely it was to

▲ Jean-Louis Trintignant as Jean-Louis and Marie-Christine Barrault as Françoise

see each other, saying, "And yet, our paths cross right here, how strange." And Jean-Louis replies, "On the contrary. Our ordinary paths never cross. Therefore, the point of intersection must be outside those ordinary paths. I've been dabbling in mathematics on the side. It would be fun to calculate our chances of meeting in a two-month period."

Later, Vidal takes Jean-Louis to visit a friend on Christmas night. She is Maud (Françoise Fabian), a divorced doctor who is amused at Jean-Louis's certainty that he will marry a woman he just saw at Mass (Françoise, played by Marie-Christine Barrault), even though he's never spoken to her. In turn, Jean-Louis enjoys being challenged by Maud, and he stays the night, though he's careful to say no to Maud's invitation to get under the covers, insisting on sleeping on top of the bed, wrapped in

a blanket of his own. "Idiot," Maud says with a smile. Maud and Jean-Louis make a good pair, but he is determined to stick to his plan, and another coincidence occurs when he runs into Françoise on the street on the morning he leaves Maud's house.

In each of Éric Rohmer's Moral Tales, the male protagonists have a fixed theory around love, and a plan around the woman they are going to be with. But the meeting of another woman (in this case, Maud) clashes with their theory, leaving them to question their entire belief system. Jean-Louis ends up choosing Françoise; regardless, Rohmer doesn't offer any answers on what he thinks is right for his characters. As he once said, "Truth isn't found in assertions," and he himself believed in the magic of the everyday, stating, "Everything is a miracle." There were plenty of miracles on

▲ Maud and Vidal listen to Jean-Louis with amusement.

right on time, it snowed, and the snow lasted all day long, not just a few minutes."

The magic and charm of *My Night at Maud's* was contagious around the world, and this ended up being the most profitable of Rohmer's *Six Moral Tales*, experiencing rare crossover success in the United States. It was released in the United States in art house theaters in 1970 and was nominated for two Academy Awards—Best Foreign Film (before the US release) and Best Screenplay (after). Esteemed American film critics, such as Roger Ebert and Andrew Sarris, named it one of the best films of 1970. Following this hit, Rohmer became the most consistently successful of the French New Wave directors, despite being the oldest and the least flashy.

During his fifty-year career, Éric Rohmer made around twenty-six feature films, many of which he placed into series. In addition to the *Six Moral Tales* of the 1960s and '70s, Rohmer made six *Comedies and Proverbs* in the 1980s and four *Tales of the Four Seasons* throughout the 1990s. He directed his last feature in 2007, and passed away in 2010, aged eighty-nine.

Rohmer's sets, with Rohmer once explaining that he always left room for "happy accidents" to occur. Cinematographer Nestor Almendros confirmed this in his book, writing, "Some people think Rohmer is in league with the Devil." For example, on the production of *My Night at Maud's*, Almendros wrote that, "Months before, [Rohmer] had scheduled the exact date for shooting the scene when it snows. That day,

More Seasonal Delights by Éric Rohmer

La Collectionneuse (1967)
Claire's Knee (1970)
Love in the Afternoon (1972)
Pauline at the Beach (1983)
The Green Ray (1986)

Rohmer's films offer us an exceptionally vivid picture of how we navigate the twists and turns that life throws our way on a daily basis. "All the pleasure of life is in general ideas," wrote Oliver Wendell Holmes. "But all the use of life is in specific solutions." No artist has expressed this dichotomy more eloquently, or lovingly, than Éric Rohmer.

Kent Jones, film critic

ACKNOWLEDGMENTS

First and foremost, I'd like to thank my editor, the wonderful Cindy Sipala at Running Press. Thank you for your guidance and for tracking me down on opening night of the TCM Film Festival to talk about this possibility. I'm so glad that you did!

Thanks to the wider team at Running Press, and to all of those who have worked on the TCM side of the TCM Library, past and present: John Malahy, Heather Margolis, Lindsey Griffin. You've all created something very special and enduring.

Thanks to TCM researcher and fact checker extraordinaire Jeff Stafford for casting your trained eye over all my facts. And I was the recipient of insight from several authors who have previously written TCM books—thank you, Dave Karger, Eddie Muller, and Jeremy Arnold. I have also been given immense support by the TCM talent, publicity, production, and programming teams. Special thanks to TCM Imports programmer Hemrani Vyas for your expert tips on movies I could include, and to script supervisor Monica Elliot for your patience as I juggled writing my TCM intro scripts and this book at the same time!

Many of my personal friends cheered me on while writing, with the movie-obsessed ones giving me extra advice on my list of films. Meg Rich, Amirose Eisenbach, Matt Perez-Mora, Joe Amodei, Raissa Bretaña, Emily Hernandez, Chad Byrnes, Nadia Neophytou, Tom Wilhite, Willard Carroll . . . I appreciate you all. Willard, I promise I will return your DVDs soon. Thanks to my family back in Australia, and to my pet family here in America—Redford, Hayworth, and Harlow—thanks for pulling me away from my keyboard at regular intervals.

Thanks to my friends at Criterion, who (unknowingly) helped me by making almost all these movies available to watch on DVD or streaming and supplying a wealth of information about them. And finally, thank you to everyone who has supported Turner Classic Movies over the past thirty years, by watching and continuing to watch. We all appreciate you.

▲ *In the Mood for Love* (2000)

BIBLIOGRAPHY

INTRODUCTION

"Video: Roger Ebert on Empathy," by The Editors, RogerEbert.com, April 4, 2018, https://www.rogerebert.com/empathy/video -roger-ebert-on-empathy.

WINTER (EARLY YEAR)

Amelie (2001)
"*Amélie*," Box Office Mojo, https://www.box officemojo.com/title/tt0211915/?ref _=bo_se_r_1.
"*Amélie*," by Roger Ebert, RogerEbert.com, November 9, 2001, https://www.rogerebert .com/reviews/amelie-2001.
"The *Amélie* Effect," by Frédéric Bonnaud, *Film Comment*, November–December 2001, http://www.filmcomment.com/issue /november-december-2001/.
"*Amélie*—The Most Stylish Film Ever Made?," by Hannah Strong, BBC Culture, September 16, 2021, https://www.bbc.com /culture/article/20210916-amlie-the-most -stylish-film-ever-made.
"Audrey Tautou: How the French Learned to Love the Star of *Amélie*," by Kim Willsher, *The Guardian*, April 13, 2013, https://www .theguardian.com/film/2013/apr/14/audrey -tautou-french-love-amelie.

"Audrey Tautou: 'I Didn't Want This Power,'" by Benjamin Secher, *The Telegraph*, August 7, 2011, http://www.telegraph.co.uk/culture /film/starsandstories/8681355/Audrey -Tautou-I-didnt-want-this-power.html.
"Interview: The Fabulous Destiny of Jean-Pierre Jeunet," by Andrea Meyer, *IndieWire*, November 2, 2001, https://www.indiewire .com/features/general/interview-the-fabulous -destiny-of-jean-pierre-jeunet-80679/.
"Jean-Pierre Jeunet," by David Thomson, *The Guardian*, February 18, 2010, https://www .theguardian.com/film/2010/feb/18/jean -pierre-jeunet-david-thomson.
"Michael Weaver," by Stuart Levine, *Variety*, October 31, 2007, https://variety.com /2007/film/markets-festivals/michael -weaver-1117975154/.
"*Teratohyla amelie*," AmphibiaWeb, https:// amphibiaweb.org/species/6926.
"Why Does *Amélie*'s Sweet Smell of Success Linger On?," by Phil Hoad, *The Guardian*, October 18, 2011: https://www.theguardian .com/film/filmblog/2011/oct/18/amelie -sweet-smell-success.

Ikiru (1952)
"Akira Kurosawa: Biography," Turner Classic Movies (website), https://www.tcm.com /tcmdb/person/106389%7C8004 /Akira-Kurosawa#biography.

"Akira Kurosawa, Film Director, Is Dead at 88," by Rick Lyman, *New York Times*, September 7, 1998, https://www.nytimes.com/1998/09/07/movies/akira-kurosawa-film-director-is-dead-at-88.html.

"Film: Kurosawa's Quiet, Tragic Bureaucrat," by David Thomson, *New York Times*, January 5, 2003, https://www.nytimes.com/2003/01/05/movies/film-kurosawa-s-quiet-tragic-bureaucrat.html.

The Films of Akira Kurosawa, by Donald Ritchie (Berkeley, CA: University of California Press, 1999).

"How Should We Be 'Living'? Kurosawa and Ishiguro Tackle the Question, 70 Years Apart," by Bilal Qureshi, NPR, March 6, 2023, https://www.npr.org/2023/03/06/1161482211/kazuo-ishiguro-living-ikiru-oscars.

"*Ikiru*," by Scott McGee, Turner Classic Movies (website), January 26, 2010, https://www.tcm.com/tcmdb/title/78970/ikiru#articles-reviews?articleId=290046.

"Kurosawa Akira," *Britannica*, https://www.britannica.com/biography/Kurosawa-Akira.

Showman: The Life of David O. Selznick, by David Thomson (London: Abacus, 1993).

"To the Tune of Mortality: 'The Gondola Song' in *Ikiru*," by Geoffrey O'Brien, The Criterion Collection, August 17, 2021, https://www.criterion.com/current/posts/7501-to-the-tune-of-mortality-the-gondola-song-in-ikiru.

Lady Snowblood (1973)

"*The Complete Lady Snowblood*: Flowers of Carnage," by Howard Hampton, The Criterion Collection, January 5, 2016: https://www.criterion.com/current/posts/3856-the-complete-lady-snowblood-flowers-of-carnage.

"Flower of Carnage: The Birth of *Lady Snowblood*," by Marc Walkow, *Film Comment*, January 26, 2016, https://www.filmcomment.com/blog/flower-of-carnage-the-birth-of-lady-snowblood/.

"Interview: Quentin Tarantino," by Scott Myers, *Go into the Story* (blog), The Black List, April 25, 2009, republished from *Screenwriters Monthly*, February 2004, https://gointothestory.blcklst.com/interview-quentin-tarantino-2a0e5f04eb3.

"*Lady Snowblood*," by Sean Axmaker, Turner Classic Movies (website), October 19, 2016, https://www.tcm.com/tcmdb/title/559728/lady-snowblood#articles-reviews?articleId=1268027.

"Nikkatsu at 100," by Simon Foster, SBS Television Australia, June 22, 2012, https://www.sbs.com.au/whats-on/article/nikkatsu-at-100/jc6d4eco5.

The Ascent (1977)

"*The Ascent*," by Greg Ferrara, Turner Classic Movies (website), July 21, 2009, https://www.tcm.com/tcmdb/title/490152/the-ascent#articles-reviews?articleId=248658.

"*The Ascent*: Out in the Cold," by Fanny Howe, The Criterion Collection, January 26, 2021, https://www.criterion.com/current/posts/7256-the-ascent-out-in-the-cold.

"Eclipse Series 11: Larisa Shepitko," by Michael Koresky, The Criterion Collection, August 11, 2008, https://www.criterion.com/current/posts/507-eclipse-series-11-larisa-shepitko.

"The Lady Vanishes," by Larushka-Ivan Zadeh, *The Guardian*, January 9, 2005, https://www.theguardian.com/film/2005/jan/10/russia.

Force Majeure (2014)

"Aftershock of a Decision," by Nicholas Rapold, *New York Times*, May 14, 2014, https://www.nytimes.com/2014/05/14/movies/force-majeure-explores-the-effects-of-basic-instincts.html.

"Every Man for Himself! Forget the Wife and

Kids," by Stephen Holden, *New York Times*, October 24, 2014, https://www.nytimes.com/2014/10/24/movies/force-majeure-a-dark-swedish-comedy.html.

"Interview: Ruben Östlund Talks *Force Majeure*," by Steve Macfarlane, *Slant Magazine*, January 14, 2015, https://www.slantmagazine.com/film/interview-ruben-ostlund/.

"Real Men Flee Avalanches," by Cara Buckley, *New York Times*, October 19, 2014, https://www.nytimes.com/2014/10/19/movies/ruben-ostlands-force-majeure-a-look-at-fear-and-masculinity.html.

The Girls (1968)

All Those Tomorrows, by Mai Zetterling (New York: Grove Press, 1986).

"Cannes 1968: The Year Jean-Luc Godard and François Truffaut Led Protests That Shut Down the Festival," by Damon Wise, *Deadline*, May 18, 2018, https://deadline.com/2018/05/cannes-film-festival-1968-protests-anniversary-commentary-news-1202380606/.

A Cinema of Obsession: The Life and Work of Mai Zetterling, by Mariah Larsson (Madison, WI: University of Wisconsin Press, 2019).

"Mai Zetterling: Cinema Artist," by Mariah Larsson, The Criterion Collection, December 13, 2022: https://www.criterion.com/current/posts/8017-mai-zetterling-cinema-artist.

"Review of *Flikorna*," by Simone de Beauvoir, *Le Monde*, date unknown.

"Swedish Cinema's Use of the Bechdel Test Is a Provocation That Works," by Abu Koivunen, Ingrid Ryberg, and Laura Horak, *The Guardian*, November 27, 2013: https://www.theguardian.com/commentisfree/2013/nov/27/swedish-cinema-bechdel-test-works.

In the Mood for Love (2000)

"Film Review; A Desire Soaked in Pain,

Confusion and Great Need," by Elvis Mitchell, *New York Times*, February 2, 2001, https://www.nytimes.com/2001/02/02/movies/film-review-a-desire-soaked-in-pain-confusion-and-great-need.html.

"Interview with Wong Kar-wai: *In the Mood for Love*," by Michel Ciment and Hubert Niogret, *Postif Magazine*, no. 477, 2000.

"*In the Mood for Love*," by Jeremy Arnold, Turner Classic Movies (website), December 13, 2016, https://www.tcm.com/tcmdb/title/452042/in-the-mood-for-love#articles-reviews?articleId=1281214.

"*In the Mood for Love*: Haunted Heart," by Steve Erickson, The Criterion Collection, October 2, 2012, https://www.criterion.com/current/posts/2494-in-the-mood-for-love-haunted-heart.

"Notes on *In the Mood for Love*," by Charles Yu, The Criterion Collection, November 1, 2022, https://www.criterion.com/current/posts/7976-notes-on-in-the-mood-for-love.

"Wong Kar-Wai: Biography," Turner Classic Movies (website), https://www.tcm.com/tcmdb/person/208829%7C0Wong-Kar-Wai#biography.

Wong Kar-Wai: Interviews, Conversations with Filmmakers, edited by Silver Wai-ming Lee and Mickey Lee (Jackson, MS: University Press of Mississippi, 2017).

Wings of Desire (1987)

"A Beginners Guide to New German Cinema," by Darby Delaney, Film School Rejects, June 29, 2018, https://filmschoolrejects.com/beginners-guide-to-new-german-cinema/.

"'Every Person Is a Universe': Wim Wenders on *Wings of Desire*," by Lou Thomas, BFI, July 4, 2022, https://www.bfi.org.uk/interviews/every-person-universe-wim-wenders-wings-desire.

"On *Wings of Desire*," by Wim Wenders, The Criterion Collection, November 9, 2009, https://www.criterion.com/current

/posts/1290-on-wings-of-desire.

"Wim Wenders: Biography," by Bryce Coleman, Turner Classic Movies (website), https://www.tcm.com/tcmdb/person/204209%7C0/Wim-Wenders#biography.

"*Wings of Desire*," by Felicia Feaster, Turner Classic Movies (website), November 23, 2005, https://www.tcm.com/tcmdb/title/95968/wings-of-desire#articles-reviews?articleId=111419.

"*Wings of Desire* Review—Wim Wenders' Elegiac Hymn to a Broken Cold-War Berlin," by Peter Bradshaw, *The Guardian*, June 22, 2022, https://www.theguardian.com/film/2022/jun/22/wings-of-desire-review-wim-wenders-elegiac-hymn-to-a-broken-cold-war-berlin.

"*Wings of Desire*: Watch the Skies," by Michael Atkinson, The Criterion Collection, November 3, 2009, https://www.criterion.com/current/posts/1288-wings-of-desire-watch-the-skies.

Jeanne Dielman, 23 Commerce Quay, 1080 Brussels (1975)

"Breathing Through Cinema: The Films of Chantal Akerman," by Carson Lund, Harvard Film Archive, September 2017, https://harvardfilmarchive.org/programs/breathing-through-cinema.

"Brilliant and Radical, Chantal Akerman Deserves to Top *Sight and Sound*'s Greatest Films Poll," by Peter Bradshaw, *The Guardian*, December 1, 2022, https://www.theguardian.com/film/2022/dec/01/sight-and-sound-female-directed-greatest-film-of-all-time-chantal-akerman-jeanne-dielman-23-quai-du-commerce-1080-bruxelles.

"Chantal Akerman Obituary," by Jonathan Romney, *The Guardian*, October 8, 2015, https://www.theguardian.com/film/2015/oct/08/chantal-akerman.

"Chantal Akerman, Whose Films Examined Women's Inner Lives, Dies at 65," by Rachel Donadio and Cara Buckley, *New York Times*, October 6, 2015, https://www.nytimes.com/2015/10/07/arts/chantal-akerman-belgian-filmmaker-dies-65.html.

"The Greatest Film of All Time: *Jeanne Dielman, 23 Quai du Commerce, 1080 Bruxelles*," by Laura Mulvey, BFI, December 1, 2022, https://www.bfi.org.uk/sight-and-sound/features/greatest-film-all-time-jeanne-dielman-23-quai-du-commerce-1080-bruxelles.

"*Jeanne Dielman*, Three Decades Later: A Q&A with Chantal Akerman," by Dan Callahan, *Slant Magazine*, January 22, 2009, https://www.slantmagazine.com/film/q-a-with-chantal-akerman-jeanne-dielman-three-decades-later/.

"*Jeanne Dielman, 23 Commerce Quay, 1080 Brussels*," by Fernando F. Croce, Cinepassion, https://www.cinepassion.org/Reviews/j/JeanneDielman.html.

"*Jeanne Dielman, 23 Commerce Quay, 1080 Brussels*," by Noel Vera, Critic After Dark, October 23, 2015, https://criticafterdark.blogspot.com/2015/10/jeanne-dielman-23-quai-du-commerce-1080.html.

"*Jeanne Dielman, 23 Commerce Quay, 1080 Brussels*: Mystery and Insight in Everyday Work," by Benjamin Wang, *Film Inquiry*, May 11, 2017, https://www.filminquiry.com/jeanne-dielman-23-quai-du-commerce-1080-bruxelles-1975-review/.

"Keeping a Distance: Chantal Akerman's *Jeanne Dielman*," by Janet Bergstrom, *Sight and Sound*, BFI, June 4, 2021: https://www.bfi.org.uk/sight-and-sound/features/keeping-distance-chantal-akerman-jeanne-dielman.

"A Matter of Time: *Jeanne Dielman, 23, Quai du Commerce, 1080 Bruxelles*," by Ivone Margulies, The Criterion Collection, August 17, 2009: https://www.criterion.com/current/posts/1215-a-matter-of-time-jeanne-dielman-23-quai-du-commerce-1080-bruxelles.

"Postscript: Chantal Akerman," by Richard Brody, *New Yorker*, October 6, 2015, https://www.newyorker.com/culture/richard-brody/postscript-chantal-akerman.

"Revealed: The Results of the 2022 *Sight and Sound* Greatest Films of All Time Poll," BFI, December 1, 2022, https://www.bfi.org.uk/news/revealed-results-2022-sight-sound-greatest-films-all-time-poll.

The St. James Women Filmmakers Encyclopedia: Women on the Other Side of the Camera, edited by Amy L. Unterburger (Detroit: Visible Ink Press, 1999).

"Tales of Ordinary Sadness: Melancholy in the Cinema of Chantal Akerman," by Joseph Earp, *Bright Wall/Dark Room*, April 2017, https://www.brightwalldarkroom.com/2017/04/10/tales-of-ordinary-sadness-melancholy-in-the-cinema-of-chantal-akerman/.

SPRING

Ali: Fear Eats the Soul (1974)

"*Ali: Fear Eats the Soul*," by David Sterritt, Turner Classic Movies (website), March 24, 2017, https://www.tcm.com/tcmdb/title/74693/ali-fear-eats-the-soul#articles-reviews?articleId=1303371.

"*Ali: Fear Eats the Soul*: One Love, Two Oppressions," by Chris Fujiwara, The Criterion Collection, October 2, 2014, https://www.criterion.com/current/posts/1067-ali-fear-eats-the-soul-one-love-two-oppressions.

"*Fear Eats the Soul* (1974)," Greatest Films of All Time, *Sight and Sound*, BFI, https://www.bfi.org.uk/film/34034fba-0e65-50d1-b5ec-c56d9ae17fd6/fear-eats-the-soul.

"The Films of Rainer Werner Fassbinder: A Retrospective," by the Playlist Staff, *IndieWire*, July 29, 2011, Internet Archive Wayback Machine, http://web.archive.org/web/20231018134346/www.indiewire.com/features/general/the-films-of-rainer-werner-fassbinder-a-retrospective-117182/.

Love Is Colder Than Death: The Life and Times of Rainer Werner Fassbinder, by Robert Katz (New York: Random House, 1987).

"Rainer Werner Fassbinder," *Britannica*, https://www.britannica.com/biography/Rainer-Werner-Fassbinder.

"Rainer Werner Fassbinder: Biography," Turner Classic Movies (website), https://www.tcm.com/tcmdb/person/60092%7C0/Rainer-Werner-Fassbinder#biography.

Rainer Werner Fassbinder Retrospective, Goethe-Institut Exhibition Booklet.

"Six Films by Douglas Sirk," by Rainer Werner Fassbinder, *New Left Review*, May–June 1975, https://newleftreview.org/issues/i91/articles/rainer-werner-fassbinder-six-films-by-douglas-sirk.

Bicycle Thieves (1948)

"The Essentials—*The Bicycle Thief*," by Frank Miller, Turner Classic Movies (website), January 21, 2011, https://www.tcm.com/tcmdb/title/68597/the-bicycle-thief#articles-reviews?articleId=373180.

The Film Encyclopedia, 7th ed., by Ephraim Katz with Ronald Dean Nolen (New York: HarperCollins Reference, 2012).

The Oxford Companion to Film, edited by Liz-Anne Bawden (New York: Oxford University Press, 1976).

The Screen; Vittorio De Sica's *The Bicycle Thief*, a Drama of Post-War Rome, Arrives at World," by Bosley Crowther, *New York Times*, December 13, 1949, https://www.nytimes.com/1949/12/13/archives/the-screen-vittorio-de-sicas-the-bicycle-thief-a-drama-of-postwar.html.

"Vittorio De Sica," *Britannica*, https://www.britannica.com/biography/Vittorio-De-Sica.

"Vittorio De Sica: Biography," Turner Classic Movies (website), https://www.tcm.com/tcmdb/person/46765%7C152035/Vittorio-De%20Sica#biography.

My Brilliant Career (1979)

"Armstrong, Gillian," by Helen Carter, *Senses of Cinema*, October 2002, https://www.sensesofcinema.com/2002/great-directors/armstrong/.

"At Tea With: Gillian Armstrong; a Lucky Director's Daring Career," by Ruth Reichl, *New York Times*, March 8, 1995: https://www.nytimes.com/1995/03/08/garden/at-tea-with-gillian-armstrong-a-lucky-director-s-daring-career.html.

"Film: Australian *Brilliant Career* by Gillian Armstrong: The Cast," by Janet Maslin, *New York Times*, October 6, 1979, https://www.nytimes.com/1979/10/06/archives/film-australian-brilliant-career-by-gillian-armstrongthe-cast.html.

"Gender Matters Results 2021/2022," by Screen Australia, Screen Australia, October 13, 2022, https://www.screenaustralia.gov.au/sa/screen-news/2022/10-13-gender-matters-results-2021-22.

"Gillian Armstrong and Her Brilliant, Free-Spirited Protagonists Redefined the Modern Movie Heroine," by David Edelstein, *Vulture*, January 9, 2020, https://www.vulture.com/2020/01/gillian-armstrong-redefined-the-modern-movie-heroine.html.

"Gillian Armstrong: I Used to Think, 'I Did It, Why Can't All the Other Women?,'" by James Robert Douglas, *The Guardian*, August 29, 2016, https://www.theguardian.com/film/2016/aug/30/gillian-armstrong-i-used-to-think-i-did-it-why-cant-all-the-other-women.

"Miles Franklin," *Britannica*, https://www.britannica.com/biography/Miles-Franklin.

"*My Brilliant Career*," by Stephanie Zacharek, Turner Classic Movies (website), June 19, 2012, https://www.tcm.com/tcmdb/title/84287/my-brilliant-career#articles-reviews?articleId=495919.

"*My Brilliant Career*: Unapologetic Women," by Carrie Rickey, The Criterion Collection, May 2, 2019, https://www.criterion.com/current/posts/6328-my-brilliant-career-unapologetic-women.

The St. James Women Filmmakers Encyclopedia: Women on the Other Side of the Camera, edited by Amy L. Unterburger (Detroit: Visible Ink Press, 1999).

Daisies (1966)

"An Audience for Free Spirits in a Closed Society," by Nicolas Rapold, *New York Times*, June 29, 2012, https://www.nytimes.com/2012/07/01/movies/daisies-from-the-czech-director-vera-chytilova-at-bam.html.

"Criterion Shines Light on Masterful *Daisies*," by Marya E. Gates, RogerEbert.com, November 7, 2022, https://www.rogerebert.com/streaming/criterion-shines-light-on-masterful-daisies.

"*Daisies*," by Greg Ferrera, Turner Classic Movies (website), August 1, 2013, https://www.tcm.com/tcmdb/title/72093/daisies#articles-reviews?articleId=659998.

"*Daisies*: Giggling Generals; One and Two," by Carmen Gray, The Criterion Collection, November 1, 2022, https://www.criterion.com/current/posts/7979-daisies-giggling-generals-one-and-two.

"'Everything That Well-Behaved Young Ladies Aren't Supposed to Do': Věra Chytilová and the Czechoslovak New Wave," by Caitlyn Christensen, *Sampsonia Way*, July 19, 2016, http://archive.sampsoniaway.org/interviews/2016/07/19/%E2%80%9Ceverything-that-well-behaved-young-ladies-aren%E2%80%99t-supposed-to-do%E2%80%9D-vera-chytilova-and-the-czechoslovak-new-wave/.

"In Memoriam: Věra Chytilová (1929–2014)," by Meredith Slifkin, *Film Comment*, March 19, 2014, https://www.filmcomment.com/blog/in-memoriam-vera-chytilova/.

"Peter Hames on Vera Chytilová," by Simon Hitchman, New Wave Film.com, February 2015, https://newwavefilm.com/interviews/hames-on-chytilova.shtml.

The St. James Women Filmmakers Enyclopdia: Women on the Other Side of the Camera, edited by Amy L. Unterburger (Detroit: Visible Ink Press, 1999).

"This Film's Going Bad: Collaborative Cutting in *Daisies*," by Dylan Rainforth, *Senses of Cinema*, August 2007, https://www.sensesofcinema.com/2007/cteq/daisies/.

"Vera Chytilova Dies at 85; Made Daring Films in Czech New Wave," by Margalit Fox, *New York Times*, March 22, 2014, https://www.nytimes.com/2014/03/23/nyregion/vera-chytilova-dies-at-85-made-daring-czech-films.html.

Spring in a Small Town (1948)

"A Century of Chinese Cinema: an Introduction," by Noah Cowan, BFI, May 28, 2014, https://www.bfi.org.uk/features/century-chinese-cinema-introduction.

"Fei Mu," by Jasper Mäkinen, *Senses of Cinema*, October 2019, https://www.sensesofcinema.com/2019/great-directors/fei-mu/.

"History of Shanghai," *Britannica*, https://www.britannica.com/place/Shanghai/History.

"Mu Fei's *Spring in a Small Town* Dwells Among WWII's Ruins," by Michael Barrett, *PopMatters*, August 9, 2007: https://www.popmatters.com/mu-fei-spring-small-town-1948.

"Second Sino-Japanese War," *Britannica*, https://www.britannica.com/event/Second-Sino-Japanese-War.

"*Spring in a Small Town* (1948)," BFI, https://www.bfi.org.uk/film/f993a5b6-935b-5b23-a1b1-4f616f2abd03/spring-in-a-small-town.

"*Spring in a Small Town*," Film at Lincoln Center, https://www.filmlinc.org/films/spring-in-a-small-town/.

"*Spring in a Small Town* Review—Powerful, Exquisite Drama," by Peter Bradshaw, *The Guardian*, June 19, 2014, https://www.theguardian.com/film/2014/jun/19/spring-in-a-small-town-review-exquisite-drama.

"An Undiscovered Master: Fei Mu," Film at Lincoln Center, https://www.filmlinc.org/series/an-undiscovered-master-fei-mu/.

Dilwale Dulhania Le Jayenge (1995)

"Bollywood," *Britannica*, https://www.britannica.com/topic/Bollywood-film-industry-India.

Bollywood: The Films! The Songs! The Stars! (New York: D.K., 2017).

"Dilwale Dulhania Le Jayenge": A Modern Classic, by Anupama Chopra (Noida, Uttar Pradesh, India: HarperCollins India, 2016).

"*Dilwale Dulhania Le Jayenge*: The Record-Breaking Bollywood Rom-Com Celebrating 1000 Weeks in Cinemas," by Scott Jordan Harris, RogerEbert.com, December 18, 2014, https://www.rogerebert.com/features/dilwale-dulhania-le-jayenge-the-record-breaking-bollywood-rom-com-celebrating-1000-weeks-in-cinemas.

"Here's What Makes Bollywood Movies So Special," by Elena Nicolaou, Oprah Daily, July 30, 2020, https://www.oprahdaily.com/entertainment/a33396048/what-is-bollywood/.

"India's Love Story with a Movie Still on the Big Screen After 27 Years," by Mujib Mashal and Suhasini Raj, *New York Times*, January 19, 2023, https://www.nytimes.com/2023/01/19/world/asia/bollywood-ddlj-maratha-mandir.html.

"25 Years of *Dilwale Dulhania Le Jayenge*, Bollywood's Best Love Story," by Neha Prakash, *Marie Claire*, October 7, 2020, https://www.marieclaire.com/culture/a34252535/dilwale-dulhania-le-jayenge-movie-oral-history/.

Cinema Paradiso (1988)

"*Cinema Paradiso*," by Felecia Feaster, Turner Classic Movies (website), March 24, 2006, https://www.tcm.com/tcmdb/title/70942/cinema-paradiso#articles-reviews?articleId=121606.

"*Cinema Paradiso*," by Roger Ebert, RogerEbert
.com, March 16, 1990, https://www.roger
ebert.com/reviews/cinema-paradiso-1990.

"*Cinema Paradiso*: An Ode to Movies," by
Patrick Hayes, MovieWeb, September 3,
2022, https://movieweb.com/cinema
-paradiso-meaning/.

"Giuseppe Tornatore: Biography," Turner Classic
Movies (website), https://www.tcm.com
/tcmdb/person/517449%7C0/Giuseppe
-Tornatore#biography.

An Angel at My Table (1990)

"*An Angel at My Table*," by Margarita Landazuri,
Turner Classic Movies (website), March 8,
2014, https://www.tcm.com/tcmdb/title
/67350/an-angel-at-my-table#articles
-reviews?articleId=963811.

"*An Angel at My Table*: Alone, Naturally," by
Amy Taubin, The Criterion Collection,
September 19, 2005: https://www.criterion
.com/current/posts/771-an-angel-at-my
-table-alone-naturally.

"*Angel at My Table* a Superb Rendering of an
Inner Life," by Dave Kehr, *Chicago Tribune*,
June 21, 1991, https://www.chicagotribune
.com/1991/06/21/angel-at-my-table-a
-superb-rendering-of-an-inner-life/.

"A Brief History of New Zealand Cinema," by
Noël de Souza, Golden Globe Awards,
October 21, 2021, https://goldenglobes
.com/articles/brief-history-new-zealand
-cinema/.

*Hollywood on the Riviera: The Inside Story of the
Cannes Film Festival*, by Cari Beauchamp
and Henri Béhar (New York: William
Morrow, 1992).

"New Again: Jane Campion," by Katharine
Dieckmann and Michael Tabb, *Interview
Magazine*, May 30, 2012, https://www
.interviewmagazine.com/film/new-again
-jane-campion.

Late Spring (1949)

"The Enigmatic 'Pillow Shots' of Yasujiro Ozu,"
by Leigh Singer, BFI, September 8, 2023,
https://www.bfi.org.uk/features/enigmatic
-pillow-shots-yasujiro-ozu.

"*Late Spring*," by Margarita Landazuri, Turner
Classic Movies (website), March 28, 2013,
https://www.tcm.com/tcmdb/title
/487647/late-spring#articles-reviews
?articleId=602020.

"Screen: Japanese Life: *Late Spring* by Ozu Opens
at New Yorker," by Vincent Canby, *New York
Times*, July 22, 1972, https://
www.nytimes.com/1972/07/22/archives
/screen-japanese-lifelate-spring-by
-ozu-opens-at-new-yorker.html.

"Why Would Ozu Cut to a Vase at the End of
This Scene?," by Jason Hellerman, No Film
School, November 11, 2020, https://
nofilmschool.com/ozu-vase.

"Yasujiro Ozu: Ten Essential Films," by Jasper
Sharp, BFI, December 12, 2019, https://
www.bfi.org.uk/lists/yasujiro-ozu-10
-essential-films.

Pan's Labyrinth (2006)

"Guillermo del Toro," *Britannica*, https://
www.britannica.com/biography/Guillermo
-del-Toro.

"Guillermo del Toro, Alejandro G. Iñárritu and
Alfonso Cuarón Discuss Career Highs and
Lows, Friendships and Death in Three
Amigos Conversation," by Michaela Zee,
Variety, January 10, 2023: https://variety
.com/2023/scene/news/three-amigos
-guillermo-del-toro-alejandro-g-inarritu
-alfonso-cuaron-netflix-1235481669/.

"Guillermo del Toro: Biography," Turner Classic
Movies (website), https://www.tcm.com
/tcmdb/person/47842%7C0/Guillermo
-Del-Toro#biography.

"How Mexico Conquered the Oscars," by León
Krauze, *Slate*, January 30, 2019, https://slate.
com/culture/2019/01/three-amigos
-directors-alfonso-cuaron-guillermo-del-toro
-alejandro-gonzalez-inarritu.html.

"*Pan's Labyrinth*: Guillermo del Toro on the Making of *Pan's Labyrinth*," by Warner Bros. Entertainment, YouTube, video, September 30, 2019, https://www.youtube.com/watch?v=8-G8pKiuG8Q.

"*Pan's Labyrinth*: The Heart of the Maze," by Michael Atkinson, The Criterion Collection, October 18, 2016, https://www.criterion.com/current/posts/4262-pan-s-labyrinth-the-heart-of-the-maze.

"The 100 Best Movies of the Past 10 Decades: *Pan's Labyrinth*," *Time*, July 26, 2023, https://time.com/collection/100-best-movies/6296100/pans-labyrinth-2006/.

All About My Mother (1999)

"*All About My Mother* Reviews," quote by Ella Taylor from *L.A. Weekly*, October 3, 2002, Rotten Tomatoes, https://www.rottentomatoes.com/m/all_about_my_mother/reviews?type=top_critics.

"*All About My Mother* (1969)," by Rebecca Kumar, Turner Classic Movies (website), February 22, 2022, https://www.tcm.com/tcmdb/title/442676/all-about-my-mother#articles-reviews?articleId=021578.

"*All About My Mother*: Matriarchal Society," by Emma Wilson, The Criterion Collection, January 18, 2020, https://www.criterion.com/current/posts/6795-all-about-my-mother-matriarchal-society.

"*All About My Mother* Wins Foreign Language Film: 2000 Oscars," by Oscars, YouTube, video, December 20, 2012, https://www.youtube.com/watch?v=Gqk-vogchFk.

"The Explosion of Color That Followed a Dictator," by Andrew Dickson, BBC, August 20, 2019, https://www.bbc.com/culture/article/20190816-the-explosion-of-colour-that-followed-a-dictator.

"'I Make Fiction Films Because I Like Representation': Director Pedro Almodovar on *All About My Mother*," by Adam Pincus, *Filmmaker Magazine*, July 6, 2019, https://filmmakermagazine.com/107627-i-make-fiction-films-because-i-like-representation-director-pedro-almodovar-on-all-about-my-mother/.

"La Movida Madrileña: the Punk Movement That Changed Madrid's Art Scene Forever," by Tom Seymour, Culture Trip, June 8, 2020, https://theculturetrip.com/europe/spain/articles/la-movida-madrilena.

"An Ode to Pedro Almodovar's *All About My Mother* on Its 20th Anniversary," by Rebecca Bodenheimer, RogerEbert.com, March 6, 2020, https://www.rogerebert.com/features/an-ode-to-pedro-almodovars-all-my-mother-on-its-20th-anniversary.

"Pedro Almodóvar and His 'Cinema of Women,'" by Julie Bloom, *New York Times*, December 2, 2016, https://www.nytimes.com/2016/12/02/movies/pedro-almodovar-and-his-cinema-of-women.html.

"Pedro Almodóvar: Biography," Turner Classic Movies (website), https://www.tcm.com/tcmdb/person/2782%7C0/Pedro-Almod%C3%B3var#biography.

"Tea with the FT: Pedro Almodóvar," by Raphael Abraham, *Financial Times*, January 2, 2015, https://www.ft.com/content/568f623a-8f4e-11e4-b080-00144feabdc0#axzz3NwLV1AbR.

Went the Day Well? (1942)

"Alberto Cavalcanti," *Britannica*, https://www.britannica.com/biography/Alberto-Cavalcanti.

"Alberto Cavalcanti: Biography," Turner Classic Movies (website), https://www.tcm.com/tcmdb/person/31013%7C5820/[alberto]-Cavalcanti#biography.

"History," Ealing Studios, https://ealingstudios.com/about-ealing/history-3/.

"Edgar Wright: How Martin Scorsese Helped Me Through Lockdown," by Mark Kermode, *The Guardian*, October 24, 2021, https://www.theguardian.com/culture/2021/oct/24/edgar-wright-mark

-kermode-martin-scorsese-lockdown
-films-interview-last-night-soho.

"*Went the Day Well?*," BFI: https://www.bfi
.org.uk/film/6b8f6196-c88b-5e44
-a96f-330f7110fd81/went-the-day-well.

"*Went the Day Well?*" by David Skerrit, Turner
Classic Movies (website), February 14, 2014,
https://www.tcm.com/tcmdb
/title/75467/went-the-day-well#articles
-reviews?articleId=955226.

The Passion of Joan of Arc (1928)

"Carl Theodor Dreyer," *Britannica*, https://
www.britannica.com/biography/Carl
-Theodor-Dreyer.

"Carl Theodor Dreyer: Biography," Turner Classic
Movies (website), https://www.tcm
.com/tcmdb/person/361400%7C26985/
Carl-Th.-Dreyer#biography.

"*The Passion of Joan of Arc*," by James Steffen,
Turner Classic Movies (website), August 17,
2004, https://www.tcm.com/tcmdb/title
/328534/the-passion-of-joan-of-arc#articles
-reviews?articleId=81387.

"Realized Mysticism in *The Passion of Joan of
Arc*," by Carl Theodor Dreyer, The Criterion
Collection, November 8, 1999, https://www.
criterion.com/current/posts/69
-realized-mysticism-in-the-passion-of-joan
-of-arc.

"A Restored *Passion of Joan of Arc* Still a
Transcendent Masterpiece," by J. Hoberman,
New York Times, November 22, 2017: https://
www.nytimes.com/2017/11/22
/movies/the-passion-of-joan-of-arc-new
-digital-restoration-film-forum.html.

"Silent Rapture in Winston-Salem," The
Criterion Collection, October 18, 2018,
https://www.criterion.com/current/posts
/5988-silent-rapture-in-winston-salem.

"Where to Begin with Carl Dreyer," by Alex
Barrett, BFI, February 3, 2016, https
//www.bfi.org.uk/features/where-begin
-carl-dreyer.

La Dolce Vita (1960)

"Federico Fellini: Biography," Turner Classic
Movies (website), https://www.tcm.com
/tcmdb/person/60684%7C50893/Federic
o-Fellini#biography.

"Federico Fellini, Film Visionary, Is Dead at
73," by Peter B. Flint, *New York Times*,
November 1, 1993, https://www.nytimes
.com/1993/11/01/obituaries/federico
-fellini-film-visionary-is-dead-at-73.html

Federico Fellini: Ringmaster of Dreams 1920–1993,
by Chris Wiegand (Los Angeles: Taschen,
2003).

"*La Dolce Vita*," *Britannica*, https://www
.britannica.com/topic/La-Dolce-Vita.

"*La dolce vita*: Tuxedos at Dawn," by Gary
Giddins, The Criterion Collection,
October 21, 2014, https://www.criterion
.com/current/posts/3335-la-dolce-vita
-tuxedos-at-dawn.

"Party Time in Fellini Land," by Michael Joshua
Rowin, The Criterion Collection, June 22,
2020, https://www.criterion.com/current
/posts/6997-party-time-in-fellini-land.

Black Girl (1966)

"*Black Girl* [1966]—A Thoughtful Microcosmic
Tale of Neocolonialism," by Arun Kumar,
High on Films, November 14, 2017, https://
www.highonfilms.com/black-girl
-1966-neocolonialism/.

"*Black Girl* (1966): Vocal Cinema," by Benjamin
Wang, *Film Inquiry*, March 17, 2017,
https://www.filminquiry.com/black-girl
-1966-review/.

"*Black Girl*: Self, Possessed," by Ashley Clark,
The Criterion Collection, January 23, 2017,
https://www.criterion.com/current
/posts/4402-black-girl-self-possessed.

"In Praise of Mbissine Thérèse Diop in Ousmane
Sembène's *Black Girl*," by Sarah Jilani, BFI,
December 15, 2016: https://www.bfi.org.uk/

features/praise-mbissine-therese
-diop-ousmane-sembenes-black-girl.
"La Noire de . . . : Sembène's *Black Girl* and Postcolonial Senegal," by Sylvia Cutler, College of Humanities, Brigham Young University, February 3, 2015, https://humanities.byu.edu/la-noire-de-sembenes-black-girl-and-postcolonial-senegal/.
"Ousmane Sembene's *Black Girl* Turns 50," by A. O. Scott, *New York Times*, May 18, 2016, https://www.nytimes.com/2016/05/18/movies/ousmane-sembenes-black-girl-turns-50.html.

The Young Girls of Rochefort (1967)
"Criterion's 'The Essential Jacques Demy,'" by Peter Sobczynski, RogerEbert.com, August 4, 2014, https://www.rogerebert.com/streaming/criterions-the-essential-jacques-demy.
"How Does My Queen? Interview with Catherine Denueve," by Arnaud Desplechin, *Film Comment*, November–December 2008.
"*The Young Girls of Rochefort*: Not the Same Old Song and Dance," by Jonathan Rosenbaum, The Criterion Collection, July 24, 2014, https://www.criterion.com/current/posts/3236-the-young-girls-of-rochefort-not-the-same-old-song-and-dance.
The Young Girls Turn 25, by Agnès Varda, Ciné-tamaris, 1993.

Purple Noon (1960)
"Alain Delon: Biography," Turner Classic Movies (website), https://www.tcm.com/tcmdb/person/48245%7C8617/Alain-Delon#biography.
"The Essential Patricia Highsmith," by Sarah Weinman, *New York Times*, March 8, 2023, https://www.nytimes.com/article/best-patricia-highsmith-books.html.
"'The Kind of Film You Make Passionately': René Clément on *Purple Noon*," by Olivier Eyquem and Jean-Claude Missiaen, *L'avant-scène:*

Cinéma, February 1, 1981, republished on The Criterion Collection in English, translated by Nicholas Elliott, December 5, 2012: https://www.criterion.com/current/posts/2587-the-kind-of-film-you-make-passionately-ren-clment-on-purple-noon.

Cléo From 5 to 7 (1962)
Agnès Varda, by Kelley Conway (Urbana, IL: University of Illinois Press, 2015).
Agnès Varda: Interviews, edited by T. Jefferson Kline (Jackson, MS: University Press of Mississippi, 2013).
"Agnès Varda Is Dead at 90; Influential French New Wave Filmmaker," by John Anderson, *New York Times*, March 29, 2019, https://www.nytimes.com/2019/03/29/obituaries/agnes-varda-dead.html.
"Agnès Varda Receives an Honorary Award at the 2017 Governors Awards," by Oscars, YouTube, video, November 12, 2017, https://youtube.com/watch?v=N5vFXOqNCso.
The Cinema of Agnès Varda: Resistance and Eclecticism (Director's Cuts), by Delphine Bénézet (New York: Columbia University Press, 2014).
"*Cléo from 5 to 7*," by Molly Haskell, The Criterion Collection, May 15, 2000, https://www.criterion.com/current/posts/87-cl-o-from-5-to-7.
"*Cléo from 5 to 7*," by Rob Nixon, Turner Classic Movies (website), August 1, 2013, https://www.tcm.com/tcmdb/title/71067/cleo-from-5-to-7#articles-reviews?articleId=659844.
"*Cléo from 5 to 7*: Passionate Time," by Adrian Martin, The Criterion Collection, January 21, 2008, https://www.criterion.com/current/posts/499-cleo-from-5-to-7-passionate-time.
"*La Pointe Courte*: How Agnès Varda 'Invented' the New Wave," by Ginette Vincendeau, The Criterion Collection, January 21, 2008:

https://www.criterion.com/current
/posts/497-la-pointe-courte-how-agn
-s-varda-invented-the-new-wave.

To Desire Differently: Feminism and the French Cinema, by Sandy Flitterman-Lewis (New York: Columbia University Press, 1996).

"What to Stream This Weekend: Agnès Varda's Chronicle of a Parisian Pop Star's Dread-Filled Afternoon," by Richard Brody, *New Yorker*, April 5, 2019, https://www .newyorker.com/culture/the-front-row /what-to-stream-this-weekend-agnes-vardas -chronicle-of-a-parisian-pop-stars-dread -filled-afternoon-in-cleo-from-5-to-7.

La Ciénaga (2001)

"*La Ciénaga*," by Margarita Landazuri, Turner Classic Movies (website), October 3, 2014, https://www.tcm.com/tcmdb/title/532817 /la-cienaga#articles-reviews ?articleId=1036620.

"*La Ciénaga*," by Roger Ebert, RogerEbert.com, October 19, 2001, https://www.rogerebert .com/reviews/la-cienaga-2001.

"La Ciénaga: What's Outside the Frame" by David Oubiña, Criterion Collection, January 26, 2015, https://www.criterion .com/current/posts/3444-la-cinaga-whats -outside-the-frame.

Pierrot le Fou (1965)

"Jean-Luc Godard: Biography," Turner Classic Movies: https://www.tcm.com/tcmdb /person/72527%7C80903/Jean-luc -Godard#biography.

"Jean-Luc Godard Death: Iconoclastic Filmmaker Ended his Life by Assisted Death in Switzerland, Aged 91," by Maanya Sachdeva and Inga Parkel, *The Independent*, September 13, 2022, https://www .independent.co.uk/arts-entertainment /films/news/jean-luc-godard-assisted -death-b2166538.html.

"Jean-Luc Godard, 91, Is Dead; Bold Director Shaped French New Wave," by Dave Kehr and Jonathan Kandell, *New York Times*, September 13, 2022, https://www.nytimes .com/2022/09/13/movies/jean-luc-godard -dead.html.

Godard on Godard, edited by Jean Barboni and Tom Milne (New York: Da Capo Press, 1985).

"*Pierrot le Fou*," by Greg Ferrara, Turner Classic Movies (website), August 21, 2015, https:// www.tcm.com/tcmdb/title/86685 /pierrot-le-fou#articlesreviews?article Id=1117791.

"*Pierrot Le Fou*—Jean-Luc Godard's 1965 Masterpiece," by Sean Axmaker, Turner Classic Movies (website), November 2007, https://www.tcm.com/tcmdb/title/86685 /pierrot-le-fou#articles-reviews?article Id=187441.

"*Pierrot le fou*: Self-Portrait in a Shattered Lens," by Richard Brody, The Criterion Collection, September 22, 2009, https://www .criterion.com/current/posts/525-pierrot -le-fou-self-portrait-in-a-shattered-lens.

A Third Face: My Tale of Writing, Fighting and Filmmaking, by Samuel Fuller (New York, Applause, 2002).

Beau Travail (1999)

"*Beau Travail*," by Greg Ferrara, Turner Classic Movies (website), October 29, 2013, https:// www.tcm.com/tcmdb/title/442735 /beau-travail#articles-reviews?article Id=770467.

"*Beau Travail*: A Cinema of Sensation," by Girish Shambu, The Criterion Collection, September 15, 2020, https://www.criterion .com/current/posts/7097-beau-travail-a -cinema-of-sensation.

"*Beau Travail*: A Military Ballet Under the Sun," by Stephen Holden, *New York Times*, September 28, 1999, https://archive .nytimes.com/www.nytimes.com/library /film/092899ny-beau-film-review.html.

"*Beau Travail* Finds the Rhythm of Life (and Dances Away the Pain)," by Gia Kourlas, *New York Times*, September 28, 2020,

https://www.nytimes.com/2020/09/28/arts
/dance/Beau-Travail-Denis-Lavant.html.

"*Cinema and Sensation: French Film and the Art of Transgression*," book review by Saige Walton, *Senses of Cinema*, April 2009: https ://www.sensesofcinema.com/2009/book -reviews/cinema-and-sensation/.

"The Fearless Cinema of Claire Denis," by Alice Gregory, *New Yorker*, May 21, 2018, https:// www.newyorker.com/magazine /2018/05/28/the-fearless-cinema-of-claire -denis.

"Greta Gerwig on *Beau Travail*," Adventures in Moviegoing, The Criterion Channel, https:// www.criterionchannel.com/beau -travail/videos/greta-gerwig-on-beau-travail.

"How Bernardo Montet Infused *Beau Travail* with His 'Choreographic Thought,'" by Hillary Weston, The Criterion Collection, October 1, 2020, https://www.criterion.com/ current/posts/7126-how-bernardo -montet-infused-beau-travail-with-his -choreographic-thought.

Parasite (2019)

"Bong Joon-Ho," *Britannica*, https://www. britannica.com/biography/Bong-Joon-Ho.

"Bong Joon-Ho Looked to Hitchcock When Making *Parasite*: 'He Always Gives Me Very Strange Inspiration,'" by Yohana Desta, *Vanity Fair*, October 11, 2019, https ://www.vanityfair.com/hollywood/2019/10 /bong-joon-ho-parasite-interview.

"Bong Joon Ho's Path from Seoul to Oscar Dominance," by Chloe Sang-Hun, *New York Times*, February 13, 2020, https ://www.nytimes.com/2020/02/13/world /asia/bong-joon-ho-south-korea.html.

"How Bong Joon Ho Invented the Weird World of *Parasite*," by David Sims, *The Atlantic*, October 15, 2019, https://www.theatlantic .com/entertainment/archive/2019/10 /bong-joon-ho-parasite-interview/600007/.

"The Makings of Bong Joon Ho," by Tony Rayns, BFI, February 12, 2020, https

://www2.bfi.org.uk/news-opinion/sight -sound-magazine/interviews /bong-joon-ho-career-story.

"*Parasite* Earns Best-Picture Oscar, First for a Movie Not in English," by Kyle Buchanan and Brookes Barnes, *New York Times*, February 9, 2020: https://www.nytimes .com/2020/02/09/movies/parasite-movie -oscars-best-picture.html.

"*Parasite*: Notes from the Underground," by Inkoo Kang, The Criterion Collection, October 30, 2020, https://www.criterion .com/current/posts/7158-parasite-notes -from-the-underground.

Monsieur Hulot's Holiday (1953)

The Films of Jacques Tati, by Brent Maddock (Metuchen, NJ: The Scarecrow Press, 1977).

"Jacques Tati," *Britannica*, https://www.britannica .com/biography/Jacques-Tati.

"Jacques Tati: Biography," Turner Classic Movies (website), https://www.tcm.com/tcmdb /person/189266%7C0/Jacques-Tati #biography.

Jacques Tati: Frame by Frame, by James Harding (London: Secker & Warburg, 1984).

Jacques Tati: His Life and Art, by David Bellos (London: Harvill Panther, 2001).

"Jacques Tati: The Director Who Made David Lynch Fall in Love with Humanity," by Joe Williams, *Far Out Magazine*, September 14, 2023, https://faroutmagazine.co.uk/the -director-who-made-david-lynch-love -humanity/.

"Jacques Tati: Things Fall Together," by David Cairns, The Criterion Collection, November 4, 2014, https://www.criterion. com/current/posts/3339-jacques-tati-things -fall-together.

Les Vacances de Monsieur Tati, by Stéphane Pajot (Le Château d'Olonne, France: Editions d'Orbestier, 2003).

"*M. Hulot's Holiday*," by David Ehrenstein, The Criterion Collection, January 5, 2004, https://www.criterion.com/current

/posts/11-m-hulot-s-holiday.

"*Mr. Hulot's Holiday*," by Jay Carr, Turner Classic Movies (website), August 11, 2008, https://www.tcm.com/tcmdb/title/83708/mr-hulots-holiday/#articles-reviews?articleId=208644.

"Scatterbrained Angel: The Films of Jacques Tati," by James Quandt, The Criterion Collection, October 27, 2014, https://www.criterion.com/current/posts/3336-scatterbrained-angel-the-films-of-jacques-tati.

Swept Away (1974)

"The Disorder of Things: A Lina Wertmüller Retrospective," Harvard Film Archive, https://harvardfilmarchive.org/programs/the-disorder-of-things-a-lina-wert-muller-retrospective.

"Grotesque Poetry: A Conversation with Lina Wertmüller," by Hillary Weston, The Criterion Collection, April 12, 2017, https://www.criterion.com/current/posts/4498-grotesque-poetry-a-conversation-with-lina-wertmuller.

"Lina Wertmüller," Turner Classic Movies (website), https://www.tcm.com/tcmdb/person/204382%7C0/Lina-Wertmuller#overview.

"Lina Wertmüller, Italian Director of Provocative Films, Dies at 93," by William Grimes, *New York Times*, December 9, 2021, https://www.nytimes.com/2021/12/09/movies/lina-wertmuller-dead.html.

"Lina Wertmüller on What Being the First Female Director Nominated for an Oscar Means to Her," by Henry Chu, *Variety*, February 28, 2018, https://variety.com/2018/film/features/director-lina-wertmuller-oscar-1202710625/.

"*Swept Away by an Unusual Destiny in the Blue Sea of August*," by Roger Ebert, RogerEbert.com, February 20, 1976, https://www.rogerebert.com/reviews/swept-away-by-an-unusual-destiny-in-the-blue-sea-of-august-1976.

"*Swept Away*—The Original 1974 Version Is Featured in the New Lina Wertmüller Collection," by Jay S. Steinberg, Turner Classic Movies (website), October 18, 2005, https://www.tcm.com/tcmdb/title/92119/swept-away#articles-reviews?articleId=104933.

"Wertmüller, Lina 1926–," Encyclopedia.com, https://www.encyclopedia.com/people/literature-and-arts/film-and-television-biographies/lina-wertmuller.

Picnic at Hanging Rock (1975)

The Cinema of Australia and New Zealand, edited by Geoff Mayer and Keith Beattie (London: Wallflower Press, 2007).

"The Extraordinary Story Behind *Picnic at Hanging Rock*," by Janelle McCulloch, *The Age*, March 30, 2017, https://www.theage.com.au/lifestyle/the-extraordinary-story-behind-picnic-at-hanging-rock-20170328-gv7upc.html.

"Peter Weir," *Brittanica*, https://www.britannica.com/biography/Peter-Weir.

"Peter Weir Confirms His Retirement from Directing: 'I Have No More Energy,'" by Leonard Pearce, The Film Stage, March 18, 2024, https://thefilmstage.com/peter-weir-confirms-his-retirement-from-directing-i-have-no-more-energy/.

"*Picnic at Hanging Rock*," Criterion Collection, April 9, 2024

"*Picnic at Hanging Rock*," by Nathaniel Thompson, Turner Classic Movies (website), August 12, 2010, https://www.tcm.com/tcmdb/title/86665/picnic-at-hanging-rock#articlesreviews?articleId=345404.

"*Picnic at Hanging Rock*: What We See and What We Seem," by Megan Abbott, The Criterion Collection, June 20, 2014, https://www.criterion.com/current/posts/3202-picnic-at-hanging-rock-what-we-see-and-what-we-seem.

"Screen: Australian Hawthorne Romance: From Down Under," by Vincent Canby, *New York Times*, February 23, 1979, https://www.nytimes.com/1979/02/23/archives/screen-australian-hawthorne-romancefrom-down-under.html.

L'Avventura (1960)

Antonioni's *"Blow-Up,"* by Philippe Garner (Göttingen, Germany: Steidl, 2011).

International Dictionary of Films and Filmmakers, edited by Nicholas Tomas (Detroit: St James Press, 1991).

"*L'Avventura*," by Felicia Feaster, Turner Classic Movies (website), April 23, 2003, https://www.tcm.com/tcmdb/title/81006/lavventura#articles-reviews?articleId=25864.

"*L'Avventura*: A Present Absence," by Geoffrey Nowell-Smith, The Criterion Collection, December 1, 2014, https://www.criterion.com/current/posts/99-lavventura-a-present-absence.

"*L'Avventura*: The Film That Redefined the Cinema," by Robert Koehler, *Sight and Sound*, BFI, September 28, 2023, https://www.bfi.org.uk/sight-and-sound/features/l-avventura-michelangelo-antonioni-1960-greatest-films-poll.

"Michaelangelo Antonioni: Biography," Turner Classic Movies (website), https://www.tcm.com/tcmdb/person/4724%7C112262/Michelangelo-Antonioni#biography.

"Michelangelo Antonioni Receiving an Honorary Oscar," by Oscars, YouTube, video, October 30, 2013, https://www.youtube.com/watch?v=EW1-zJbsf-k.

"Note on *L'Avventura*," by Pauline Kael, Scraps from the Loft, April 8, 2021, https://scrapsfromtheloft.com/movies/lavventura-pauline-kael/.

FALL

Metropolis (1926)

The Encyclopedia of Science Fiction Movies, edited by Phil Hardy (London: Octopus Books, 1984).

"The Essentials—*Metropolis*," by Frank Miller, Turner Classic Movies (website), March 5, 2014, https://www.tcm.com/tcmdb/title/5892/metropolis#articles-reviews?articleId=962144.

The Faber Companion to Foreign Films, by Ronald Bergan and Robyn Karney (Boston: Faber and Faber, 1992).

The Film Encyclopedia, 7th ed., by Ephraim Katz with Ronald Dean Nolen (New York: HarperCollins Reference, 2012).

Fritz Lang: The Nature of the Beast, by Patrick McGilligan (New York: St. Martins Press, 1997).

"Metropolis," *Britannica*, https://www.britannica.com/topic/Metropolis-film-1927.

"*Metropolis* (1927)," BFI, https://www.bfi.org.uk/film/bda6ff8a-ed7e-5942-980d-c2910c0120ec/metropolis.

Must-See Sci-Fi: 50 Movies That Are Out of This World, by Sloan De Forest (Philadelphia: Running Press, 2018).

Science Fiction in the Cinema, by John Baxter (London: A. S. Barnes, 1969).

"The Story of Fritz Lang's *Metropolis*," by Chuck Frownfelter, Cinema Scholars, December 25, 2022, https://cinemascholars.com/the-story-of-fritz-langs-metropolis-1927/.

"What Is German Expressionism in Film? Defining the Style," Studio Binder, March 18, 2020: https://www.studiobinder.com/blog/german-expressionism-film/.

The Rules of the Game (1939)

The Faber Companion to Foreign Films, by Ronald Bergan and Robyn Karney (Boston: Faber and Faber, 1992).

"Jean Renoir: Biography," Turner Classic Movies (website), https://www.tcm.com/tcmdb/person/160204%7C80577/Jean-Renoir#biography.

"Jean Renoir, Director of *Grand Illusion* Film, Dies," by Paul Montgomery, *New York Times*,

February 14, 1979, https://www
.nytimes.com/1979/02/14/archives/jean
-renoir-director-of-grand-illusion-film
-dies-outlook-like.html.

"*The Rules of the Game*," by Brian Cady, Turner Classic Movies (website), November 25, 2022, https://www.tcm.com/tcmdb/title /88741/the-rules-of-the-game#articles -reviews?articleId=12766.

"*The Rules of the Game*: Everyone Has Their Reasons," by Alexander Sesonske, The Criterion Collection, November 15, 2011, https://www.criterion.com/current /posts/308-the-rules-of-the-game-everyone -has-their-reasons.

"What Makes a French Comedy One of the Greatest Films of All Time?," by Ben Kenigsberg, *New York Times*, January 7, 2021, https://www.nytimes.com /2021/01/07/movies/jean-renoir-rules -of-the-game.html.

The Double Life of Véronique (1991)

"Cannes: What the Heck is the Ecumenical Jury?," by Scott Roxborough, *Hollywood Reporter*, May 21, 2022, https://www.holly woodreporter.com/movies/movie-news /cannes-2022-ecumenical-jury -explained-1235151825/#!.

"The Depths of What We Cannot Know: On *The Double Life of Véronique*," by Jessica Ritchey, RogerEbert.com, March 30, 2016, https:// www.rogerebert.com/features/the -depths-of-what-we-cannot-know-on-the -double-life-of-veronique.

"*The Double Life of Véronique*," by Michael Atkinson, Turner Classic Movies (website), August 24, 2006, https://www.tcm.com /tcmdb/title/73503/the-double-life-of -veronique#articles-reviews?articleId =143798.

"*The Double Life of Véronique*: Through the Looking Glass," by Jonathan Romney, The Criterion Collection, February 1, 2011, https://www.criterion.com/current /posts/457-the-double-life-of-veronique -through-the-looking-glass.

"Have You Ever Felt Strangely As If You Were Somewhere Else?," by Roger Ebert, RogerEbert.com, February 25, 2009: https:// www.rogerebert.com/reviews /the-double-life-of-veronique-1991-1.

"Kieślowski's Muse," by Peter Cowie, The Criterion Collection, February 1, 2011, https://www.criterion.com/current/ posts/1734-kieslowski-s-muse.

"Krzysztof Kieślowski: Biography," Turner Classic Movies (website), https://www.tcm .com/tcmdb/person/101802%7C0/Krzysztof -Kieslowski#biography.

"A Short History of Polish Cinema," by Andrew Pulver, *The Guardian*, April 6, 2011: https:// www.theguardian.com/film/film blog/2011/apr/06/short-history-of-polish -cinema.

"10 Great Polish Films," by Michael Brooke, BFI, April 2, 2015, https://www.bfi.org.uk /lists/10-great-polish-films.

"Where to Begin With Krzysztof Kieślowski," by Michael Brooke, BFI, March 27, 2023, https://www.bfi.org.uk/features/where -begin-with-krzysztof-kieslowski.

Day for Night (1973)

"*Day for Night*," by David Sterritt, Turner Classic Movies (website), May 13, 2013, https:// www.tcm.com/tcmdb/title/72411 /day-for-night#articles-reviews?article Id=626496.

"*Day for Night*: Are Movies Magic?," by David Cairns, The Criterion Collection, August 17, 2015, https://www.criterion.com /current/posts/3659-day-for-night-are -movies-magic.

"François Truffaut: Biography," by Richard Harland Smith, Turner Classic Movies (website), https://www.tcm.com/tcmdb /person/194455%7C52096/ Fran%C3%A7ois-Truffaut#biography.

"François Truffaut, New Wave Director, Dies,"
by Eric Pace, *New York Times*, October 22,
1984, https://www.nytimes.com/1984
/10/22/obituaries/francois-truffaut
-new-wave-director-dies.html.

"Godard vs. Truffaut," interview with Dudley
Andrew, The Criterion Collection,
August 19, 2015, https://www.criterion.com/
current/posts/3661-godard-vs-truffaut.

Truffaut: A Biography, by Antoine de Baecque and
Serge Toubiana (Berkeley, CA: University of
California Press, 2000).

Devi (1960)

"*Devi*: Seeing and Believing," by Devika Girish,
The Criterion Collection, October 26, 2021,
https://www.criterion.com/current
/posts/7585-devi-seeing-and-believing.

"Durga Puja," *Britannica*, https://www.britannica
.com/topic/Durga-Puja.

"Satyajit Ray, 70, Cinematic Poet, Dies," by Peter
B. Flint, *New York Times*, April 24, 1992,
https://www.nytimes.com/1992
/04/24/movies/satyajit-ray-70-cinematic
-poet-dies.html

"Satyajit Ray's Encounter with Jean Renoir,"
SatyajitRay.org, https://satyajitray.org
/encounter-with-jean-renoir/.

Cure (1997)

"A Brief History of Japanese Horror," by Rob
Buscher, The Rikumo Journal, October 30,
2017, https://journal.rikumo.com/journal
/paaff/a-brief-history-of-japanese-horror.

"*Cure*: Erasure," by Chris Fujiwara, The Criterion
Collection, October 18, 2022, https://www.
criterion.com/current/posts
/7959-cure-erasure.

"Looking Back at Kiyoshi Kurosawa's *Cure*,"
by Seongyong Cho, RogerEbert.com,
November 8, 2022, https://www.rogerebert
.com/far-flung-correspondents/looking
-back-at-kiyoshi-kurosawas-cure.

The Vanishing (1988)

"About," Sluizer Films BV, http://www
.georgesluizer.com/01-About.htm.

"George Sluizer on *The Vanishing*," The Criterion
Collection, October 28, 2014, https://www.
criterion.com/current/posts/3348-george-
sluizer-on-the-vanishing.

"*The Vanishing* (1988)," by Nathaniel
Thompson, Turner Classic Movies (website),
November 29, 2011, https://www.tcm.com/
tcmdb/title/94684
/the-vanishing#articlesreviews?article
Id=461428.

"*The Vanishing* Review/Film; How Evil Can
One Person Be?," by Janet Maslin, *New York
Times*, January 25, 1991, https://
www.nytimes.com/1991/01/25/movies
/review-film-how-evil-can-one-person-be.html.

"*The Vanishing*: The End of the Road," by
Scott Foundas, The Criterion Collection,
October 29, 2014, https://www.criterion
.com/current/posts/3340-the-vanishing-the
-end-of-the-road.

Peeping Tom (1960)

"Fancy a Quickie?," by Matthew Sweet, *The
Guardian*, January 2, 2007, https://www
.theguardian.com/film/2007/jan/02/features
.features11.

A Life in Movies, by Michael Powell (New York:
Faber & Faber, New York, 1986).

"Michael Powell: Biography," Turner Classic
Movies (website), https://www.tcm.com
/tcmdb/person/154725%7C111805
/Michael-Powell#biography.

Million Dollar Movie, by Michael Powell (New
York: Random House, 1995).

"*Peeping Tom*," by Roger Ebert, RogerEbert.com,
May 2, 1999, https://www.rogerebert.com
/reviews/great-movie-peeping-tom-1960.

"*Peeping Tom*," by Felicia Feaster, Turner Classic
Movies (website), August 22, 2005, https://
www.tcm.com/tcmdb/title/86435/peeping

-tom#articles-reviews?articleId=102783.

"*Peeping Tom*," by Laura Mulvey, The Criterion
Collection, November 15, 1999, https://
www.criterion.com/current/posts
/65-peeping-tom.

"The *Peeping Tom* Controversy Explained: How
Martin Scorsese Helped Save a Forgotten
Gem," by Devin Meenan, *Film Inquiry*,
September 11, 2022, https://www.slashfilm
.com/994834/the-peeping-tom-controversy
-explained-how-martin-scorsese-helped
-save-a-forgotten-gem/.

"'Scorsese Says *The Red Shoes* Is in His DNA':
Thelma Schoonmaker on Her Life and
Work with Michael Powell and His Friend
Marty," by Nadia Khomami, *The Guardian*,
December 8, 2023, https://www.theguardian
.com/film/2023/dec/08/thelma
-schoonmaker-interview-the-red-shoes
-michael-powell-martin-scorsese.

The Orphanage (2007)

"Geraldine Chaplin: Biography," by Shawn
Dwyer, Turner Classic Movies (website),
https://www.tcm.com/tcmdb/person
/32231%7C60621/Geraldine-Chaplin
#biography.

"The Ghost Down the Hall Is Scary in Spanish,
Too," by A. O. Scott, *New York Times*,
December 28, 2007, https://www.nytimes
.com/2007/12/28/movies/28orph.html.

"J. A. Bayona: Biography," Cinetown.org, https://
cinetown.org/people/profile
/jabayona.

"J. A. Bayona and Sergio Sánchez on *The
Orphanage*: The RT Interview," by Alex Vo,
Rotten Tomatoes, January 9, 2008, https://
editorial.rottentomatoes.com/article
/ja-bayona-and-sergio-sanchez-on-the
-orphanage-the-rt-interview/.

"Juan Antonio Bayona, *The Orphanage*," by Nick
Dawson, *Filmmaker Magazine*,
December 28, 2007, https://filmmaker
magazine.com/1296-juan-antonio
-bayona-the-orphanage/.

"The Jury of the 77th Festival de Cannes," Juan
Antonio Bayona bio, Festival de Cannes,
April 29, 2024, https://www.festival-cannes
.com/en/press/press-releases/the-jury-of
-the-77th-festival-de-cannes/.

*Death of a Cyclist (*1955)

"*Death of a Cyclist*," by Felicia Feaster, Turner
Classic Movies, August 1, 2006, https
://www.tcm.com/tcmdb/title/645363
/death-of-a-cyclist#articles-reviews?article
Id=141992.

"*Death of a Cyclist*," by Rebecca Naughten, Eye
for Film, November 14, 2014, https
://www.eyeforfilm.co.uk/review/death-of
-a-cyclist-1955-film-review-by-rebecca
-naughten.

"*Death of a Cyclist*: Creating a Modern Spanish
Cinema," by Marsha Kinder, The Criterion
Collection, April 21, 2008, https://www
.criterion.com/current/posts/550-death-of
-a-cyclist-creating-a-modern-spanish-cinema.

"Juan Antonio Bardem: Biography," Turner
Classic Movies (website), https://www
.tcm.com/tcmdb/person/9721%7C90432
/Juan-Antonio-Bardem#biography.

"Juan Antonio Bardem: Brave Director Whose
Films Mocked the Repression of Franco's
Spain," by Ronald Bergan, *The Guardian*,
November 2, 2002, http://film
.guardian.co.uk/News_Story/Guardian
/0,4029,824602,00.html.

Elevator to the Gallows (1958)

"*Elevator to the Gallows*," Miles Davis (website),
https://www.milesdavis.com/film/elevator
-to-the-gallows/.

"*Elevator to the Gallows* (aka *Fanatic*)," by
Jay Carr, Turner Classic Movies (website),
August 15, 2007, https://www.tcm.com
/tcmdb/title/75606/elevator-to-the-gallows
#articles-reviews?articleId=180494.

"*Elevator to the Gallows*: Louis Malle on the
Ground Floor," by Terrence Rafferty,
The Criterion Collection, April 24, 2006,

https://www.criterion.com/current/posts
/420-elevator-to-the-gallows-louis-malle
-on-the-ground-floor.

The Faber Companion to Foreign Films, by Ronald
Bergan and Robyn Karney (Boston: Faber
and Faber, 1992).

Louis Malle, by Hugo Frey, French Film Directors
(Manchester, UK: Manchester University
Press, 2004).

Malle on Malle, edited by Philip French (London:
Faber and Faber, 1996).

"Miles Davis Improvises the Score to *Elevator
to the Gallows*," The Criterion Collection,
February 7, 2018, https://www.criterion
.com/current/posts/5369-miles-davis-
improvises-the-score-for-elevator-to-the-
gallows.

Review: *Elevator to the Gallows*: A Legendary
Louis Malle Film Returns to the Big Screen,"
by Kenneth Turan, *Los Angeles Times*,
August 11, 2016, https://www
.latimes.com/entertainment/movies/la
-et-mn-elevator-gallows-review-20160805
-snap-story.html.

Pale Flower (1964)

"All Our Yesterdays: The Past Is Always Present
in the Films of Masahiro Shinoda," by Tom
Mes, *Film Comment*, September–October
2010.

"*Crazed Fruit*: Imagining a New Japan—The
Taiyozoku Films," by Michael Raine, The
Criterion Collection, June 27, 2005, https://
www.criterion.com/current/posts
/373-crazed-fruit-imagining-a-new-japan
-the-taiyozoku-films.

"Five Unmissable Films from the Japanese New
Wave Movement," by James Balmont,
AnOther Magazine, November 29, 2021,
https://www.anothermag.com/design-living
/13734/five-unmissable-films-from-the
-japanese-new-wave-movement.

"Noir Blooms in the Rainy Night," by Roger
Ebert, RogerEbert.com, May 16, 2011,
https://www.rogerebert.com/reviews/great

-movie-pale-flower-1964.

"*Pale Flower*," by Jeremy Arnold, Turner Classic
Movies (website), April 25, 2019, https://
www.tcm.com/tcmdb/title/558241
/pale-flower#articlesreviews?article
Id=1484407.

"*Pale Flower*: Loser Take All," by Chuck Stephens,
The Criterion Collection, May 17, 2011,
https://www.criterion.com/current/posts
/1860-pale-flower-loser-take-all.

Babette's Feast (1987)

"*Babette's Feast*," by Nathaniel Thompson, Turner
Classic Movies (website), November 8, 2013,
https://www.tcm.com/tcmdb/title
/67854/babettes-feast/#articles-reviews
?articleId=906478.

"*Babette's Feast*: 'Mercy and Truth Have Met
Together,'" by Mark Le Fanu, The Criterion
Collection, July 22, 2013, https://www
.criterion.com/current/posts/2842-babette
-s-feast-mercy-and-truth-have-met-together.

"*Babette's Feast* Wins Foreign Language Film:
1988 Oscars," by Oscars, YouTube, video,
January 31, 2014, https://www.youtube
.com/watch?v=QRYzlBodJwE.

"Gabriel Axel: Biography," Turner Classic Movies
(website), https://www.tcm.com
/tcmdb/person/7347%7C56827/Gabriel-
Axel#biography.

"Interview with Gabriel Axel," by Jill Forbes,
Sight & Sound, Spring 1988.

"Stéphane Audran, Star in Oscar-
Winning *Babette's Feast*, Dies at 85,"
by Neil Genzlinger, *New York Times*,
March 27, 2018, https://www.nytimes.
com/2018/03/27/obituaries/stephane
-audran-who-starred-in-babettes
-feast-dies-at-85.html.

"Then and Now: *Babette's Feast* Reviewed," by
Sam Wigley, BFI, December 14, 2012,
https://www.bfi.org.uk/features/then-now
-babettes-feast-reviewed.

WINTER (YEAR END)

Fanny and Alexander (1982)

"Bergman: From Tormented Childhood to Film Icon," Reuters, August 9, 2007, https://www.reuters.com/article/idUSL30329741/.

"Fanny and Alexander," by James Steffen, Turner Classic Movies (website), October 25, 2006, https://www.tcm.com/tcmdb/title/74540/fanny-and-alexander#articles-reviews?articleId=136022.

"Fanny and Alexander: Bergman's Bildungsroman," by Rick Moody, The Criterion Collection, November 8, 2011, https://www.criterion.com/current/posts/347-fanny-and-alexander-bergman-s-bildungsroman.

"Fanny and Alexander Review—Ingmar Bergman's Dark Fusion of Shakespeare and Dickens," by Peter Bradshaw, The Guardian, December 1, 2022, https://www.the guardian.com/film/2022/dec/01/fanny-and-alexander-review-ingmar-bergmans-dark-fusion-of-shakespeare-and-dickens.

"Fanny and Alexander: In the World of Childhood," by Stig Björkman, Criterion, November 2011: https://www.criterion.com/current/posts/346-fanny-and-alexander-in-the-world-of-childhood.

"Ingmar Bergman," Britannica, https://www.britannica.com/biography/Ingmar-Bergman.

"Ingmar Bergman, Master Filmmaker, Dies at 89," by Mervyn Rothstein, New York Times, July 30, 2007, https://www.nytimes.com/2007/07/30/movies/30cnd-bergman.html.

Paris Pick-Up (1962)

"Frederic Dard: Shunned by Critics, Loved by Readers as San-Antonio: A Conjurer with French Language," by Katherine Knorr, New York Times, June 10, 2000, https://www.nytimes.com/2000/06/10/news/ritanni-dardshunned-by-critics-loved-by-readers-as-sanantonio-a.html.

"French Theatre Legend Robert Hossein Dies Aged 93," RFI, December 31, 2020, https://www.rfi.fr/en/culture/20201231-french-theatre-legend-robert-hossein-dies-aged-93.

"The Greatest French Crime Writer You've Never Heard Of," by Paul French, Crime Reads, March 9, 2017, https://crimereads.com/the-greatest-french-crime-writer-you've-never-heard-of/.

"Paris Pick-Up," by Michael Bayer, Heart of Noir, https://heartofnoir.com/film/le-monte-charge-1962/.

"Paris Pick-Up," by Paul Schrader, Letterboxd, https://letterboxd.com/film/paris-pick-up/.

Black Christmas (1974)

"Black Christmas (1974)," by Richard Harland Smith, Turner Classic Movies (website), May 18, 2011, https://www.tcm.com/tcmdb/title/68859/black-christmas#articles-reviews?articleId=410638.

"Black Christmas Inspired John Carpenter's Original Halloween," by Michael Kennedy, ScreenRant, December 4, 2019, https://screenrant.com/black-christmas-halloween-movie-inspiration-john-carpenter/.

"Discover This Yuletide Slasher That Inspired John Carpenter's Halloween," by Anton Bitel, Little White Lies, November 13, 2017, https://lwlies.com/articles/black-christmas-final-girl-trope-halloween/.

"Fright Exclusive Interview: Bob Clark," by Jsyn, Icons of Fright, May 2005, Internet Archive Wayback Machine, http://web.archive.org/web/20220421201044/www.iconsoffright.com/IV_Bclark.htm.

My Night at Maud's (1969)

"Eric Rohmer: Biography," Turner Classic Movies (website), https://www.tcm.com

/tcmdb/person/164310%7C48224/Eric
-Rohmer#biography.

"Eric Rohmer: Everyday Miracles of a New Wave
Master," by Michael Newton,
The Guardian, December 26, 2014, https://
www.theguardian.com/film/2014
/dec/26/eric-rohmer-everyday-miracles
-new-wave-master.

Eric Rohmer: Realist and Moralist, by C. G. Crisp
(Bloomington, IN: Indiana University Press,
1988).

"*Les Provinciales* of Blaise Pascal," *Britannica*,
https://www.britannica.com/biography
/Blaise-Pascal/Les-Provinciales.

Magill's Survey of Cinema, Foreign Language Films,
vol. 5, edited by Frank Magill
(Englewood Cliffs, NJ: Salem Press, 1985).

A Man with a Camera, by Nestor Almendros
(New York: Farrar, Straus and Giroux, 1986).

"*My Night at Maud's*," by Lang Thompson,
Turner Classic Movies (website), May 8,
2007, https://www.tcm.com/tcmdb
/title/84377/my-night-at-mauds#articles
-reviews?articleId=88887.

"*My Night at Maud's*: Chances Are . . . ," by Kent
Jones, The Criterion Collection,
August 14, 2006, https://www.criterion.com/
current/posts/436-my-night-at-mauds
-chances-are.

▲ Marcello Mastroianni in *La Dolce Vita* (1960)

INDEX

Page numbers in **bold** refer to photographs or their captions.